PURE FIRE

CHRISTOPHER B. STRAIN

PURE

Self-Defense as Activism in the Civil Rights Era

FIRE

The University of Georgia Press | Athens and London

© 2005 by the University of Georgia Press
Athens, Georgia 30602
All rights reserved
Designed by Mindy Basinger Hill
Set in 10.5/13.5 Adobe Caslon by Bookcomp
Printed and bound by Maple-Vail
The paper in this book meets the guidelines for
permanence and durability of the Committee on
Production Guidelines for Book Longevity of the
Council on Library Resources.

Printed in the United States of America

09 08 07 06 05 c 5 4 3 2 1
09 08 07 06 05 p 5 4 3 2 1

Library of Congress Cataloging-in-Publication Data

Strain, Christopher B., 1970–
    Pure fire : self-defense as activism in the
civil rights era / Christopher B. Strain.
        p. cm.
    Includes bibliographical references and index.
    ISBN 0-8203-2686-0 (hardcover : alk.
paper) — ISBN 0-8203-2687-9 (pbk. :
alk. paper)
    1. African Americans—Civil rights—History—20th
century.   2. Civil rights movements—United
States—History—20th century.   3. Self-defense—
United States—History—20th century.   I. Title.
    E185.61.S913 2005
    323.1196'073—dc22   2004018178

British Library Cataloging-in-Publication Data available

CONTENTS

ACKNOWLEDGMENTS

This book (which uses the terms "black" and "Afro-American" to capture the spirit of protest in the civil rights movement) is based on archival findings, supplemented by autobiography and oral testimony; where appropriate, as in the first chapter, I have used secondary sources. The second chapter treats Martin Luther King's own writings as primary sources and discusses the historiographical questions in so doing; it also delves deeply into archival material from Dr. King's papers, collected at Boston University. The third chapter relies on Robert Williams's papers, collected at the Bentley Library of the University of Michigan; the fourth chapter on Malcolm X's own sermons and speeches; the fifth on newspapers and interviews; the sixth on the McCone Commission papers, collected at the Bancroft Library of the University of California at Berkeley; and the seventh on autobiography, oral history, and the newly created Black Panther Party Papers, collected and housed at Stanford University. The book also utilizes published oral histories such as Howell Raines's *My Soul Is Rested* and Henry Hampton's *Voices of Freedom*, full of firsthand testimony by activists. In many cases I prefer these interviews to those that I have conducted myself for two simple reasons. If it is true—as someone wittier than I once observed—that the older we get, the more we remember things that never happened, then interviews conducted in the 1960s and 1970s might be more accurate and more revealing than those conducted forty years after the fact. But more importantly, many of the individuals considered in this study were public figures, interviewed extensively during the heyday of their activism, and the notion put forth in this book—that self-defense played a crucial role in the civil rights movement—is readily documented through a variety of existing sources. Much of the story, as it were, has been here all along, partially concealed in pre-existing histories, interviews, and memoirs, winking up at historians like diamonds in the rough.

A number of people deserve thanks for their contributions to this book, which evolved from a Master's thesis at the University of Georgia, to a Ph.D. dissertation at the University of California at Berkeley, to its present form. My dissertation committee—Leon Litwack, Waldo Martin, and Ronald Takaki—shaped this book in its early phases, as they also shaped me as a scholar and as a person. I emulate each of them, and I hope that this book reflects some of what they have imparted to me. Bob Pratt and

Bill McFeely taught me how to think, write, and grow as a historian. Much of what I know about history (and about life) I learned under their tutelage, whether in LeConte Hall, Weaver D's, or the Georgia Bar. Tim Tyson deserves special thanks for his guidance and encouragement. He spent much time and effort responding to e-mail queries, reading drafts, and mentoring me as a graduate student at a distant university when I had no legitimate claim to his mentorship. His support has been invaluable.

Greta de Jong and Hasan Jeffries each provided excellent comments after taking time from their busy schedules in the spring of 2003 to read the manuscript. Jeff Ogbar deserves a special thanks, as do Sallie Brown, Clayborne Carson, Joanne Grant, the late Jim Kettner, the members of my dissertation group at Berkeley, my colleagues and students at the Harriet L. Wilkes Honors College of Florida Atlantic University, and the staffs at the following archives: the Bentley Historical Library at the University of Michigan; the Bancroft Library at UC Berkeley; the Manuscripts, Archives and Rare Books Division of the Schomburg Center for Research in Black Culture at the New York Public Library; the Moorland-Spingarn Research Center at Howard University; the Department of Special Collections at Stanford University; the Department of Special Collections at Boston University; and the Rare Book, Manuscript, and Special Collections Library at Duke University.

My friends have read bits and pieces of the manuscript in various stages of completion. They have listened and perused, edited and critiqued, questioned and answered; they have also gently torn me away from the manuscript when I have needed a break and a little perspective. I would like to thank them for helping in this regard. J. P. Daughton, Lara Smith, Jen Milne, Greg Delaune, and Sara Krier have all been particularly quick with a critical eye, a kind word, a hot meal, a cold drink, or a big hug when needed. The editorial staff at the University of Georgia Press has worked professionally and tirelessly to make this manuscript a book. Thanks also to Yani Bailes and Amy Broderick for lending their ideas for the dust jacket. Finally, I would like to thank my parents and grandparents—Dan and Jean Strain, Ed and Betty Barry, and my academic mentor, Mattie Lou Strain— and my uncle Ed Barry Jr. for their constant love and support. All of these people and more have facilitated the completion of this book; however, I alone am responsible for any limitations of structure, articulation, and style herein.

PURE FIRE

White reporter: "Why do you teach black supremacy and hate?"

Malcolm X: "To pour on pure fire in return."

INTERVIEW, 1964

INTRODUCTION

PURE FIRE

For much of its history, the southern United States could be a terrible and terrifying place for black people to live. In the antebellum period, slavery relegated Africans in America to a life under the lash. From the end of Reconstruction to the middle of the twentieth century, white racists engineered and fine-tuned the mechanisms of racial separation and applied them enthusiastically in order to institutionalize inequality; they also systematized a program of racial violence, including assaults and lynchings, to ensure their place above black people in the region's social hierarchy. Implicit and extreme violence held the mechanisms of segregation in place through the 1960s. As historian Fred Powledge has noted: "Perhaps the most important characteristic of American race relations in the early 1950's was the degree to which terror reigned in the black community and in the black mind. Black Southerners lived in a police state, a place where violence—officially sanctioned violence—could be visited upon them in a moment, and for no reason at all. . . . And the oppressors could do anything they wanted and get away with it." Another historian has similarly observed, "Negroes were so far outside the human family that the most inhuman actions could be visited upon them. . . . Black life could be snuffed out on whim, you could be killed because some ignorant white man didn't like the color of your shirt or the way you drove a wagon."[1]

It was not until the 1950s that cracks began to appear in the South's racial order, and civil rights activists used nonviolent tactics in the 1960s to widen these cracks into rifts of civil rights reform. During this period, nonviolent activists challenged jim crow segregation in the United States by rendering ineffective the stultifying violence that had come to define the region. Leading the nation to a new understanding of responsible citizenship and biracial unity, these activists offered black and white Americans alike a new way of living their lives: not only as citizens of a multicultural nation-state but also as members of what Dr. Martin Luther King Jr. called a "beloved community" in which diverse peoples could come together and live in harmony. They also helped to mask the deep scars left on the South by the region's "peculiar institution," slavery. Activists, utilizing nonviolence as a protest tactic, a way of life, or both, blazed a trail toward a better way of human interaction. But to many—perhaps most—black people striving for freedom and equality in the southern United States, it seemed much more in keeping with traditional American ideals to strike back at those who kept swinging at them, or shoot back at those who kept shooting at them. Accordingly, the question of whether or not to defend oneself became a critical question for the students, ministers, and others—mostly black, some white—engaged in civil rights protests.

That black people might actually defend themselves was a terrifying notion to southern whites, who depended on terrorism to preserve their own wealth and power and to maintain the system of laws and social practices they had constructed to confine black people to menial jobs. Self-defense by black Americans in the 1960s represented more than a glitch in the matrix of southern white supremacy, black subordination, and segregation. Afro-Americans had been denied the basic constitutional and human right to self-defense in both the time of slavery and the jim crow era, and the practice of armed self-defense in the civil rights movement signaled an effort to assert that right, just as the struggles for desegregation, voting rights, and economic justice were attempts to assert other constitutional and human rights. Therefore, self-defense was more than a tactic used alongside nonviolence. It was an essential part of the struggle for citizenship itself. Scholars have written extensively about nonviolence (the abstention from violence as a matter of principle) and nonviolent direct action (the application of nonviolence in social protest) in the Afro-American civil rights movement.[2] The so-called violent trends of the latter stages of the civil rights movement, 1965–68, have also been thoroughly discussed.[3] Coincidentally there exists a rich literature related to violence, nonviolence, and the relation of each to political activism and social change.[4] This body of literature has tended to frame the use of violence as a tactic to achieve other goals. It is important to note that this study consciously moves beyond these previous dialogues in an attempt to chart a new direction in civil rights studies and protest studies. Rather than plow old ground, I hope to survey this terrain in a new way.

Until recently, civil rights scholars have tended to treat the civil rights movement in two distinct phases: pre-1965 and post-1965.[5] Many accounts of the civil rights movement have also tended to dichotomize any discussion of the struggle for black equality in terms of violence and nonviolence: descriptive categories for antithetical modes of protest, with nonviolence being normative.[6] The prevailing consensus has maintained that nonviolence shaped and directed the movement up until roughly 1965, when the civil rights struggle was thrown off course by frustration, impatience, disillusionment, and combativeness and "turned" violent. Under this paradigm, a clear dichotomy would seem to exist between the pre-1965, nonviolent movement and the post-1965, violent movement.

Recent scholarship has provided a powerful and necessary indictment of these earlier analyses.[7] These newer studies indicate that while very little violence (intentionally destructive or injurious force) occurred in the civil rights movement on the part of Afro-Americans, some black activists and onlookers did advocate the use of self-defense (defined as the act of repelling an attack) in securing civil rights. The surfeit of such stories in recent years has complicated our understanding of the civil rights movement as a self-described nonviolent movement. Of even more interest are those activists who accepted nonviolence, defined as the abstention from violence as a matter of principle, while contradictorily professing a belief in self-defense.

At least three conclusions may be drawn from this new wave of scholarship. First, the traditions of armed self-defense and nonviolence co-existed in the civil rights movement, with each yielding influence to the other. Second, the pre-1965/post-1965 dichotomy created by journalists and earlier historians is a false one, as is the violent/nonviolent dichotomy commonly used to describe the movement. The year 1965 did *not* mark a clear change between an earlier nonviolent movement and a later violent one, and thus violence as a category of black protest in the 1960s represents one side of a classic "either-or" fallacy and also a red herring. Third, by criticizing activists who asserted Afro-Americans' right to protect themselves, journalists and scholars have perpetuated a historical double standard regarding the use of violence by black and white Americans (i.e., whites can, blacks cannot). The dichotomies that journalists, scholars, and even activists themselves have constructed (pre-1965 versus post-1965, nonviolence versus violence, integration versus separation, Martin versus Malcolm, and others) have greatly obscured the centrality of self-defense in the struggle for black equality.

The issue of armed self-defense extended far beyond the realm of civil rights demonstrations and organized protest. It was a question that, in some form or another, informed the daily actions and behaviors of many, many Afro-Americans faced with the menace of violent aggression by white supremacists. Exactly what role did self-defense play in the civil rights movement during the years 1955–1968? In answering this question, it is important to examine the mindset of black Americans employing self-defense during the late 1950s and early 1960s—*before* the right to self-defense became something of an assumption by those emboldened by the rhetoric and ideology of Black Power. Accordingly, this book is an exercise in intellectual history: the history of an idea, as reflected in both events and people. In a sense, it picks up where two period studies, Harold Cruse's *Crisis of the Negro Intellectual* and James Robert Ross's *The War Within: Violence or Nonviolence in the Black Revolution* leave off.[8] "Very little attention has been paid to the possibility," Charles Payne has suggested more recently, in *I've Got the Light of Freedom: The Organizing Tradition and the Mississippi Freedom Struggle,* "that the success of the movement in the rural South owes something to the attitude of local people toward self-defense."[9] I have attempted to offer a corrective by situating the ideas of activists such as Robert F. Williams of Monroe, North Carolina, and Charles Sims of the Deacons for Defense and Justice—black men who advocated armed self-defense during the early and middle phases of the modern civil rights movement—into a broader historical context, and to consider how the issue impinged on notions of personhood, black advancement, citizenship, and "American-ness."

Self-defense as an expression of "American-ness" has resounded in constitutional theory and American law. Closely tied to matters of political theory and the nature of man, the right to self-defense derives from a number of sources, including Greek and Roman law, natural law theory, English common law, and the writings of various philosophers.[10] Both Hobbes and Locke concluded that self-defense is a fundamental *natural right* inherent in people as human beings. The right to self-defense antedated the United States Constitution, but the Framers included it nonetheless, along with other "inalienable" rights discussed in the Declaration of Independence. British citizens living in the colonies symbolized the importance of this right with the colonial-era Gadsden flag, which depicted a rattlesnake coiled to strike and the slogan "Don't Tread on Me."

The American Revolution and the creation of the new republic sharpened the distinctions between civil liberties, civil rights, and human rights; over two hundred years later, the differences are still clear. For example, no one, especially an agent of the government, is allowed to violate civil liberties that, as prerogatives of individuals, are wholly free from governmental action. Civil liberties protect the individual against his or her government. Examples include the freedoms of religion, speech, the press, and assembly. In this sense, civil liberties are more akin to human rights, which exist in people in a state of nature, apart from government. Other individual prerogatives, protected against state action with supplementary enforcement powers granted to the federal government, are civil rights, such as the right to vote. Civil rights protect individuals against other individuals, including governmental officials participating in discriminatory practices based upon race, color, creed, or national origin. As one constitutional scholar has noted, civil liberties "actually comprise the 'negative' side of democracy, freedom from restrictions, rather than the 'positive' side, popular participation in the selection of government and in government decisions [i.e., civil rights]."[11]

But second-class citizenship and the methodical denial of civil rights historically blurred this distinction with regard to Afro-Americans—as did the complicated dialectic between means and ends. Interestingly, self-defense as practiced by civil rights activists and other black Americans in the 1950s and 1960s assumed qualities of not only human rights but also civil rights and civil liberties; in this way, the practice of self-defense became an unlikely path toward full citizenship and full "American-ness."

Self-defense is fundamentally a matter of legal and ethical concern. The Model Penal Code, a standardized American legal reference drafted in 1962, declares that "the use of force upon . . . another is justifiable when the actor believes that such force is immediately necessary." Throughout history, philosophers, legal scholars, and even some pacifists have tended to agree that self-defense is permissible; controversies surrounding it have centered on whether the impending violation was sufficient to trigger a legitimate response. Self-defense is traditionally understood as a legal "defense of justification" rather than a "defense of excuse" (insanity, for example). A person who is otherwise guilty of an egregious wrongdoing such as murder has, in the eye of the law, done nothing wrong if he or she is justified in self-defense. Justifiable self-defense requires three conditions: imminence, necessity, and proportionality. The attack must be imminent, which means that it is about to happen and the time for defense is now. A pre-emptive strike against a feared aggressor is illegal force used too soon, and retaliation against an assailant who has already harmed but no longer poses a threat is illegal force used too late; therefore, justifiable self-defense must be neither too soon nor too late. If a defender confronts an attacker who has not yet posed or no longer poses an imminent threat, he or she in effect becomes the attacker.[12]

Justifiable self-defense also presumes that self-defense is a necessity, that the defendant has no other means of escape from the assailant. Finally, the defense must be proportional to the attack: a defender who shoots someone who has punched him risks being accused of using excessive force, thereby negating the claim to self-defense.

It is interesting to me how the personal and largely apolitical issue of self-defense morphed into a highly public and political issue for black Americans in the 1960s. The increased politicization of self-defense by black Americans during this period paralleled the development of a heightened awareness of political, social, and economic deprivation. Must self-defense be self-consciously political to be considered activism? From a strictly prescriptive viewpoint, the answer remains yes; however, because the issue of self-defense was racialized from the earliest days of American history, and because black persons were traditionally denied that right, one could easily argue that *any* assertion of self, or of self-protection, by black Americans represented a blow against racism and bigotry. Activism is usually characterized as public demonstration: marches, protests, boycotts, and the like. Similarly, self-defense is usually understood to be an apolitical act of resistance. However, it seems clear that, in the context of the struggle for black equality, self-defense assumed important constitutional and political roles in black empowerment—even though it was often an individual act of defiance, free from formal coordination, collective action, or overtly political aims.

The personal and localized act of defending oneself from harm can simulate the perquisites of open political challenge under certain circumstances. This study describes those circumstances. Self-defense by black Americans in the mid-twentieth century frequently assumed characteristics of what Raymond and Alice Bauer identified as "day to day resistance" in the nineteenth century.[13] Indeed, the issue of self-defense traces the trajectory of how the personal became the political in Afro-American history.

Had some cats on the police force I was raised up with, and they knew that if they hit me they were gon' have to do me in bad, 'cause I was gon' fight back. And I still fight right now, at my age. Don't push me. My time is not long, not put on this earth to stay forever, and the time I'm here, I'm gon' be treated right.

CHARLES SIMS, BOGALUSA, LOUISIANA, 1975

CHAPTER 1
GON' BE TREATED RIGHT
Self-Defense in Black History

The issue of self-defense became a focal point in the civil rights movement, symbolic of the many crucial challenges that black Americans faced; in this way, it acted as a catalyst for civil rights agitation in the 1960s. When viewed in the limited context of strategy and tactics within the civil rights movement, self-defense seems to have been a peripheral issue, related to how activists might best achieve certain aims, such as desegregation or voting rights. However, when viewed within the larger context of Afro-American history, self-defense comes into clear focus as a dominant, recurring motif.

The issue of self-defense has been a central theme in Afro-American history since its earliest days. Like other Americans, people of African descent living in the United States have, through the generations, found need to resort to self-defense. Unlike other Americans, although slaves and free persons of color apparently had some de jure claim to justifiable self-defense in the early republic, the inconsistent application of these legal precedents amounted to a de facto denial of the right of black persons to protect themselves.

The complex and organic law of slavery in the American colonies developed in part from cases dealing with assaults by whites on blacks, as in two cases before the North Carolina Supreme Court, the landmark *State v. Mann* (1824) and *State v. Jowers* (1850), and with assaults by blacks on whites. These cases set legal precedents in defining slaves as humans and as chattel. *State v. Mann* effectively denied slaves the right to defend themselves when it authorized a master's use of force to subdue a runaway slave; *State v. Jowers* maintained that "insolence" was insufficient justification for a white man's assault on a free black. In 1821, the Mississippi Supreme Court held in *State v. Jones* that under the common law a person could be convicted for killing a slave. Slaves were people, under this ruling, and killing a person was murder.[1]

However, black people defending themselves against white aggressors represented a threat to the social order: a black person who raised his or her hand in self-protection against a white person threatened a blow not simply to an individual person, but to the way things were, particularly in the South. Such strictly defined social relations reached back to the colonial period, long before the Civil War. White colonists knew that compulsion sustained slavery and that slavery sustained the South. They did not like to contemplate that violent resistance could consequently destroy the South and the "Southern way of life." They were very much vested in the idea of denying the possibility of black insubordination and insurrection on any level; therefore, black persons could rarely be permitted to defend themselves against those whites who would harm them.

At its most basic level, slavery was a social relationship grounded in force.[2] By definition, it necessitated coercion. In North America and the Caribbean, British colonists compelled Africans to work for them; without fair compensation, force was necessary. Of course, slaves did not always accept this situation passively. Their responses took many different forms. They feigned illness, slowed the pace of their work, fought back, committed suicide and homicide, and emancipated themselves through flight. They deliberately created problems of discipline. They arranged "accidents" as a means of retribution without having to accept the blame. They subverted white authority through arson and theft. Their acts of resistance threatened not only property but also safety and had the potential to undermine the very institution that enslaved them.

Self-defense was one such act of resistance. Sometimes slaves responded reflexively against abusive masters, reacting to physical assault by defending themselves. Self-defense was seldom a viable alternative for slaves, who risked life and limb in choosing it, but it did happen with some frequency: it was paradoxically the first and last appeal for those grievously threatened. The book *Before Freedom Came: African-American Life in the Antebellum South*, by Edward Campbell and Kym Rice, recounts several vignettes, culled from the WPA slave narratives of the 1930s, of slaves resorting to self-defense in the eighteenth and nineteenth centuries. These stories dramatize how the issue of self-defense has played a fundamental role in African-American history since its earliest days. For example, the authors retell how the overseer of a plantation in Mississippi attempted to beat a slave named Mose. Tied to the ground with stakes, Mose ripped loose and attacked the overseer with one of the stakes before he was beaten unconscious. He was later auctioned off. Another slave exacted revenge for the murder of her little sister by attacking her mistress, "Old Polly." After Polly tried "to give [her] a lick out in the yard," she picked up a rock "about as big as half your fist and hits her right in the eye and busted the eyeball, and tells her that's for whippin' my baby sister to death. You could hear her holler for five miles."[3]

A slave in Oklahoma, fed up with the indignities of servitude, turned on his owners one day and "just killed all of 'em he could." Even older slaves fought back. After her young master whipped her, an elderly mammy in Mississippi took a pole from her loom and beat him "nearly to death," shouting, "I'm goin' to kill you. These black titties sucked you, and then you come out here to beat me!"[4]

Female slaves, in particular, relied on self-defense. They faced the added threat of sexual predation by their masters, and many would not succumb. Because they could not rely on their men folk for protection, and because they had no recourse to any formal justice system when attacked by white men (or by black men, for that matter), self-defense became definitive to black womanhood under slavery. To illustrate, an overseer in Arkansas decided to whip a slave woman named Lucy to make an example of her; however, as her son remembered, "She jumped on him and like to tore him up." Word spread that Lucy would not be beaten. She was sold, but never again whipped.[5]

Slaves repeatedly choked down the temptation to fight back. Most often, they would channel this impulse into other forms of resistance, such as those noted above. Because self-protection was a non-option as far as most blacks and virtually all whites were concerned, slaves rarely fought back with direct, physical force; to do so meant death or perhaps something worse. Accordingly, the ability of slaves to endure physical abuse reflected a singular perseverance and strength of will.

As slavery sank its roots deep in American soil, the idea of self-defense became racialized in the United States to the point that a severe double standard existed: that is, white persons could legally defend themselves but black persons could not. For obvious reasons, slaves were prohibited from owning firearms. The discriminatory enforcement of laws regulating the carrying of weapons in eighteenth-century America often left blacks, free and slave alike, unarmed in hostile environments where whites remained free to carry firearms.

Because of the historical antagonisms between different races in America, gun ownership was always laden with racialized meanings. White settlers of British North America needed guns not only to combat other European colonists with imperial designs, but also to defend themselves from Native Americans resentful of their encroachment. An armed white population was also crucial in maintaining control over an enslaved black underclass. Guns thus became symbols of freedom. Whites seemed to have all the guns and whites, after all, were "free." By the turn of the nineteenth century, custom and legal sanction had confirmed black people as non-citizens in the South, as well as in other parts of the United States. By asserting the right to defend themselves they were, in fact, reiterating their claim to full citizenship. In this way, the idea of self-defense became critical in the black quest for civil rights.[6]

David Walker, a fiery pamphleteer, issued an initial call for self-defense in 1830. His *Appeal* represents the first, and the most unequivocal, call for self-defense in black history. Born the son of a male slave and a free black woman in North Carolina in 1785, Walker inherited his mother's free status; she did not dissuade the righteous anger that compelled her son to speak out against slavery, and that anger eventually compelled him to leave the

South. Walker counseled that if slaves struck for their freedom, then they should "kill or be killed." He implored:

> Now, I ask you, had you not rather be killed than to be a slave to a tyrant, who takes the life of your mother, wife and dear little children? Look upon your mother, wife and children, and answer God Almighty! and believe this, that it is no more harm for you to kill a man who is trying to kill you than it is for you to take a drink of water when thirsty; in fact; the man who will stand still and let another murder him, is worse than an infidel, and, if he has common sense, ought not to be pitied.[7]

In blunt language, Walker insisted upon self-defense as the only course of action in attaining freedom.

Similarly, abolitionist constitutionalists argued that slavery, involving the total abridgement of basic rights, violated the basic guarantee of equal rights essential to republicanism. This breach in social contract permitted the ultimate right of resistance central to the American liberal political tradition. In other words, slaves were well justified—constitutionally speaking—in taking up arms to secure their freedom.

Henry Highland Garnet, a black Presbyterian minister and one of the country's most militant spokespersons for equal rights and antislavery, survived by defending himself. As a boy, he had carried a knife when walking through the streets of New York to the African Free School. Later, after he had been admitted to the Noyes Academy in Canaan, New Hampshire, local farmers moved to evict him and his fellow students one evening by hitching an oxen team to the school building and attempting to pull it down. Garnet reportedly took a shotgun and "blazed through the window" into the darkness beyond. He and the twelve other students made their escape in a wagon.[8]

Garnet made compelling arguments for the moral justification of violent resistance to slavery. God asked men and women to respect the Sabbath and to respect his laws; but, Garnet argued, slavery made this impossible. Slavery put man, created in God's image, in direct conflict to his will; therefore, man was obligated to destroy slavery. "Neither God nor angels or just men, command you to suffer for a single moment," he told the National Convention of Colored Citizens in Buffalo, New York, in 1843. "Therefore it is your solemn and imperative duty to use every means, both moral, intellectual, and physical that promises success. . . ." Death in resistance was superior to life in obeisance.[9]

Frederick Douglass, the most outspoken and well-known abolitionist, debated Garnet in 1843 at the same convention. Garnet called for slave insurrections while Douglass, adhering to the nonviolent principles of his white mentor and fellow abolitionist, William Lloyd Garrison, challenged Garnet and argued that moral suasion was the only effective way to end slavery. But Douglass's rhetoric regarding violence and the justifiable use of force would change over the coming years. Douglass did not need much convincing that self-defense was empowering: his own experience had told him as much. Like Garnett, Douglass had effectively defended himself as a youth. In his autobiography, Douglass described a series of beatings by Edward Covey, the "Negro Breaker" to whom the sixteen-year-old Douglass was hired out for insolence. After the young Douglass complained to his master about his mistreatment and received no quarter, he resolved to defend himself and resist any ill treatment in the future. A confrontation loomed, and the following Monday when Covey finally attacked him, Douglass resisted and prevailed, defeating Covey. Douglass would later observe that the fight with Covey signified "the turning point in my life as a slave. It rekindled in my breast the smoldering embers of liberty. It . . . revived a sense of my own manhood. . . . It recalled to life my crushed self-respect, and my self-confidence, and inspired me with a renewed determination to be a free man."[10]

Douglass had trouble reconciling his faith in self-defense and his faith in Garrisonian abolitionism. After all, how could one be nonresistant while advocating self-defense? Garrison, enamored with the perfectibility of the human spirit, could not recommend violence as a means to end slavery because he recognized a divine presence in all people, realized through moral rectitude. Violence, as Garrison understood it, was itself evil, and would not only compromise moral reform but corrupt it as well; therefore, moral suasion and nonresistance were essential tools of social reform. Such an argument offered little to slaves, who were more likely to feel shame in nonresistance to oppression than in violation of an abstract moral objective. Whatever their moral strength, docility and stoicism were somewhat contemptible in the face of involuntary servitude. Accordingly, Douglass could not embrace Garrisonian pacifism as it related to nonresistance: it became increasingly difficult for him to express convictions plausible to most black folks yet consistent with Garrison.[11]

While he never acknowledged Garnet's influence on his own thinking, several factors pushed the adult Douglass toward a more public advocacy of self-defense in the antebellum period. These factors included the series of national Negro conventions between 1843 and 1855, his meetings with John Brown between 1847 and 1859, the Compromise of 1850 and Fugitive Slave Act, the Dred Scott case, his split with Garrison, and the establishment of his own paper, *The North Star*. It seems clear that Douglass did not change his thinking with regard to self-defense so much as he simply allowed his admiration of self-defense to become public over time. But it was his reticence about violence, in part, that prevented him from joining John Brown in his assault on Harper's Ferry in 1859.

Historians have disagreed about Douglass's views on violence. Biographer William McFeely has written that Douglass "had little taste for violence." The opponents of abolition "made every effort to get Douglass . . . to come out in favor of violence," McFeely has written, but "he countered with equal determination not to play into their hands."[12] But if Douglass had a distaste for violence, it did not prevent him from writing, "Every slavehunter who meets a bloody death in his infernal business is an argument in favor of the manhood of our race," in his essay "Is It Right and Wise to Kill a Kidnapper?" or from depicting how slaves might use their broken fetters to kill slavers in his 1852 novella, "The Heroic Slave." Waldo Martin maintains that Douglass "believed in, counseled, and acted upon the natural compulsion to self-defense."[13] Nathan Huggins has argued that Douglass's thoughts on violence were characterized by "a subtle drifting away, marked by changes in perspective" on Garrison's views; he has also suggested that Douglass "never had qualms about violence, he merely lacked the means." However, there is much evidence to suggest that Douglass truly appreciated the uncompromising morality of Garrison's approach.[14]

When presented with a large cane in 1853, Douglass noted that "a good stick" could be as useful as a good speech "and often more effective."

There are among the children of men, and I have gained the fact from personal observation, to be found representatives of all the animal world, from the most savage and ferocious to the most gentle and docile. Everything must be dealt with according to its kind. What will do for the Lamb will not do for the Tiger. A man would be foolish if he attempted to bail out a leaking boat with the Bible, or to extinguish a raging fire by throwing in a Prayer Book. Equally foolish would he look if he attempted to soften a slave-catcher's heart without first softening his head.[15]

Douglass hoped he would never have need of the cane, but resolved that if he ever met "a creature requiring its use," he would use the cane "with stout arm and humane motive."[16] For slave hunters he recommended, *"A good revolver, a steady hand, and a determination to shoot down any man attempting to kidnap."*[17]

Douglass was perhaps able to reconcile his dual admiration of Garrison and self-defense by understanding self-defense as the logical extension of self-reliance. In fact, his rhetoric and writings were peppered with references to the importance of self-reliance. On the lecture circuit, he often delivered a speech about "Self-Made Men" who were not examples of economic success but paragons of self-respect and dignity, and this speech was apparently one of his most popular lectures. "He who does not think himself worth saving from poverty," he spoke, "will hardly be thought worth the efforts of anybody else." He revered Benjamin Franklin's maxim that "God helps those who help themselves," and argued that self-reliance was the basis of not only individual initiative but also Afro-American manhood. "Personal independence," he maintained, "is the soul out of which comes the sturdiest manhood." It was not a great leap from self-reliance to self-defense, which Douglass seemed to have understood as a fundamental expression of relying upon oneself. "The practice of carrying guns," he would later suggest during the Civil War, "would be a good one for the colored people to adopt, as it would give them a sense of their own manhood."[18] A fascination with self-made men and self-reliance is hardly surprising from a former slave who freed himself and thereby created his own luck.

Furthermore, Douglass may have recognized self-defense not as "violence," per se, but as a unique subcategory of violence: a limited, measured kind of force, moderated by its own moral considerations. For some of his fellow black reformers, like Henry Highland Garnet and Martin Delany, the choice seemed to be as simple as "stay and die or resist and escape," but Douglass never used such simplistic rhetoric: aggression he generally opposed, self-defense he felt was justified. Most white abolitionists were pacifists, who did not believe force should ever be used, even against evil.

Most black abolitionists, including Robert Purvis, James Forten, Charles Lenox Remond, did not agree, perhaps because, as Waldo Martin has noted, whites became abolitionists out of choice, and blacks were abolitionists out of necessity. Regardless, Douglass's understanding and appreciation of self-defense is emblematic of the uncomfortable tradition of self-defense in Afro-American history.

Interestingly, the words of white abolitionists echoed those of their black brethren. Cassius M. Clay, a Kentucky abolitionist, argued in 1844 that moral power lost none of its force if backed by "cold steel" and "the flashing blade," "the pistol and the Bowie knife"; alone, moral power "stands by and sees men slain." Many northern abolitionists criticized Clay for his remarks; a few lauded him. Steeped in southern notions of personal honor, Clay insisted that "so long as the spirit is inferior to matter, so long will the sensibilities of the soul, the cherished sanctity of the heart, the love of character, and an inviolable good name, become eminently the subjects of *self-defence* [sic]." Abolitionists in places like Kentucky were few in number and faced serious opposition. Clay affirmed the right of abolitionists to protect their civil liberties when threatened. "Thanks to bowie knives and pistols," he told an audience in Iowa, "a man may speak some truth in Kentucky, if he has friends enough, and they [are] well enough armed. . . ." Claiming self-defense, he fatally stabbed one of his proslavery opponents at an election campaign meeting in Madison County, Kentucky, in 1849.[19]

Southerners like Clay lived their lives according to circumscribed, behavioral patterns of honor. Notions of honorable behavior, requiring men to challenge any affront to their character, dominated the white South. These patterns came to influence Afro-American culture as well. Despite the willingness of both blacks and whites to defend themselves, a double standard existed in which white southerners were expected to defend themselves against impudent slaves, but black southerners were forbidden to do so against sadistic masters.[20]

A few black persons slipped through this double standard of jurisprudence. One case illustrated how black folks sometimes enjoyed the same legal considerations as whites. In 1854, "J. Jack" found himself on trial for the murder of a white man, Goodwin Parker. Parker and his companions had visited Jack at night at his father's house; the two men quarreled; Parker was stabbed and killed. Jack was able to plead self-defense largely because of a gaping gash in his head "which penetrated his skull" and "appeared to have been made with a hatchet, an axe or a hammer." The deceased was found with a hatchet in his hand. Evidence of threats against the defendant were originally ruled out; however upon appeal, Judge Caton, referring to the "sacred right of self-preservation," determined that "the evidence in the case tends very strongly to show that the deceased made an assault upon the prisoner, and that the homicide was committed in necessary self-defense." Were it not for the ugly wound, Jack's plea of self-defense would likely have gone unheard.[21]

Traditionally, self-defense had been interpreted as a quintessential human right; however, by the middle of the nineteenth century, it had assumed qualities, with regard to black Americans, of not only civil rights but also civil liberties. Under common law and natural-rights theory, private citizens were always entitled to use deadly force to protect themselves; however, in the antebellum South, Afro-Americans—by law, part-persons and part-chattel—were not citizens in any sense of the word. Therefore, self-defense represented a critical missing link in establishing black citizenship: by confirming their right to self-defense, black Americans could cinch their status as human beings at the same time that they cinched their status as citizens of the United States.

To illustrate, Chief Justice Taney indicated in his opinion regarding the famous Supreme Court case *Dred Scott v. Sandford* (1857) that the Constitution did not protect the right of black Americans, slave or free, to possess firearms. According to Taney, regarding black people as American citizens would "give to persons of the negro race, who were recognized as citizens in any one State of the Union, the right to enter every other State whenever they pleased . . . and it would give them the full liberty of speech in public and in private upon all subjects upon which its own citizens might speak, to hold public meetings upon political affairs, and to keep and carry arms wherever they went."[22] Such freedoms were unthinkable to Taney and to many southerners, who proved as domineering as ever after the Civil War supposedly decided the question of slavery.

Indeed, for many former slaves, emancipation changed their lives little. A freedwoman named "Katie Darling" recalled that "missy whip me after the war jist like she did 'fore. She has a hun'erd lashes up for me now."[23] There is much evidence that white violence, both organized and individual, increased in the post-emancipation South, and the response by black folks was varied.[24] Running away became less and less viable for three major reasons. First, there was nowhere to run. With the semi-sweet successes of Reconstruction, many freedmen suspected that the North was little better than the South with regard to its racial assumptions (later, with the Great Migration of southern blacks to urban enclaves in the north, these suspicions were confirmed for many). Second, pride prohibited many freedmen from continuing to turn the other cheek. Emancipation loosed in the freed slaves a reluctance to absorb insult and marked a new behavioral dynamic between blacks and whites in America. Third, by the 1860s, people of African descent living in the newly reconstituted United States had come to see America as their home. The transition from African to Afro-American was long since complete, and black Americans yearned to reap the benefits of the war fought, in large part, over, for, and by them. While they continued to look to Africa as a place of spiritual sustenance, the reality of relocation became less and less attractive with time. Indeed, serious attempts at colonization and repatriation died with the end of the Civil War. Only Marcus Garvey's "Back to Africa" movement stirred a brief flurry of interest in the 1920s, but even then the idea of Afro-Americans' returning to their mother country seemed fanciful to most blacks and whites alike.

Southern state legislatures passed measures following the Civil War aimed at disarming the newly freed slaves. These measures were part of a larger body of legislation in 1865 and 1866 known as the "Black Codes." These codes aimed to reduce freedmen to the former conditions of slavery. Defenders of these codes argued that they were designed for the protection of the Negroes, to instill in them a sense of responsibility which they, as slaves, did not have. Critics charged that it was a deliberate attempt to perpetuate slavery.[25]

Mississippi provides a typical example of restrictions of this kind. The Mississippi state constitution provided that "[e]very citizen has a right to bear arms, in defence of himself and the State." After the Civil War, however, the Mississippi state legislature enacted a statute "that no freedman, free negro or mulatto . . . not licensed so to do so by the board of police of his or her county, shall keep or carry firearms of any kind."[26] In Florida, "bowie-knives" and "dirks" were prohibited (on penalty of forfeiture of the weapon plus a whipping or the pillory or both); the equivalent statute in South Carolina specifically targeted military weaponry ("pistols" and "muskets"), rather than shotguns or rifles used for hunting.[27] To enforce such measures, bands of armed whites traversed the countryside and forcibly robbed freedmen of their arms. By insuring citizenship rights for freedmen, the Fourteenth Amendment aimed, in part, to stop such outrages; in fact, such provisions in Mississippi's Black Codes were cited in the Thirty-nineth Congress in support of the need for the Civil Rights Act of 1866 and the Fourteenth Amendment.[28]

In these congressional debates, the right to self-defense, universally understood to be protected by commonlaw, was seen less as a human right than a civil one; that is, the right to bear arms became, during the debates, a function of one's citizenship. For example, Representative Henry J. Raymond, a Republican from New York, explained: "Make the colored man a citizen of the United States and he has every right which you or I have as citizens of the United States under the laws and constitution of the United States. . . . He has a defined *status*; he has a country and a home; a right to defend himself and his wife and children; a right to bear arms. . . ."[29] Such rationale reiterated the relationship of civil rights, race, and guns. If blacks were citizens, then they were Americans. If they were Americans, then they could own firearms as white folks could. If Raymond were correct, then it meant a veritable army of legally armed black citizens in the midst of white southerners still haunted by the slave uprisings of yesteryear. Many white folks blanched at the mere thought of such a scenario. Raymond's message was clear: it would behoove white people to oppose diligently any moves toward black citizenship.

What Raymond forecast was anathema to many legislators who, fearing an armed black populace, attempted to align skin color with citizenship. For example, Senator Thomas A. Hendricks, a Democrat from Indiana, opposed the amendment precisely because "if this amendment be adopted we will then carry the title [of citizenship] and enjoy its privileges in common with the negroes, the coolies, and the Indians."[30] It was not a great leap from this interpretation of the Fourteenth Amendment to the notion of the United States as a "white man's country," an assumption underlying most of the arguments of white supremacists at that time.

Southern critics of the Fourteenth Amendment did not claim that its wording was unclear; rather, they objected to its "breadth" in "conferring on the Negro the kind of rights to be found in the first eight amendments," in addition to the right to vote.[31] Simply put, many legislators, southern and northern alike, feared Negroes with guns.[32] Opponents to the amendment objected on the basis that preexisting legislation already guaranteed blacks the rights of citizenship, excepting suffrage; regardless, the southern states were compelled to ratify it as a condition for reentering the Union.

The Fourteenth Amendment served a dual purpose with regard to bearing arms. First, it affirmed the personal right of the freedmen to own firearms. The right to keep and bear arms was interpreted as a basic right of citizenship upon which no state could infringe. In this way, as some constitutional scholars have noted, the Fourteenth Amendment incorporated the Second Amendment.[33] Second, it thwarted the attempt of the defeated southern states to maintain militias. By defining the Fourteenth Amendment in terms of *individual* (not state) rights, its framers checked the powers of states'-rights advocates.[34]

No sooner had the Fourteenth Amendment become law than forces in the South began its methodical undoing. In the 1870s, white southern nationalists, or "Redeemers," clung to the mythologized glory of the Old South and labored to replicate the freedman's former state of servitude. A new wave of violence swept the South. Part of that violence involved the disarming of black citizens by nightriders.[35]

The most notorious example of this vigilantism resulted in *United States v. Cruikshank* (1876), a Supreme Court case involving a mob of whites who had broken up a freedmen's political meeting, disarmed them, prevented them from voting in a state election, and murdered fifty-nine of them in what became known as the Colfax Massacre. The *Cruikshank* decision, completely subverting the Fourteenth Amendment and the Enforcement Act of 1870, overturned the conviction of the white transgressors in federal courts and held that the Bill of Rights was not incorporated by the Fourteenth Amendment, except as such rights related to the national government. It marked an enormous setback for black civil rights.[36]

The era immediately following Reconstruction gave rise to the laws of segregation, known as the "jim crow" system; it remains the most intense period of interracial violence in American history, characterized by lynching and terrorism by the Ku Klux Klan.[37] Practically all outspoken Afro-American leaders during this period advocated self-defense on some level. T. Thomas Fortune, the preeminent Afro-American editor of the early twentieth century, urged black citizens to use physical force to defend themselves and retaliate for outrages. In an early editorial in the *Boston Globe*, he warned that if Negroes became convinced that neither state nor federal government would protect them, they would "show the very same disposition to fight for their rights as any other people." He felt black men tended to be too servile and docile. "We do not counsel violence," he said, "we counsel manly retaliation. We do not counsel a breach of the law, but in the absence of law . . . we maintain that every individual has every right . . . to protect himself." Sometimes it might be necessary to use force "to assert their manhood and citizenship."[38]

Similarly, Ida B. Wells-Barnett, whose anti-lynching campaign stemmed from the deaths of three of her friends in Memphis, advised in *Southern Horrors and Other Writings* (1892) "a Winchester rifle should have a place of honor in every black home. . . . [I]t should be used for that protection which the law refuses to give. When the white man who is always the aggressor knows he runs as great risk of biting the dust every time his Afro-American friend does, he will have greater respect for Afro-American life.[39]" Her first action after the Memphis lynchings was to arm herself. "I had bought a pistol the first thing after Tom Moss was lynched, because I expected some cowardly retaliation from the lynchers," she recalled in her autobiography. She felt that she had better "die fighting against injustice" than to "die like a dog or a rat in a trap." She had already determined "to sell my life as dearly as possible" if attacked. She felt it would "even up the score a bit" if she could take one lyncher with her. "The more the Afro-American yields and cringes and begs," she maintained, "the more he has to do so, the more he is insulted, outraged and lynched."[40]

In 1889, John E. Bruce, a prominent black journalist, articulated the need for self-defense. He wrote:

Under the present condition of affairs the only hope, the only salvation for the Negro is to be found in a resort to force under wise and discreet leaders. . . . The Negro must not be rash and indiscreet either in action or in words but he must be very determined and terribly earnest, and of one mind to bring order out of chaos and to convince southern rowdies and cutthroats that more than two can play at the game with which they have amused their fellow conspirators in crime for nearly a quarter of a century.[41]

That same year, Buddie Shang, an elderly black man and former slave belonging to John Randolph, was walking along a canal embankment in Lacyburg, Virginia, when he became involved in an altercation with another man. Whether by accident or intent, the shotgun he was carrying discharged; the load of shot missed his foe and blasted through the shack of a white man, Lewis Nichols. Enraged, Nichols emerged from his shack and began to throw bricks at Shang, who fired again, killing Nichols. Shang was arrested, tried for murder, and acquitted by an all-white jury on the basis of self-defense; it took the jury only three minutes to acquit. In 1912, Shang died peacefully at the age of ninety-seven in Lacyburg. Perhaps because of his ties to Randolph, a prominent Virginian, or perhaps because he was well-liked as a local shoeshine man, Buddie Shang got away with killing a white man in self-defense. Clearly, fame or fortune or a combination of both sometimes played a role in whether or not a black person could legally claim self-defense. In 1891, two years after Buddie Shang's trial, Moses Fleetwood Walker, a black baseball player retired from the Negro League, was assaulted while walking home from church on a Sunday afternoon. He killed his attacker with a knife in self-defense. To the cheers of fans present at the trial, a jury acquitted him, too.[42]

That black people owned guns in the South in the late nineteenth and early twentieth century is readily apparent.[43] What happened when they used them to protect themselves is less clear. Some scholars have speculated that lynching itself rose to such a fever pitch during this period precisely because a new generation of black Americans who had not known the deference required of slavery had come of age. They have argued that an increasing willingness among blacks to resist mob action in the 1890s increased the cost of lynching to whites and thereby reduced its frequency. Others have noted that the relatively frequent occurrence of black resistance coincided with the end of the lynching era, perhaps signifying a deterrence factor. In some instances, resistance dissuaded southern mob violence. Sheriffs willing to use their side arms to protect their black prisoners foiled more than one lynching.[44]

Two dramatic examples in Georgia in 1899 punctuated the need for self-defense. The first illustrates how armed resistance could be successful. A white woman named Matilda Hope gave birth to a mulatto child in McIntosh County, Georgia, in 1899. She claimed to have been raped by her black neighbor Henry Delegale. Without hesitation, Delegale surrendered to the sheriff after being accused, preferring custody to a possible lynching. The following morning the sheriff decided to relocate Delegale from Darien to Savannah, "for safekeeping." Sensing imminent disaster, the local black community protested, rallying to keep Delegale in Darien. The sheriff asked Georgia Governor Allen Candler to intervene by providing troops to quell the black "insurrection." The state militia arrived and escorted Delegale to Savannah; he was later found not guilty of the accused rape and released. The incident became known as the Darien Insurrection of 1899.[45]

But the Darien Insurrection represented the exception, not the norm. The second example from Georgia in 1899, the Sam Hose lynching, typified the savage and extralegal response black persons living in the South could expect when accused of wrongdoing. White citizens attacked, lynched, burned, dismembered, and otherwise violated a black man wrongly accused of rape. Sam Hose came to symbolize the bestial ferocity of southern chivalry run amuck.[46] The lynching of Sam Hose so outraged one black man, Robert Charles, that he exacted his own revenge in New Orleans the following year. An altercation with one police officer turned into an armed rampage in which Charles killed seven white people (four of them police officers) and wounded twenty others with his Winchester rifle. His actions, in turn, prompted a serious race riot in which at least a dozen black people were killed and dozens more injured. Robert Charles was eventually shot down by a mob of armed white men, buried in an unmarked grave, and dismissed as a "crazy nigger."[47]

A vexing case in 1904 illustrated how questions of race often automatically trumped the facts in any altercation between blacks and whites. As Roy Martin and other white teammates from Kansas City High School practiced outside at Kerr Park, a group of black boys, including Louis Gregory, cut across the ball field on their way to plink cans and shoot "varmints" at the creek just beyond the park. An altercation ensued; within minutes, Martin lay dead, and Gregory was jailed as his killer. Louis, who was crippled, allegedly fired at Martin in self-defense; however, the *Kansas City Star* ran a different story, painting the black boys as the aggressors. The following day eighty or so black students found their entrance to the high school blocked by approximately seven hundred white students. The school was closed, the students were sent home. That evening, a group of black citizens armed with Winchester rifles and revolvers surrounded the jail where Gregory was being held. The *Star* reported the incident as a race riot. At his trial, Gregory pleaded self-defense; however, he was found guilty of first-degree murder and sentenced to life in prison. It is still unclear exactly what happened at the park.[48]

The Darien Insurrection, the Sam Hose lynching, and the jailing of

Louis Gregory again prompted black intellectuals to consider seriously the implications of self-defense. The year after Gregory's trial, W. E. B. DuBois and fellow black intellectuals launched the Niagara Movement, advocating agitation rather than accommodation. Soon after, in 1909, DuBois and other black and white Progressives (turn-of-the-century reformers) organized the National Association for the Advancement of Colored People (NAACP), which began its fight for justice in the courts. The NAACP's first legal battle was a self-defense trial: the Pink Franklin case. Franklin, a black farmhand, had been awoken at 3:00 A.M. by an apparent intruder; Franklin killed the intruder. The intruder turned out to be a police officer serving a warrant for a civil charge. Franklin's plea of self-defense was disavowed, and the NAACP took the case all the way to the Supreme Court, which ruled against Franklin. Joel Spingarn (after whom the NAACP's Spingarn Medal is named) vowed, along with his brother Arthur, to fight similar cases as they arose, and the NAACP continued to lobby for the legal claim of Afro-Americans to self-defense.

In the wake of the Pink Franklin case, black leaders continued to advocate self-defense. As editor of the *Crisis*, the NAACP's publication, W. E. B. DuBois published at least two images of resistance, each a cartoon illustrating blacks defending themselves. The first, entitled "Woman to the Rescue" and published in 1919, depicts a mother swinging a club labeled "Federal Constitution" at Gorgon-like vultures labeled "GRANDFATHER CLAUSE," "JIM CROW LAW," and "SEGREGATION." The second, entitled "For the Children!" and published in 1934, depicts hooded Klansmen peeking over a hill. The Klansmen carry flags labeled "LYNCHING," "PEONAGE," and "SEGREGATION." Striding toward the hill is a determined black sharecropper, gripping a rifle in one hand and pulling his son along with the other.[49] These images, cloaked in allegory, conveyed DuBois's own intellectual gravitation toward forceful resistance, but his commitment was more than rhetorical. In 1916, during the Atlanta riot, DuBois rushed home to guard his house and protect his family: he did so by keeping watch on the porch with a rifle across his lap.

Following the Chicago race riot of 1919, DuBois offered his most adamant call for self-defense in a mildly entitled essay, "Let Us Reason Together," published in the *Crisis*. The editorial argued in favor of self-defense and armed resistance as whites, fearful of competition for jobs and housing, lashed out at black citizens enjoying a cultural renaissance in America's cities after World War I.

Today we raise the terrible weapon of Self-Defense. When the murderer comes, he shall no longer strike us in the back. When the armed lynchers gather, we too must gather armed. When the mob moves, we propose to meet it with bricks and clubs and guns. But we must tread here with solemn caution. We must never let justifiable self-defense against individuals become blind and lawless offense against all white folk. We must not seek reform by violence. We must not seek Vengeance. "Vengeance is Mine," saith the Lord. . . . We must defend ourselves, our homes, our wives, and children against the lawless without stint or hesitation, but we must carefully and scrupulously avoid on our own part bitter and unjustifiable aggression against anybody.

DuBois noted that the line between "just resistance" and "angry retaliation" was slim, but "grim and sober consideration" would enable democratic justice to prevail. He concluded by declaring, "If the United States is to be a Land of Law, we would live humbly and peaceably in it—working, singing, learning, and dreaming to make it and ourselves nobler and better; if it is to be a Land of Mobs and Lynchers, we might as well die tomorrow."[50] As DuBois called for self-defense in prose, a poet eloquently and powerfully called for it in verse; the two writers articulated the same sentiment. Published in 1919, "If We Must Die" by Claude McKay equated assertion of self with martyrdom and elevated them both in the name of uplifting the race. The poem concludes:

Though far outnumbered let us show us brave,
And for their thousand blows deal one death-blow!
What though before us lies the open grave?
Like men we'll face the murderous, cowardly pack,
Pressed to the wall, dying, but fighting back![51]

McKay remembered the days following World War I when he wrote the poem not with a smile but with a shudder. "We did not separate from one another gaily to spend ourselves in speakeasies and gambling joints," he recalled, "We stuck together, some of us armed, going from railroad station to our quarters. . . . We stayed in our quarters all through the dreary ominous nights, for we never knew what was going to happen."[52]

Self-defense had a place in popular music as well. The ballad "Frankie and Johnnie," popular in the late nineteenth and early twentieth centuries, immortalized one famous self-defense case involving the revenge of a black woman seeking retribution against her two-timing lover. The folksong was based on an actual murder, reported in the *St. Louis Post-Dispatch* on October 20, 1899. Twenty-two-year-old Frankie Baker, "an ebony-hued cake-walker" shot "Johnnie" Albert Britt on Targee Street in St. Louis on October 15, 1899. Released by the authorities, Baker claimed that she had used self-defense in fending off a knife attack. The many renditions of the popular ballad, portrayed in song, art, and film, confirmed its status as a bawdy classic in American folk culture during the first years of the twentieth century.[53] During these same years, famed bluesman Huddie Ledbetter, better known as "Leadbelly," killed a man in a fight over a woman. Like an Old-West gunslinger, he reportedly did not draw his pistol in an altercation in 1917 until his black adversary had already drawn his own gun. Leadbelly claimed self-defense, but after languishing in jail for months, he pled guilty to one count of murder and one count of assault to murder. The judge sentenced him to thirty years of hard labor; had the blues singer killed a white man, he probably would have been executed. The event contributed to Leadbelly's mystique, and secured his place as a legend in blues music.[54]

Organized religion also condoned resorting to arms for self-defense, as did black print media. Bishop John Hurst maintained that black people should practice Christian virtues. "If while exercising these virtues, however," he warned, "his assailants . . . persist in molesting him, let him do what self-respecting people should do—namely use his gun with effect and impose respect." Newspapers such as the New York *Commoner* similarly advised: "Let every Negro arm himself, and swear to die fighting in defense of his home, his rights, and his person."[55]

Overtures of self-defense, more often than not, backfired and intensified violence. For example, on May 21, 1921, a young shoe shiner, Dick Rowland, was arrested after being accused of accosting a woman in an elevator shaft in downtown Tulsa. The following day the *Tulsa Tribune* ran an editorial suggestively entitled, "To Lynch a Negro Tonight." A white mob gathered outside the jail in an attempt to lynch Rowland. A group of fifty to seventy-five armed black men, dressed in their World War I Army fatigues, confronted the racists, but they were overwhelmed. For the next several days, gangs of armed whites went into the predominately Afro-American Greenwood section of town, where they burned houses and black-owned businesses and shot hapless bystanders; a private plane circled overhead, bombing the neighborhood with dynamite. Scores of black people died.[56]

Following a similar incident in Rosewood, Florida, in early January, 1923, a posse of Klan members using bloodhounds tracked down Sam Carter, an alleged accomplice in an alleged rape by a man named Jesse Hunter. The mob shot Carter after extracting a confession. Angry black neighbors armed themselves and fought the Klan; three whites and two blacks died in the ensuing melee. Twenty-five black combatants barricaded themselves in a house, where they staved off attack. Four more died (and more might have had the Klan not run out of ammunition), including Sylvester Carrier and his mother, Sarah. According to a newspaper account, one more member of the Carrier family died on Saturday, January 26, when the mob dragged James Carrier to the graveyard, "made him stand on the newly dug graves of his brother and mother . . . while they riddled his body with shots." Fearing further reprisals, black citizens of Rosewood hid in the nearby swamps as the mob, still unsatisfied, burned almost the entire town to the ground.[57]

What happened in Rosewood was a riot. "Race riots" in the nineteenth and early twentieth centuries were fundamentally different from those of the late twentieth century. One hundred years ago, a race riot meant whites wantonly killing and destroying property in a local black community, rather than a frustrated uprising by black persons themselves. Many riots followed a similar pattern, as DuBois explained in an editorial for the *New York World* in 1919. Since the days of slavery, whites had customarily regarded large congregations of blacks with suspicion, and they took proactive steps to break up such "meetings." "Somebody goes and shoots at the Negroes secretly," DuBois wrote, "and at the slightest sign of resistance the whole organization of the black belt is called into being." This organization consisted of "all the law officers of the county and all the white men near and in neighboring counties and states, armed to the teeth." In one such incident, sharecroppers who had gathered in Hoop Spur, Arkansas, to discuss how to market their cotton were attacked without provocation. They returned the fire of their white attackers and killed one of them. The incident escalated until over sixty black persons had been killed, one thousand arrested, one hundred twenty-three indicted; of these, twelve were sentenced to death and fifty-four to terms of imprisonment in the penitentiary.[58]

The Rosewood and Hoop Spur incidents symbolized the back-biting, double-edged nature of armed self-defense in Afro-American history: it was a necessity, but also something to be avoided. Self-preservation dictated that one fight back, but it also dictated that one avoid annihilation. Throughout this period, southern laws, customs, and morés ensured neither police protection nor assurance of pardon for a black person faced with the dilemma of defending himself or herself against violent attack. Self-defense could bring down the white power structure, including the full weight of the judicial and legal systems, upon a person's head, as well as set into motion the extralegal mechanisms of repression such as mob vigilantism and lynching. The possibility of retribution pertained not only to the person defending himself but also to that person's household and community. But for many, the honor and self-esteem gained in self-defense counterbalanced these risks.

It is important to note that, in the 1920s, the largest mass-movement of black people in history endorsed armed self-defense and, in fact, created a quasi-military organization. The United Negro Improvement Association (UNIA), under the leadership of the black nationalist, Marcus Garvey, embraced military discipline embodied by uniformed men on horseback called the Universal African Legion. With several hundred chapters in the South in the 1920s, the UNIA popularized the notion of self-defense by black Americans, and in doing so may have inadvertently helped the NAACP in its legal battles in support of black self-defense.[59]

For example, in 1925, one couple, aided by the nation's best-known and most successful trial lawyer, took a stand and beat the odds. Thinking Detroit would be a good place to raise their one-year-old daughter, Dr. Ossian Sweet and his wife Gladys moved into a two-story house in a white neighborhood on Detroit's eastside in June 1925. That night, a crowd of angry whites gathered outside their new home to "welcome" them to the neighborhood; the following night a larger crowd appeared, throwing rocks through the windows. Fearing for their lives, the Sweets fired through the open windows; the fusillade killed one man, Leon Breiner, and wounded another. Dr. Sweet; his two brothers, Otis and Henry; Gladys; and seven friends were arrested and charged with conspiracy to commit murder in the first degree. The NAACP, continuing its crusade to make black self-defense legitimate, hired Clarence Darrow, who had recently finished the biggest case of his career, the Scopes trial in Tennessee. The prosecution argued to the all-white jury that the Sweets fired the shot that killed Breiner; the defense responded that it remained unclear who killed Breiner, and even if they had, it was nevertheless self-defense. The fair-minded judge and the eloquent defense attorney counterbalanced the racial hysteria that surrounded the case: the first trial ended in a hung jury and a second jury—also all-white—took less than four hours to deliver a "not guilty" verdict. It was a landmark ruling.[60] The NAACP, aided by the Communist Party, USA, continued to defend self-defense throughout the 1930s.

In the early years of World War II, wild rumors of armed insurrection and domestic insurgency circulated through white southern communities. For example, white southerners told one another that Afro-Americans in Charleston, South Carolina, were hoarding ice picks; whether the ice picks were to be used for self-protection or mass murder was equally unnerving to whites who believed the report. In Memphis, Tennessee, local black citizens were allegedly ordering cartons of pistols and rifles from the Sears and Roebuck Company catalog. Black farmers were supposedly practicing paramilitary drills outside of New Orleans. Black women, working as domestic servants, were said to be joining "Eleanor Clubs" in which they diabolically plotted subterfuge within the very homes of their white employers; the clubs were named after Eleanor Roosevelt, the liberal wife of President Franklin Delano Roosevelt. Shrouded in half-truths and hearsay, the rumors likely stemmed from a fear that newly empowered Afro-Americans would no longer stay in their place. The black populace had begun to stir in the early 1940s, as blacks served in the armed forces, gained greater economic power, and enjoyed higher standards of living. As the war broke out, black Americans rallied to the motto "Double V"—victory against fascism abroad, and victory against jim crow at home—and began to demand equal treatment, integration of the armed services, fair wages, and the right to vote. This new militancy alarmed white southerners, who curiously responded by passing along whispers of black mutiny. The rumors pointed not only to the irrational fears of white southerners but also to a new awareness among whites that black southerners could and would defend themselves; they may also have stemmed from the very real preparations by a few black southerners to strike a blow for racial justice.[61]

In the 1940s, the Communist Party aided Afro-Americans through the Civil Rights Congress (CRC), a left-wing legal defense organization founded in 1946. Led by William L. Patterson, the CRC gained notoriety for its legal defense of wrongly accused black citizens, its support of Communists accused of "un-American" activities, and its petition of the United

Nations that charged the United States with a campaign of genocide against its own black citizens. The CRC came into existence following a dramatic armed confrontation between black and white Tennesseeans. On February 25, 1946, armed black citizens in Columbia, Tennessee, prevented the lynching of James Stephenson, a nineteen-year-old black Navy veteran involved in a round of fisticuffs with a white repairman at a local appliance store. That night, after Stephenson had fled for the safety of Chicago, black residents of "The Bottom" shot and wounded four police officers when the officers tried to enter this predominately black section of town. The following morning, the Tennessee Highway Patrol stormed the district, wrecking various establishments and beating whomever they found. By the end of the day, more than one hundred black persons, mostly men, had been jailed; two days later, highway patrolmen killed two of the detainees at the jail cell. The NAACP and the Communist Party rallied to the defense of those involved.[62]

One of the CRC's most publicized trials was a high-profile case in 1947 that definitively illustrated the dilemma of self-defense by black Americans. Rosa Lee Ingram, a Georgia tenant farmer and widowed mother of eleven children, was convicted and sentenced to death, along with two of her sons, for the murder of a neighboring white tenant farmer, John Stratford. The white farmer allegedly initiated the altercation on Ingram's property in November 1947 by striking her with the butt of a rifle; he may also have sexually harassed her. Ingram's son intervened, wrested the gun from Stratford, and struck a blow to his head that proved to be fatal. Black citizens, white liberals, and white radicals rallied to the aid of Ingram and her sons, whose plight was publicized by the black press and Communist newspapers, but a speedy and questionable trial resulted in their conviction. The prosecution's pursuit of the death penalty in what seemed a clear-cut case of self-defense seemed particularly galling, as did the conviction of all three defendants when the responsibility for Stratford's death lay with only one of Ingram's sons. The case spawned a number of radical women's organizations linked to the CRC campaign; these organizations—including the Sojourners for Truth and Justice, initiated by Charlotta Bass, Shirley Graham DuBois, Louise Thompson Patterson, Alice Childress, and Rosalie McGee—were founded mostly by black women with ties to the Communist Party. Woody Guthrie, the legendary folksinger, lamented the miscarriage of justice in his song "The Ballad of Rosa Lee Ingram." In September 1959, Ingram and her sons were freed after spending eleven years in a Georgia prison.[63]

Afro-American history is replete with examples of people who talked self-defense and people who lived it. There was a profound difference between those who spoke rhetorically about the virtues of self-defense, and those who could and did act on it—often only once. Clearly, black persons living in the southern United States lived in an extraordinarily hostile environment, a violent world in which a weapon could mean the difference between life and death. By the middle of the twentieth century, many had come to believe, no doubt correctly, that their ability to survive in such an environment depended critically on being adequately armed.

On the verge of the civil rights era, self-defense remained not only a key link between civil rights, human rights, and citizenship but also a major theme in Afro-American history. It was foremost in the minds of black leaders in the eighteenth, nineteenth, and early twentieth centuries, and it represented an everyday reality for many working-class and middle-class black folks. Among white Americans it was a notorious practice, symbolic of black intractability; among black Americans, the same notoriety made it talismanic, highly regarded in folk culture and legend. Self-defense would become a critical issue in the civil rights movement, given forward momentum by two seminal events in the years 1954 and 1955: the Supreme Court's *Brown v. Board of Education* decision and the murder of Emmett Till.

On May 17, 1954, Chief Justice Earl Warren delivered the Court's unanimous decision regarding segregated schools in Topeka, Kansas. In a statement that stands as one of the court's and the nation's legal landmarks, Warren wrote: "We conclude that in the field of public education the doctrine of 'separate but equal' has no place." The *Brown* decision overturned *Plessy v. Ferguson* (1896), which had sanctioned jim crow segregation and defined southern race relations for half a century.

After *Brown*, white southerners ensconced themselves behind the ramparts of delay and "massive resistance" to desegregation; they were aided by the inertia of the federal government and abetted by the deliberate defiance of southern state governments. White supremacists organized resistance groups such as White Citizens Councils, and the Ku Klux Klan itself rejuvenated and thrived during this period. Lynching, which had been on the decline, returned to the South. There were three such incidents in 1955, all in Mississippi. The Reverend George W. Lee was lynched after he led a voter registration campaign in Belzoni; Lamar Smith was murdered at

Brookhaven; and Emmett Till, a fourteen-year-old from Chicago who was visiting relatives in Leflore County in August, was beaten, mutilated, and shot after he was accused of whistling at a white woman. The viciousness of the Till lynching moved the public, both black and white. For many people who read about the crime in the Afro-American press and saw photos of Till's open-casket funeral in Chicago, Emmett Till's murder became a catalyst for involvement in the civil rights movement.

White resistance following the *Brown* decision and the accompanying increase in interpersonal violence toward black folks testified to the need for Afro-Americans to rely upon their own ingenuity, assertiveness, determination, and, if necessary, force in securing their own personal safety and well-being. When Martin Luther King moved to Montgomery to assume the pastorship of the Dexter Avenue Baptist Church, self-defense was a well-established tradition in Afro-American history. While he did not anticipate how immediate his need for self-protection would become, the young minister, like other black men of his generation, did not question his right to protect himself and his family against aggression from any quarter. For King, as for other black southerners, nonviolence was antithetical to lived experience.

You have heard that it was said, "An eye for an eye and a tooth for a tooth."

But I say to you, do not resist one who is evil. But if anyone strikes you on the right

cheek, turn to him the other also.

MATTHEW 5: 38–39

CHAPTER 2

THE OTHER CHEEK

The Possibilities of Nonviolence, 1955–1956

During the Montgomery Bus Boycott, Martin Luther King Jr. educated himself about nonviolent direct action and began to transform it into a transcendent response to white supremacy. He did not automatically forgo the tried-and-true practice of self-defense, but instead wrestled with the applications of applied nonviolence as an appropriately Christian approach to social and political change.

On March 2, 1955, a fifteen-year-old girl named Claudette Colvin was arrested for refusing to give up her seat on a Montgomery city bus to a white person. Virginia Durr, whose husband, Clifford, provided legal counsel for Colvin, described what happened in a letter to her friend Clark Foreman:

She was crying all the time, and the policeman hit her with a billy club on her rump and when they got her to the jail the chief or the presiding policeman said all she needed was a good "whupping" but they didn't give it to her. I asked what made her stand her ground and she said "I done paid my dime, they didn't have no RIGHT to move me." Isn't that thrilling to think that one little fifteen year old girl could have the courage to stand up to all that?[1]

Fearful that the constitutionality of Colvin's appeal might be sustained, authorities eventually dropped the charges of violating the city's segregation laws and found her guilty of assault and battery against the four men who dragged her off the bus. Durr reported, "This has created tremendous interest in the Negro community and made them all fighting mad and may help give them the courage to put up a real fight on the bus segregation issue."[2] In a similar incident that same spring in Montgomery, fourteen-year-old Mary Louise Smith was arrested for refusing to abdicate her bus seat, and the local chapter of the National Association for the Advancement of Colored People (NAACP) sought to make a test case of the incident. However, Smith became pregnant and her mother, fearing damage to the young girl's reputation when the case went to court, encouraged her to drop the case.

Local black leaders in Montgomery continued to search for the ideal test case with which to challenge the city's jim crow bus laws, and Rosa Parks provided the opportunity for which they had been looking. On the evening of Thursday, December 1, 1955, Parks paid her usual fare at the front of the bus, boarded at the "black entrance" at the rear, and took a seat near the middle, in the "no-man's land" between the black and white sections. At a later stop, when the driver picked up several white passengers, he ordered the black riders to vacate their seats and move to the back of the bus. Parks refused. Police arrested her for violating the city's public transportation laws. And, as the story goes, in doing so a tired black seamstress started a revolution.

Legend inaccurately characterizes Rosa Parks as an automaton, pushed by weariness to challenge the bus driver's abuse (when asked why she did it, she reportedly replied that her feet hurt); actually, as a Highlander Folk School participant and NAACP administrator, she had not only a consciousness of the larger struggle for black equality but also a history of social activism. In fact, Parks had been active in the Claudette Colvin case. Black community leaders rallied behind Parks to show their support for her decision not to yield to the bus company's segregation regulations. As they probed various means of mounting a protest, violent tendencies swelled and threatened to explode. Rumors circulated that local black folks were threatening to "beat the hell out of a few bus drivers" and preparing for a fight; some expressed an urge to "give as good as we get."[3] Black community leaders such as E. D. Nixon, founder of the Montgomery branch of the NAACP, and Jo Ann Robinson, a stalwart of the Women's Political Council, realized that they had to act quickly and proactively to capitalize on the situation and to prevent bloodshed. They agreed to endorse a boycott on Monday, December 5, 1955. Although the original intent was that local black residents would decline to ride the city's buses for one day, this action grew into a nonviolent protest that lasted more than a year. In the space of a weekend, Parks, already a respected figure within the black community of Montgomery, became a symbol of the years of injustice and indignity black people had suffered there, and her friends and neighbors rallied to her cause.

Like an insect trapped in amber, Montgomery was a place entombed by its past. Known as the "Cradle of the Confederacy," it was the capital of Alabama and, on February 4, 1861, the birthplace of the Confederate States of America. The city boasted not only a large livestock market but also diversified industry, which developed after the Civil War. It also served as the marketing center for the region's fertile, black-soil farms. But one-crop farming and sharecropping had brought poverty to Montgomery and its environs in the first half of the twentieth century. The city had done its best to survive the triple ravages of the Civil War, Reconstruction, and the indomitable boll weevil, and its people remembered each vividly.

White Montgomerians, like other white southerners, generally took pride in their city's heritage and distrusted change. For black residents to challenge segregation was neither easy nor without risk. Black community leaders steered Martin Luther King Jr., the new pastor of the Dexter Avenue Baptist Church and a freshly minted Ph.D. student from Boston University, into the boycott's vacant generalship as director of the Montgomery Improvement Association (MIA), an organizing committee created to facilitate the boycott. They knew the hazards involved in overturning the status quo in Montgomery, not the least of which was incurring the wrath of the Ku Klux Klan. The black community needed someone to take the heat:

a bellwether for their cause. King, one of many people in the assemblage who would make the boycott succeed, met their needs. As a student leader and promising young scholar, he had already demonstrated considerable charisma. He had the least to lose in relation to the established, local black leadership; he was, in a political sense, expendable. He was noncontroversial because he was untouched by any political or ministerial factions within the black community. Moreover, he was an excellent public speaker. He seemed like a natural choice to lead the boycott.

Understandably apprehensive about his leadership role, King moved cautiously. Fresh from graduate school and unsure of his abilities in the real world, he did not want to jeopardize his standing with his new congregation, an atypical assemblage of professionals and faculty members from Alabama State College who suited King's needs for intellectual development and propriety. Yearning for direction, he leaned heavily on his father, Martin Luther King Sr., for advice and guidance, as he always had when faced with difficulty. A product of a privileged, middle-class upbringing, King believed, like his father, that moderate politics was the best path for Negro advancement.[4] But in taking the helm of the MIA, he took the first step in what proved to be a distinguished career in radical politics.

King did not employ nonviolent direct action in the early stages of the civil rights movement as a matter of protocol; he adopted it as a strategy of protest after reflection and deliberation. Understanding how King came to embrace nonviolence is essential to understanding the civil rights movement, which would rely heavily on nonviolent protest for its successes. King's path to nonviolence is also essential to understanding the complex role self-defense played in this struggle.

Mapping King's ontology is not a simple task. His philosophy of nonviolence synthesized the teachings of Jesus Christ and Mahatma Gandhi, but King never had the opportunity in his short life to detail his own ideas in a rigorous or systematic way. Thus, theologians and historians face the rather difficult challenge of piecing together how King understood nonviolence, and Montgomery provides a logical place to start.[5]

With much personal hardship to local black citizens, the bus boycott dragged on. After the first few mass meetings, King's friends and peers, mostly Dexter members, decided it was too dangerous to let him drive around town by himself. Recognizing the threat of white retribution, they offered to escort him to and from meetings. They organized into a corps of drivers and bodyguards, using what weapons they had; for example, the Reverend Richmond Smiley toted his tiny .25-caliber Beretta.[6]

As the activists worked out a strategy for the boycott, outside forces complicated matters. On the evening of January 30, 1956, dynamite rocked King's home. An angry crowd gathered at the scene. One man challenged a policeman who attempted to push him aside: "I ain't gonna move nowhere. That's the trouble now; you white folks is always pushin' us around. Now you got your .38 and I got mine; so let's battle it out."[7] King intervened, speaking to the crowd:

> I want you to go home and put down your weapons. We cannot solve this problem through retaliatory violence. . . . We must love our white brothers, no matter what they do to us. We must make them know that we love them. Jesus still cries out across the centuries, "Love your enemies." This is what we must live by. We must meet hate with love.[8]

But while King defused the volatile situation with a message of peace, he prepared for war. Armed sentinels guarded the parsonage at night as repair work got underway. One of King's friends from college offered to guard him personally with a shotgun. King and the Reverend Ralph David Abernathy, minister of the First Baptist Church, decided to carry sidearms. "We felt we ought to be ready," Abernathy later recalled. "I asked King if he had any means of protection for him and his family. He said the only weapon he had was a butcher knife. He asked, 'What do you have?' I said, 'The only thing I have is a razor.' We decided that we should go downtown together and buy some weapons for our protection."[9] And apparently they did. In late 1963, King would admit to having had a gun in Montgomery. "I don't know why I got it in the first place," he mused. "I sat down with Coretta one night and we talked about it. I pointed out that as a leader of a nonviolent movement, I had no right to have a gun, so I got rid of it." Despite King's insistence that he had banned firearms at the parsonage, a visitor in late February 1956 reported that King's bodyguards possessed "an arsenal."[10]

The day after the bombing, King called on Alabama governor James E. ("Big Jim") Folsom for state protection. Folsom offered to have state officers watch King's home, but King pressed further. "What we would like to have is to have you issue a permit to keep a gun in my car," he told Folsom.[11] The governor responded that he would have to speak with the sheriff about the matter. Folsom did not inform King, who had no knowledge of local gun laws, that he did not need a permit: it was perfectly legal to carry a firearm in a vehicle, so long as it was in plain view. Folsom then pigeon-holed the request, which was eventually forgotten. Accompanied by the Reverend H. H. Hubbard, King and Abernathy went to the county sheriff's office on Wednesday, February 1, 1956, to request permits to allow the night watchmen at King's home to carry guns.[12] They apparently completed the required paperwork, but authorities denied the application.[13]

That very night, a bomb exploded at E. D. Nixon's house; again, luckily no one was injured. In the aftermath of the bombings, representatives of the Fellowship of Reconciliation (FOR) rushed to Montgomery to speak with King, who found himself in need of guidance. FOR, a pacifist group founded by Quakers and Episcopalians during World War I, had followed the story from afar and sensed an opportunity to apply Gandhian strategy in Montgomery.

In early March 1956, Bayard Rustin, a FOR ambassador, and William Worthy, a black journalist, rapped on the front door of Dr. King's parsonage in Montgomery. Armed guards, protecting the home against further terror-ist attack, stood in the shadows nearby. Only a few weeks earlier, on January 30, someone had tossed a single stick of dynamite onto the King family's porch. It was now as bright as day: floodlights strung around the perimeter of the roof illuminated the yard. It was hardly a welcoming atmosphere.[14]

Rustin and Worthy had heard a lot about the young preacher, especially in regard to his dynamism, his charisma, and his presence. He had stood up to the white establishment in Montgomery, addressed impassioned crowds at local mass meetings, and successfully led a black boycott of white-owned businesses. He was, by all accounts, a special person, and they looked for-ward to meeting him.

King also anticipated the visit. Only four or five people in the United States knew—really *knew*—how to teach nonviolent direct action, and two of them were visiting his home. King was already familiar with the theory behind it; he had heard about Gandhian philosophy during his studies at Morehouse College, Crozer Theological Seminary, and Boston University. But he wanted to learn how it actually worked in practice, on the street, in everyday life. He knew he needed help in engineering the bus boycott that had paralyzed Montgomery's public transit system the past few months.

Ushered inside, Rustin took a seat on the living room sofa. Worthy sat, too, but as he lowered himself into an armchair, Rustin warned, "Watch out,

Bill! There's a gun in that chair!" Worthy asked King if he felt that firearms were compatible with a nonviolent movement. Surprised and embarrassed, King answered affirmatively, saying that he intended to harm no one unless violently attacked. The three men stayed up all night as Rustin attempted to persuade King that guns could hinder the success of their cause and that even the presence of guns ran counter to the philosophy developing behind what became the modern civil rights movement.

King defended his precaution. He was trying to practice nonviolence, he told Rustin, but he did not subscribe to the kind of pacifism championed by A. J. Muste, a labor-union organizer during the Great Depression. As a student at Crozer, King had heard Muste speak. "I was deeply moved by Dr. Muste's talk," he later wrote, "but far from convinced of the practicability of his position."[15] He had written a paper while at Crozer that challenged Muste's notions of pacifism.

Rustin, who would become King's right-hand man, was adamant. He was most bothered by King's apparent lack of philosophical commitment. Rustin's first advice to King was to get rid of the guns around his house. He also encouraged him to think of the situation in Montgomery less as a boycott and more as a protest movement, to think of the method less as passive resistance and more as nonviolence. In Rustin's mind, Montgomery held the promise of becoming an international showcase for the power of nonviolence. King was thinking in less grandiose terms; to both men, however, the boycott meant more than a choice of seats on a city bus. It symbolized a direct challenge to racial injustice in the South.

Despite his theological acumen, King apparently knew little about the practical implementation of nonviolence. "Like most people, I had heard of Gandhi," he reminisced, "but I had never studied him seriously."[16] Rev. Glenn Smiley—a white southerner, Methodist preacher, and FOR worker—remembered his first meeting with King on February 27, 1956. Arriving with an armload of books on the subject, Smiley asked King about his familiarity with nonviolent doctrine. "I said to Dr. King," he later recalled, " 'I'm assuming that you're very familiar [with] and have been greatly influenced by Mahatma Gandhi.' And he was very thoughtful, and he said, 'As a matter of fact, no. I know who the man is. I have read some statements by him, and so on, and I will have to truthfully say'—and this is almost a direct quote—'I will have to say that I know very little about the man.' "[17] King wondered whether Gandhi's methods could be transposed to the American

South. Smiley inundated him with books such as Richard Gregg's *Power of Nonviolence* (1938) to show that they could be.[18]

The Power of Nonviolence used a clever metaphor to explain nonviolence. Gregg, who had studied Gandhi's methods while living in the Mahatma's ashram in India, conceived of nonviolence as "a sort of moral jiujitsu." Jiujitsu is an Eastern martial art that relies on throwing an opponent off balance. As an unexpected reaction to attack, nonviolence, like jiujitsu, would cause an opponent to falter. The person attacked would then control the situation as the assailant was "thrown" into a reassessment of his values and moral assumptions.[19]

Smiley saw King as a skeptical initiate of nonviolence. Writing to colleagues in the Fellowship of Reconciliation soon after his arrival in Montgomery, he told them that King

> wants to do right, but is too young and some of his close help is violent. King accepts, as an example, a body guard, and asked for [a] permit for them to carry guns. This was denied by the police, but nevertheless, the place [King's house] is an arsenal. King sees the inconsistency, but not enough. He believes and yet he doesn't believe. The whole movement is armed in a sense, and this is what I must convince him to see as the greatest evil. . . . If he can *really* be won to a faith in nonviolence there is no end to what he can do.[20]

Additionally, Bayard Rustin reported to some members of the War Resisters League, a coalition of conscientious objectors and pacifists, that there existed in Montgomery "considerable confusion on the question as to whether violence is justified in retaliation to violence directed against the Negro community."[21] Both Smiley and Rustin saw King's grasp of nonviolent doctrine as tenuous and sought to educate him. "For being so new at this," Smiley wrote in another letter, "King runs out of ideas quickly and does the old things again & again. He wants help."[22]

Appropriately, the young minister turned to Mohandas K. Gandhi for inspiration. In his struggle against British imperialism in India, Gandhi had insisted that a struggle against oppression must appeal to activist and nonactivist alike, not only to a discontented minority but also to the majority of the community. He felt that a social movement relying on the tactics of nonviolence not succeed without convincing a full majority of the people that its cause is just.[23]

Gandhi had revolutionized traditional Hindu teachings.[24] The concept of God as absolute truth is ubiquitous to Hindu philosophical thought; however, Gandhi made the subtle distinction that Truth is God, rather than vice versa. Struggling for an English word to describe his conception of enlightenment and salvation, he landed on the word *nonviolence*, a term that proved somewhat puzzling to most Westerners. "To find Truth as God," he wrote, "the only means is Love, i.e. nonviolence. . . ." As one scholar has explained (quoting both Gandhi and King):

> In its active role nonviolence is a positive state of love, of doing good to the evil doers, of mercy; it "means the largest love, greatest charity." "It is the extreme limit of forgiveness." It is more akin to the Greek concept of *agapé*, of what Martin Luther King call[ed] "understanding goodwill."

Gandhi equated love and nonviolence. Violence could lead only to brutishness, never truth; therefore, it held no utility for him. His uniqueness lay in the fact that he not only preached nonviolence but also practiced it to the exclusion of almost everything else in his life.[25]

Conscientious objectors in the United States put a slightly different spin on Gandhi's teachings while remaining true to their spirit. According to Rustin, Gandhi also taught that in such an atmosphere, where the majority accepts the objectives of a social movement as valid, "protest becomes an effective tactic to the degree that it elicits brutality and oppression from the power structure."[26] In other words, it was not the abstract injustice of the segregated South that later stirred the nation's conscience, but rather the spectacle of small children escorted by bayonet-wielding troops at Little Rock, protestors in Birmingham assaulted with police dogs and high-pressure water hoses, and marchers beaten and trampled at the Edmund Pettus Bridge in Selma.

Gandhi intrigued King, who devoured his writings. He also read *War without Violence*, written by Krishnalal Shridharani in the late 1930s. Shridharani, a follower of Gandhi, conceptualized *satyagraha*—the power of truth, or "soul force" as it came to be known during the civil rights movement—as a weapon more formidable than anything oppressors could wield.[27] King would later reflect upon his reluctant acceptance of Gandhian philosophy and *satyagraha*. He wrote that, during seminary, he felt that the "turn the other cheek philosophy" and the "love your enemies philosophy" were valid "only when individuals were in conflict with other individuals";

when racial groups and nations were in conflict "a more realistic approach seemed necessary." As he "delved deeper into the philosophy of Gandhi," his "skepticism concerning the power of love gradually diminished," but he confessed to having "merely an intellectual understanding and appreciation of the position, with no firm determination to organize it in a socially effective situation." *Satyagraha* he explained as a combination of ideas. "Satya," he wrote, "is truth which equals love, and agraha is force; 'satyagraha,' therefore, means truth-force or love force." Promoted by the Fellowship of Reconciliation, *satyagraha* was an essential element of nonviolence.[28]

Ideologically, King was receptive to the concept of nonviolence, yet far from fully committed to it at this stage in his life. His theological acumen was formidable; like most seminary students, he had wrestled with weighty, unanswerable questions about God and human nature and good and evil, and knew something about nonviolent theory from his studies at both Crozer and Boston University. Perhaps the most potent intellectual influence on King was that of theologian Reinhold Niehbur, who emphasized that those who were oppressed could not be free if they relied on moral persuasion while eschewing power and pressure. Niehbur also criticized Gandhian nonviolence on the grounds that it was often impractical, impossible, and exclusive; he emphasized that both nonviolence and violence involved coercion, and so one was not necessarily "more moral" than the other.[29]

As the Montgomery protest unfolded, King worked through his strategy of social change. "I had come to see early," he later wrote, "that the Christian doctrine of love operating through the Gandhian method of nonviolence was one of the most potent weapons available to the Negro in his struggle for freedom."[30] King brought to the theory of nonviolence a concern with love and compassion, a benevolent worldview, and a theological background solidly grounded in Christian beliefs. To him, Jesus Christ exemplified love in its highest form, *agapé*, which transcended human difference and lent redemption to nonviolent activism. Rustin approached nonviolence from a moral but distinctly unreligious background; for him, nonviolence was a matter of right and wrong. King, by comparison, saw nonviolent direct action as an ultimate expression of faith in humanity, of charity toward all, of spiritual nonviolence—in short, of Christian love. As King explained, "Christ furnished the spirit and motivation, while Gandhi provided the method."[31]

Nonviolence, for King, worked on several basic premises. First, it connoted courage, not cowardice. It was active resistance to evil, not passive nonresistance. Second, it was redemptive, looking toward the creation of what King called "the beloved community" and what Gandhi had referred to as *sarvodaya*, the ideal society. Nonviolence sought to win over the opponent through reconciliation. Third, it attacked an unjust system itself rather than those living within that system. Hate the evil deed, King would say, not the evildoer. Fourth, it required "a willingness to accept suffering without retaliation." Unearned suffering was redemptive. Finally, nonviolence eradicated not only physical violence but "violence of the spirit": it created peace and spread love. One can actually see the development of King's philosophy of nonviolence by reading his notations in the margins of his copy of William Stuart Nelson's article "Satyagraha: Gandhian Principles of Non-Violent Non-Cooperation," published in the Autumn–Winter issue, 1957–58, of the *Journal of Religious Thought*. Here King first jotted down his notions of the supremacy of truth and of nonviolence as a way of life; he also recorded how nonviolence avoids both external and internal violence, and how it distinguishes between evil and the evildoer.[32]

Additionally, certain universal truths informed King's method of protest. He believed that people, within their own destinies, are good and free. He believed that God is both "toughminded" and "tenderhearted": a powerful but loving God. He believed that humankind fell from God's grace when Adam and Eve overstepped the bounds of their freedom and that individuals continued to create problems for themselves when their actions impinged on the freedom of others. He believed that an imbalance of justice (toughmindedness) and love (tenderheartedness) causes disharmony. And he believed that persons must be respected because God loves them as individuals; that is, people are sacred.[33]

King's appeal to Christian sensibilities allowed his words to germinate in the South, a bastion of religious conservatism and Christian belief. Here, the union of Christianity and black protest was strong. The South provided the ideal setting for his message, and the black church provided the ideal vehicle for his strategy of nonviolent protest. He recognized not only the centrality of religion in southern black life and culture, but he also recognized the church as the vanguard of social revolution in the South; he saw that religion gave meaning and significance to spirituality and community.[34] King worked within the larger Afro-American tradition of protest through religious channels. Furthermore, the rhetoric of Christianity made his words more palatable to otherwise hostile white southerners; that is, if it did not convert them to King's position, it at least eased some of their fears.[35]

In adopting nonviolence, King followed in the footsteps of William Whipper, Frederick Douglass, the NAACP, and the National Urban League, all of whom had emphasized nonviolence and moral suasion as the most practical methods for achieving integration and basic constitutional rights for black Americans. Most notably, CORE had effectively used nonviolence in its campaigns against racial discrimination. In other words, King was not the first black American to recognize the merits of nonviolence in addressing black needs. Nonetheless, his faith in nonviolence ran counter to the pervasive, if sometimes unspoken, sentiment among black Americans that freedom should come "by any means necessary." There existed a persistent and undeniable strain in Afro-American thought and history that championed the effectiveness of self-defense. King disregarded this tradition with great effect. Nonviolence, for him, made self-defense obsolete. But if he quickly became convinced of the virtues of nonviolence, others needed more convincing.

Even the most committed leaders in Montgomery took time to sanction nonviolence. In his autobiography, Ralph Abernathy would later quote King as saying: "An eye for an eye and a tooth for a tooth will only end up in a blind generation and a toothless people."[36] Abernathy recalled when things "turned ugly" in Montgomery.

> We began to get threatening phone calls, many of them obscene. Virtually every one of MIA's known leaders received such calls; and no matter how often you told your wife that anyone making anonymous threats would be too cowardly to carry them out, you never quite convinced her or yourself. You knew that in the past blacks had been gunned down from cover of darkness or else dragged to obscure wooded areas by masked men and then lynched. So violence was always a very real possibility, even when your demands were modest and expressed in the most moderate of terms.[37]

Abernathy's first impulse when threatened was to arm himself.

Others relied on self-protection, too. Rosa Parks's husband kept a gun by his bed because of the threats and harassments his wife endured as an indicted boycott leader.[38] King recalled in *Stride toward Freedom* that members of the executive board of the MIA would occasionally approach him in private to advocate a "more militant" approach. Some felt that "at least a modicum of violence" would convince whites that they "meant business and were not afraid." He told the story of a member of his church who suggested that they should "'kill off' eight or ten white people" to show they were no longer afraid.[39]

If King was tempted, he did not show it. Aware of some dissent, he remained convinced of the power of nonviolence. To Bayard Rustin's question, "What is the attitude in the Negro community?" in Montgomery in the fall of 1956, King replied:

> The people are just as enthusiastic now as they were in the beginning of the protest. They are determined never to return to jim crow busses. The mass meetings are still jammed and packed and above all the busses are still empty. Every now and then we will hear some complaint, but the vast majority of the people are dedicated to sacrificing and sticking out to the finish. I think also there is a growing commitment to the philosophy of nonviolence on the part of the Negro community. Even those who were willing to get their guns in the beginning are gradually coming to see the futility of such an approach.[40]

"I still believe that love is the most durable power in the world," he preached on November 6, 1956, just seven days before the U.S. Supreme Court's decision against Alabama's bus segregation laws.[41]

A milestone of success, the Montgomery bus boycott represented a shining moment for King. Activists in Montgomery showed that nonretaliatory action for a cause could promote solidarity, build morale, and even bring victory against segregationist forces. King decided, under the tutelage of activists such as Rustin, that justice could prevail without force, without hatred, and without firearms. With nonviolence, King replaced his pistol with a powerful weapon that effectively "outgunned" his adversaries. The boycott exposed the true power of nonviolence, which did not depend solely on the moral force of protest or love but used love as a fulcrum: a means of levering the majority culture toward justice and equality.[42] It was also in Montgomery that King committed himself not simply to attacking jim crow segregation but to changing the racial preconceptions of white Americans.[43]

In Montgomery, King realized that moral suasion alone did not suffice. In subsequent protests, he sought to upset the complacency of middle-class, white America. Indeed, he consciously designed his method of social protest to generate change by initiating conflict within the existing political system. His demonstrations were designed to provoke and aggravate; that is, his politics of confrontation sought to generate a crisis. They were intended to prod a hesitant government to restructure its legal system and to coerce an indifferent society to look inward and reconsider its values and ideals. King's methods were not designed to mollify or conciliate.

The American public tended to equate nonviolent direct action with passive resistance and self-defense with violence; this confusion helped to translate the issue at the heart of the struggle for black equality into a false dichotomy of "violence versus nonviolence." King advocated a much more proactive and confrontational stance than the term "passive resistance" implied. The term, which connotes noncooperation with, or inert resistance to, a government or occupying power, devalued King's novel and powerful approach to social protest. Similarly, many white Americans interpreted self-defense not as a responsive kind of armed resistance but as aggression.

Television and print media reinforced these perceptions when they lumped black behavior into one of these two categories. Activists seemingly had to choose either to petition their grievances in a deferential, nonthreatening way or to lash out violently at the symbols of white supremacy. There was no middle ground. Journalists used words such as "nonviolence" and "pacifism" interchangeably, just as they described self-defense by activists as "violence."[44]

The "violent/nonviolent" dichotomy circumscribed the role of violence in the civil rights movement. Thinking of the struggle for black equality in such dualist terms inevitably aligned self-defense with militance; it also underscored the hostility King encountered from black critics who perceived nonviolent direct action to be soft or accommodating. Although the dichotomy provided a convenient way to discuss the actions of black activists, it was reductionist; in particular, it left little room for the role of justifiable self-defense in combating violent white supremacists.

As King envisioned it, nonviolence was simply an expression of Christian love: a rearticulation of the Golden Rule. When he began his crusade in 1955, self-defense, as an accepted part of the American character, represented the normative reaction for an individual faced with antagonistic behavior. King offered Afro-Americans a means of supplanting this tradition with a far more conciliatory response. Nonviolence became—in large part due to the selflessness of those Montgomerians involved in the bus boycott—the normative method of civil rights protest.

The question of protecting himself from harm King relegated to the realm of faith. From the beginning, he had resolved that what he was doing was extremely dangerous and, in giving his care to God, he had devoted himself to a greater cause. The issue was not his life, "but whether Negroes would achieve first-class treatment on the city's buses." His safety was a distraction from more important issues; dwelling on it was "too great a burden to bear." King concluded that violence, "even in self-defense," ultimately created more problems than it solved. The beloved community, "where men can live together without fear," was within reach, but only through "a refusal to hate or kill" in order to "put an end to the chain of violence"; the beloved community would require "a qualitative change in our souls" and "a quantitative change in our lives."[45]

Given that King was attracted to the Hegelian synthesis as "the best answer to many of life's dilemmas," it is curious that he was not more vocal on the subject of self-defense, which was a true hybrid, a combination of violence and nonviolence.[46] It was responsive and answering, not aggressive. It was (by definition) reactive, not offensive. In this sense, self-defense was not "violence," but a kind of unique subcategory of violent behavior, moderated by ethical considerations. It was "good violence" in that it was morally justifiable. But King did not concentrate on the ethics of self-defense because, in his view, the moral imperative of nonviolence was so much greater.

Many black people, impressed with the results of nonviolent direct action, questioned their own ability to adhere to its stringent demands. Others remained skeptical about its efficacy. J. Pius Barbour, editor of the *National Baptist Voice*, wrote a letter to King (addressing him by his childhood name) that simply asked:

Dear Mike,
Can you overthrow a social system without violence?
                    Your friend,
                    J. Pius Barbour[47]

Such questions prompted a highly pitched debate within the civil rights community over the merits of self-protection during 1957–1962.

The Montgomery Bus Boycott succeeded handily. The boycott ignited a generation of young black Americans who had no plans to live under segregation as their parents had done. It demonstrated that legal challenge, as the NAACP practiced with partial success, was not the only method for bringing results. It allowed individual black citizens to get involved and make a difference. It also affirmed nonviolent direct action as a viable method in the struggle for black equality. But the precedent set by the Montgomery bus boycott was soon to come under assault on a number of fronts.

In other communities there were Negroes who had their skulls fractured, but not a single demonstrator was even spat upon during our sit-ins. We had less violence because we'd shown the willingness and readiness to fight and defend ourselves. . . . We appeared as people with strength, and it was to the mutual advantage of all parties concerned that peaceful relations be maintained.

ROBERT WILLIAMS, DESCRIBING SIT-IN CAMPAIGNS IN MONROE,

NORTH CAROLINA, 1962

CHAPTER 3

PEOPLE WITH STRENGTH

Questioning the Nonviolent Ideal, 1957–1962

The most outspoken critic of nonviolent direct action as a method of protest in the struggle for black equality was Robert Williams. Williams, who headed the local chapter of the NAACP, paid for his advocacy of self-defense with persecution and exile. His life served as a testament to the fear the practice of self-defense by determined black southerners could induce in white southerners.

By the middle of 1956, Martin Luther King's opinions regarding nonviolence and self-defense had shifted radically from his earlier opinions. He understood nonviolence as a noble and righteous passport to civil rights reform and, while he may have continued to view self-defense as manly and righteous in its own way, he also now viewed it as counterproductive in the larger struggle for black equality. In the next few years, King's way of thinking was challenged as the civil rights movement broadened. Not everyone involved in the struggle for black equality subscribed to the sensibilities girding nonviolence, and disagreements with King's methods rippled through the movement. These were not always personal responses to King, but part of a larger dialogue regarding the best path toward black equality. During the late 1950s and early 1960s, some activists, as well as many concerned persons on the periphery of the movement, felt that the efficacy of nonviolence was yet to be established and proven in an American context. A number of these critics publicly expressed reservations about nonviolence; interestingly, each of these objections seemed to center on the question of self-defense.

For example, P. L. Prattis, a columnist for the *Pittsburgh Courier*, took aim at King in 1957 in a five-part series on the virtues of nonviolence. A black man writing for a leading black newspaper, Prattis was not only a respected journalist but also director of the Youth Education Project and a member of the Pennsylvania House of Representatives. He saw nonviolence as little more than a "diversionary tactic," and wondered how relevant it could really be to the plight of Afro-Americans in Montgomery. "I do not know of any instance where a racial group or minority, so situated as we are here in the United States, has ever won full freedom or full citizenship by simply using the tactic of nonviolence," he wrote. He lauded the rebellious Hindustani for "twisting the lion's tail" in India in the 1930s, and he admired nonviolence as "a most valuable tactic" in liberating the Indian subcontinent from British domination; but the American South, he surmised, was quite different from the Near East. "Figuratively, he [the Negro] must be prepared when the occasion demands to put his fist in somebody's face if he is going to win respect."[1]

He wondered, while listening to King being cheered at a convention of the National Council of Negro Women in Washington, how many of those present, "would actually offer his life, his home, or his church." Black folks, he felt, were not able to adhere to true nonviolence—that is, the kind Gandhi advocated. "The zeal, self-sacrifice, and training necessary to make a program of peaceful resistance . . . simply does not seem to exist among Negroes, North or South," Prattis stated. "Nor is there the unity required." He felt that King overestimated his people's capacity to persevere. "Despite his most extraordinary achievements in one community [Montgomery], the

Negroes there are not united behind him." Comparing his own people with Native Americans, he wrote: "We like to gloat that the American Negro has lived and the American Indian has died. This is not true. Indians fought almost to extinction, but in so doing they won respect." He predicted his own actions in a tight situation.

> What am I going to do if the white man strikes me? I am going to kick him in his teeth, regardless of what Dr. King exhorts. If my white fellow Americans are decent with me, I'll meet them more than half-way. But I'm not going to let them boot me around and then expose more surface. I don't think such behavior will win them from or for my people.
>
> I'll be a bit patient, but all the time I'll know that glory and freedom in this world await those who fight. The white man bleeds just like anybody else. He'll stop, think and listen if he has learned that he will and must account for every blow he strikes.

In conclusion, he asked, "Is it better to be tolerated and despised, or hated and respected?" For Prattis, the answer was obvious.[2]

The *Pittsburgh Courier* columnist pinpointed the greatest objection of most black people toward nonviolence: while nonviolent direct action might work effectively within the context of organized social protest, nonviolence itself did not transfer well into other facets of daily life. Self-sacrifice might help to desegregate a public facility, but who was willing, in his own neighborhood, away from the newspaper reporters and flashbulbs, to sacrifice his own family without a fight? Of course, practically no one involved in challenging jim crow would have suggested abnegating self-defense in one's own home, but a number of black Americans, listening to Martin Luther King and the other apostles of nonviolence, failed to distinguish the practice of nonviolence in a private sphere from the practice of nonviolence in a public sphere. The result was a substantial backlash against King's methods of protest. As Robert F. Williams would explain, claiming to voice the views of many black persons toward nonviolence, "All those who dare to attack are going to learn the hard way that the Afro-American is not a pacifist; that he cannot forever be counted on not to defend himself. . . . Those who doubt that the great majority of Negroes are not pacifists, just let them slap one. Pick any Negro on any street corner in the United States of America and they'll find out how much he believes in turning the other cheek."[3]

During the five-year period 1957–1962, the locus of civil rights activity shifted away from Martin Luther King and his organization, the Southern Christian Leadership Conference (SCLC), founded in 1957 to continue civil rights agitation after the Montgomery bus boycott. In the fall of 1957, for example, the nation's attention locked onto Little Rock, Arkansas, where Governor Orval Faubus vowed to block the desegregation of the all-white Central High School. In what proved to be the most serious domestic crisis of Dwight Eisenhower's presidency, "Ike" ordered 1100 army paratroopers from the 101st Airborne Division into Little Rock and federalized the Arkansas National Guard to ensure desegregation. For the first time since Reconstruction, federal troops were sent into the South to protect the civil rights of black Americans.[4]

In the wake of the Little Rock crisis, the question of how to deal with rabid segregationists seemed open for debate within the pantheon of civil rights leadership. Some national figures such as W. E. B. DuBois openly challenged the nonviolent ideal. Indeed, DuBois held many reservations about the viability of nonviolence in the South. He felt that rehabilitating the racial prejudice of white southerners was largely impossible. As he pointed out, from the end of Reconstruction until the 1950s, the nation had widely refused to regard the killing of a black person in the South as murder, or the violation of a black girl as rape. Airing these views, DuBois criticized Martin Luther King in a review of Lawrence Reddick's *Crusader Without Violence*, an early biography of King. The review, published in the *National Guardian* in 1959, described Reddick's portrayal of King as "interesting and appealing but a little disturbing." DuBois said, "His [King's] application of this philosophy in the Montgomery strike is well-known and deserves wide praise, but leaves me a little in doubt. I was sorry to see King lauded for his opposition to the young colored man in North Carolina who declared that in order to stop lynching and mob violence, Negroes must fight back."[5] DuBois used the book review as a means of critiquing not only Reddick's writing but also King's policy. Interestingly, DuBois also interpreted nonviolence as "submission," which reinforced the notion that nonviolent direct action was not a valid form of protest.

The "young colored man in North Carolina" to whom DuBois referred was Robert F. Williams, an ex-Marine from Monroe, North Carolina. The words and deeds of Robert F. Williams signified a departure from the precedent set in Montgomery and a return to traditional methods of self-protection in the face of white aggression. King quickly learned that his own personal conviction—that suffering unanswered violence could wear down and ultimately defeat an enemy—defied the logic and common sense of many black Americans. Such self-sacrifice struck many as a most implausible proposition, requiring extraordinary courage and willpower. Some, like Robert Williams, regarded it as debasing and not so much as a moral imperative as a political tactic; others regarded it as simply impossible. Williams led the attack against "cringing, begging Negro ministers" committed to "turn-the-other-cheekism"; he was one of the few, like Prattis and DuBois, who publicly challenged the idea that blacks should rely on nonviolent tactics. He argued:

> Nonviolence is a very potent weapon when the opponent is civilized, but nonviolence is no repellent for a sadist. I believe Negroes must be willing to defend themselves, their women, their children and their homes. They must be willing to die and to kill in repelling their assailants. Negroes *must* protect themselves, it is obvious that the federal government will not put an end to lynching; therefore it becomes necessary for us to stop lynching with violence.
>
> It is instilled at an early age that men who violently and swiftly rise to oppose tyranny are virtuous examples to emulate. I have been taught by my government to fight. Nowhere in the annals of history does the record show a people delivered from bondage by patience alone.[6]

Williams respected what he called "pure pacifism," but saw it as less effective than displaying a "willingness to fight." By endorsing self-defense, Williams claimed he could not be nonviolent.

Robert Franklin Williams was born the son of a boilermaker's helper in Monroe, North Carolina, on February 26, 1925.[7] Williams's childhood was not unlike that of other black children in small, Southern towns. After completing a National Youth Administration training course at the age of eighteen, he went to Detroit to work as a machinist and to help pay off his father's debts. Williams's tenure in Detroit marked the beginning of an incessant search for steady employment and fulfillment: his migratory quest carried him all over the United States. After a hitch in the Army, another in the Marines, and countless jobs in Michigan, New Jersey, New York, and California (as well as North Carolina), he returned to Monroe in 1955. "When I got out of the Marine Corps," Williams remembered, "I knew I wanted to go home and join the NAACP."[8] His experience in the armed services, tainted by segregation and discriminatory practices, spurred him to political activism. His ardor found outlet in Monroe's anemic chapter of the NAACP.

At mid-twentieth century, blacks comprised about one-quarter of Monroe's population. In the late 1940s, most middle-class blacks living in Monroe were either teachers or preachers. Many belonged to the NAACP; however, the branch was still relatively small and ineffectual, more symbolic than threatening. Local whites tolerated its limited activities until 1954, when it came under attack. *Brown v. Board of Education, Topeka, Kansas* (1954), which overturned the "separate-but-equal" precedent of *Plessy v. Ferguson* (1896) and mandated school desegregation in the South, fomented stirrings for integration throughout the country; white "massive resistance" to these stirrings was swift and severe. White Citizens Councils joined forces with local Ku Klux Klan affiliates to pressure the officers and members of NAACP branches into nonaction. Economic sanctions by employers, banks, and finance companies threatened to stifle NAACP branches throughout the South; so, too, did the specter of beatings and lynchings. The Union County NAACP, like other branches, lost members and became inactive. In late 1955, when Williams joined, it was already in decline; by 1956, only six members remained.[9]

Faced with the ignominy of folding their branch, Union County NAACP officers called a meeting to elect new leadership; much to Williams's surprise, they elected him president. Dr. Albert F. Perry was elected vice-president. After the election, when only he and Perry chose to renew their memberships, Williams began a personal crusade to enroll new members. Rather than recruit professionals, to whom the NAACP had always appealed, he scoured the local pool hall. In the course of one month, he drummed up fifty members, the requisite number to keep the branch open.[10]

Williams's NAACP branch was interesting in two respects. First, it was integrated; second, it was comprised mainly of working-class black folks.[11] He had recruited an atypical, motley bunch, including construction workers, day laborers, farmers, domestics, and the unemployed. There were some white members and a few black professionals. The chapter also had a strong representation of returned veterans.[12] Williams recognized their will and determination, forged in service of their country, to fight for a better standard of living for black people in Monroe.

Williams had become aware of the ardent militancy of Monroe's black veterans during a peculiar episode in which he had participated ten years earlier: the burial of Benny Montgomery, a high-school classmate. Seriously wounded in Europe in World War II, Montgomery had returned to Monroe with a steel plate in his head after a long hospitalization. Mentally impaired, he nevertheless managed to hold down a steady job on a local dairy farm. Shortly before Williams returned from the Army in 1946, Montgomery stabbed another man to death after a drunken argument. Disregarding both his mental instability and the possibilities of psychiatric treatment and rehabilitation, an all-white jury found him guilty and sentenced him to death. Despite pleas for clemency, the governor of North Carolina refused to stay the sentence. Montgomery died in the gas chamber.[13]

His family wanted to bring him home for burial, but the chief of police visited the black undertaker and told him there would be trouble if anyone tried to bury Montgomery, especially in his Army uniform, in Monroe. Local white folks, the police chief said, would not stand for it. Black veterans learned of the threat and complained loudly. Montgomery had won medals for bravery while the chief of police had stayed home during the war, they pointed out. The veterans, Williams included, felt Montgomery had paid society's debt for killing another man and deserved a decent burial. They vowed to support the undertaker and the family.[14]

As the undertaker retrieved Montgomery's body at the state prison and prepared it for burial in his medal-bedecked uniform, the vets organized armed patrols to guard the funeral parlor and patrol the black neighborhood. Many black veterans owned souvenir guns—war trophies such as the German-made, 9mm Luger pistol Williams himself acquired in Detroit in 1948—for which ammunition was readily available. "I have come here as a concerned citizen to warn you against permitting any attempt to interfere with the burial of Benny Montgomery," a black preacher warned the police chief. "The black veterans have armed themselves and are walking the streets ready to kill."[15]

Montgomery was buried without incident. The readiness of these men to defend their fellow veteran's honor symbolized a resurgence of self-defense in the black struggle for equality. Williams would describe this event as "one of the first incidents that really started us to understanding that we had to resist, and that resistance could be effective if we resisted in groups, and if we resisted with guns."[16] Many vets, battle-hardened and worldly-wise, returned home after World War II to initiate and lead what would become the modern civil rights movement. They had experienced an egalitarianism in combat overseas unknown in the racially bisected South. They had managed their duties as servicemen with élan, and they yearned for similar satisfaction from their lives at home after the war. Whether sitting in Parisian cafés or enjoying the company of white women in London, they had tasted freedoms in Europe forbidden in their homeland. For black soldiers, the return home highlighted the irony of second-class citizenship in the U.S. For these men, after defending democracy against Nazism and fascism and observing the beginning stages of a "Cold War" against Communist totalitarianism, segregation seemed an increasingly unacceptable part of the American landscape. Most importantly, Afro-American veterans returned to the United States with a new restlessness for change.[17]

Ten years later, under Williams's leadership, some of these same veterans organized in Monroe to stand down the Klan. "Fresh out of the armed forces," they felt they could match the local police and Klansmen with their gun-handling skills. "When a man learns to use arms," Williams noted, "he gets more self-confidence in himself, and the fact that he knows what to do with arms, he knows the power of arms."[18]

With the support of local white Unitarians, Williams and his constituents began a campaign to integrate various public facilities around Monroe in 1957. They desegregated the public library "without any friction at all," according to Williams.[19] In one of his first moves as NAACP president, Williams organized a cadre of men devoted to self-defense and protection of the black neighborhood in Monroe. "Since the city officials wouldn't stop the Klan, we decided to stop the Klan ourselves," he later explained.[20]

Tensions peaked in 1957 when the group actually engaged nightriders in combat, repelling a Klan raiding party sent to terrorize Dr. A. E. Perry on the evening of October 5. Perry, vice-president of the local NAACP, had been outspoken in petitioning the city council for the construction of a swimming pool in the black section of town. Monroe's only swimming pool, built with federal funds and municipally maintained, was for whites only; black children swam in "swimming holes," unsafe ponds and drainage ditches in which several had drowned. When local Klan members threatened to "get" Perry, Williams posted watch at his house from dusk till dawn. Guards dissuaded a KKK motorcade with gunfire when the cars advanced on Perry's house.[21] The incident received little press. Only three publications reported the fight: the Baltimore *Afro-American*, the Norfolk *Journal and Guide*, and *Jet* magazine, which published a feature-length article on October 31, 1957, entitled "Is North Carolina NAACP Leader a Marked Man?"[22]

A year later, a strange drama unfolded which not only centered international attention on Monroe, but also underscored the hysterical tendencies of white Southerners when confronted with issues of race and sex. On October 28, 1958, two boys, seven-year-old David Simpson and nine-year-old Hanover Thompson, were playing with a group of white girls, including seven-year-old Sissy Sutton. As part of a game, she kissed Hanover on the cheek. Later that afternoon, Sissy told her mother about the incident. Incensed, her mother called the police, who later arrested the boys with their service revolvers drawn. The girl's father had allegedly armed himself with a shotgun and went searching for the little boys. Sissy's mother later told a reporter: "I was furious. I would have killed Hanover myself if I had the chance."[23]

Police held the boys incommunicado at the jail for questioning. Their mothers, frantic with worry over their missing children, had no idea where they were for six days, until November 4, when Judge Hampton Price found the boys guilty of assault and sentenced them to a reformatory, the Morrison Training School for Negroes, for indeterminate terms: if they behaved well, the boys might be released before they turned twenty-one.[24]

Williams was outraged. Enlisting the help of Conrad Lynn, a civil rights attorney from New York, he mounted a campaign to free the boys. Traveling widely around the United States, he publicized what became known as the "Kissing Case." Despite international pressure, the national office of the NAACP, under Roy Wilkins's leadership, hesitated to become involved. During his travels, Williams became known outside the greater Charlotte area. His tireless crusading paid off when, three months after their ordeal began, the boys came home.[25]

The following summer, in the midst of a nervous peace in Monroe, Williams began publishing his newsletter, the *Crusader*. The premiere issue was a hodge-podge of news clips and rants, including reflections on how far black Americans had progressed since slavery, on court bulletins, and on politics. One of the most interesting passages from the inaugural issue explored the notion of black manhood:

Unless a man has some measure of pride, he is not worthy of the dignity to be called MAN. A true man feels himself to be superior to no man and no man to be superior to him. A true man will protect his women, children, and home. He will not walk with a chip on his shoulder, nor will he allow himself to be subjected to slavery and oppression. The Negro is never going to be respected in this nation as a man until he shows a willingness to defend himself and his women. The so-called big men of the race are called boys by their white masters, because the master knows that he wouldn't dare treat a man the way he treats the old black boy.[26]

Williams would return to this typology again and again, comparing activism to black manhood. For him, methods of protest and the way in which blacks lobbied for social change were closely linked to the responsibilities of gender. Self-protection, for Williams, was the key to manhood. Continuing another theme in his writing, the third issue of the *Crusader* cited Jehovah in frightening capital letters:

WHEN I WHET MY GLITTERING SWORD, AND MY HAND TAKETH HOLD ON JUDGMENT: I WILL RENDER VENGEANCE UNTO MY ENEMIES, AND THOSE THAT HATE ME WILL I REQUITE.

I WILL MAKE MY ARROWS DRUNKER WITH BLOOD, AND MY SWORD SHALL DEVOUR FLESH; FROM THE BLOOD OF THE SLAIN AND OF THE CAPTIVES, FROM THE CRUSHED HEAD OF THE ENEMY.[27]

In passages such as this one, Williams displayed his knowledge of the Bible, his ability to quote scripture, and his preference for the fire-and-brimstone retribution of the Old Testament. Apocalyptic in nature, his words recalled those of Nat Turner and other nineteenth-century slaves who rebelled, claiming righteousness in the eyes of God. Early issues of the *Crusader* reflected Williams's immaturity as an essayist; but they also conveyed the righteous anger that fueled his writing.

Frustrated with the inequity of southern justice, Williams lashed out in 1959 after becoming ensnarled in two frustrating legal battles. The first trial involved a white hotel guest who had kicked a black maid down a flight of stairs for disturbing his sleep. The judge dropped all charges against the man, who failed to appear for his court date. The second trial proved even more exasperating. Williams angrily responded to the acquittal of a white man accused of attempting to rape an eight-months-pregnant black woman, Mary Ruth Reid. In an impassioned speech, he declared that Afro-Americans should "meet violence with violence":

> We cannot rely on the law. We can get no justice under the present system. If we feel that injustice is done, we must then and there on the spot be prepared to inflict punishment on these people. Since the federal government will not bring a halt to the lynching and since the so-called courts lynch our people legally, if it's necessary to stop lynching with lynching, then we must be willing to resort to that method. We must meet violence with violence.[28]

His fiery rhetoric garnered the attention of not only the national media, but also of Martin Luther King Jr., who challenged Williams's call to violence in 1959.

In an exchange published in *Liberation* magazine in 1959, King responded to Williams's ire, which included personal charges against King and his brand of nonviolence. In writing this article, King benefited from the editorial assistance of Bayard Rustin, who helped him to articulate his attitudes toward self-defense. King took a stand against Williams by attempting to rectify the paradoxical role of nonviolence within a possibly violent movement. He did so by de-emphasizing self-defense, which cut at the heart of his nonviolent message. To explain his philosophy, he divided violence into three discrete categories: pure nonviolence, self-defense, and "the advocacy of violence as a tool of advancement, organized as in warfare, deliberately and consciously." Of these three, only the third did King condemn as damaging to a "real collective struggle." He preferred nonviolence as a method of mass social protest, but readily admitted that it was the most difficult to perpetuate. He felt that the general populace could not adhere to the strict discipline required of true nonviolence. Even Gandhi, King noted, sanctioned self-defense for those unable to adopt pure nonviolence; as Gandhi had done, King refused to condemn self-defense outright. "When the Negro uses force in self-defense," King wrote, "he does not forfeit support—he may even win it, by the courage and self-respect it reflects." King's tentative regard for self-defense grew out of his pragmatism, his conception of black manhood, and especially his understanding of the Christian tradition that, under the mantra "an eye for an eye," historically permitted retaliatory violence.[29]

Williams and King had a stormy relationship. In the press, each attacked the other's approach to protest, but only to a certain extent: both realized that they were involved in the same struggle and complemented each other's efforts, and both understood that the threat of violence could be used as leverage. For example, Williams wrote: "When our people become fighters, our leaders will be able to sit at the conference table as equals, not dependent on the whim and generosity of the oppressor."[30] Williams claimed that he and King were not ideologically dissimilar. "I wish to make it clear," he wrote, "that I do not advocate violence for its own sake, or for the sake of reprisals against whites. Nor am I against the passive resistance advocated by the Reverend Martin Luther King and others. My only difference with Dr. King is that I believe in flexibility in the freedom struggle."[31]

Consistently, the two men misunderstood one another. As a spokesman for nonviolent direct action, King mistook Williams's call to "meet violence with violence" as an invitation to kill white people with impunity. He noted:

> Mr. Williams would have us believe that there is no collective and practical alternative [to violence]. He argues that we must be cringing and submissive or take up arms. To so place the issue distorts the whole problem. There are other meaningful alternatives.[32]

Williams, for his part, failed to understand the aggressiveness of King's nonviolent direct action, and he sometimes equated nonviolence and pacifism. In *Negroes With Guns*, he would later write that if student protesters could show him the gains of nonviolent methods, then he too would "become a pacifist."[33] Williams's equating nonviolence with pacifism denied nonviolent direct action its forcefulness. He characterized self-protection as the only manly response to violent attack, but King redefined nonviolence as a manly act: anyone who uses nonviolent direct action "will need ample courage and willingness to sacrifice." Nonviolence "needs the bold and the brave because it is not free from danger. It faces the vicious and evil enemies squarely."[34] The rivalry between followers of the two men became so great that the first published biography of King seemingly took its name—in a gesture meant to refute Williams—from the newsletter, the *Crusader*. Published in 1959, the hastily compiled biography was entitled *Crusader Without Violence*.

King's failure to back Williams in his tribulations in Monroe helped to ostracize Williams at a time when he most needed public sympathy. After his admonition to "meet violence with violence" in 1959, the national board of the NAACP denounced and suspended Williams.[35] Many, including

Robert A. Fraser, secretary-treasurer of the AFL-CIO, protested the suspension.[36] The branch voted to make Williams's wife, Mabel, president in his place (he was later re-elected unanimously, in absentia). Mabel's election in her husband's stead suggests that the couple were popular in Monroe and enjoyed widespread support in the local black community, but "five years ago when I started talking about self-defense," Williams confessed in 1961, "I would walk through the streets and many of my black neighbors would walk away to avoid me."[37]

Understandably, many of the black citizens of Monroe warmed slowly to his call to arms in the late 1950s. They were afraid, and rightly so: Williams posed a very real danger to them all. Repercussion for speaking out against the status quo, let alone taking steps to change it, could be swift in the South. In the past, some black citizens had lost their jobs, while others had lost their lives, and those retributive white folks bent on "justice" were not discriminating in how they allotted it. Williams was inviting censure—or worse—by his words and deeds, but there was something appealing about his example, and many in the black community saw him as more brave than insane. The respect he commanded from whites was empowering for the black people of Monroe.

White southerners lived their lives by the laws of tradition; that is, the way things had always been was the way things should be. Andrew Myers has best illustrated the reticence of Monroe's white citizenry to embrace change during this period. He has written:

> Although Monroe whites took pride in their modernity, they still happily regarded their town as an isolated, conservative, southern community. They feared the recent, rapid changes which had taken place. Their insecurity was reflected in the 1949 enactment of an alcohol prohibition law. A year later, during the height of the Red Scare, thirty-five Monroe businessmen took out a four-column advertisement in the [Monroe] *Enquirer* entitled "Americanism and Christianity or Communism and Atheism?" Soon afterwards, they replaced the courthouse weather vane with a neon cross.[38]

Clearly, whites in Monroe, like other white southerners, yearned for stability in their lives. They believed that change, if at all necessary, should take place gradually and peaceably within the existing laws and folkways. Because they believed that assimilation by blacks would disrupt the existing social and political order, they feared it. Their fear often manifested itself in strict adherence to tradition: in this case, unyielding jim crow laws. Seg-regationists, racial supremacists, and those whites otherwise unsympathetic to the goals of the movement feared agitated "nigras," running amuck.[39]

For example, when Williams formed a rifle club and spoke of the need for black people to defend themselves, white folks became alarmed. They ignored the fact that his club, the Union County Rifle Club, resembled the white rifle clubs already in existence in Monroe, just as they ignored that Williams had applied for a charter from the National Rifle Association (which he received, after passing off the organization as a white group).[40] Apparently, they did not like the idea of Afro-Americans responding to violence "with anything more vigorous than spirituals," as one writer has noted.[41] White inhabitants of Monroe became afraid, but whatever fear they felt did not outweigh their complacency with the status quo. No matter how frightened they might have been of the monumental changes brought to their world by the civil rights movement, their fear did not translate into a collective effort to change along with it. Instead, their fear hardened into an intransigent resignation to keep things as they were.

The suspension of Williams as NAACP president goaded him to make more extreme comments. In a debate moderated by A. J. Muste, famed pacifist and labor activist, he challenged Bayard Rustin and Dave Dellinger on the merits of self-defense.[42] He suggested that freedom might neces-sitate deliberate violence on the part of blacks. The NAACP permanently expelled him, but Williams continued to agitate locally, incurring the wrath of local whites; one article, published in 1961, cited four attempts on his life during the previous few years.[43]

As racial tensions mounted in Monroe, the attention of the nation again shifted to a new arena. On February 1, 1960, four black college freshmen from North Carolina A&T protested the jim-crow practices at Woolworth's in Greensboro by "sitting-in" at the drugstore's lunch counter. Like Rosa Parks's refusal to relinquish her seat, it was a minor gesture with major consequence. Within two weeks, the sit-ins spread to eleven cities in five southern states. By the end of the month, young people, conducting sit-ins all over the South, found themselves spearheading a movement to desegre-gate national chain stores in southern towns. Two months later, the Student Nonviolent Coordinating Committee (SNCC) was founded.

Meanwhile, Williams had begun stockpiling arms. Circulation of the *Crusader* grew. In April 1961—in the wake of the unsuccessful U.S. invasion of Cuba at the Bay of Pigs—he sent a telegram to the United Nations that read: "Now that the United States has proclaimed military support for people willing to rebel against oppression, oppressed colored people in the South urgently request tanks, artillery, bombs, money, use of American airfields, and white mercenaries to crush racist tyrants who have betrayed the American Revolution and Civil War. We also request prayers for this noble undertaking."[44]

Relentlessly, Williams continued to needle the sensibilities of those around him by trying to promote change. News of his efforts and of the tense atmosphere between blacks and whites there slowly seeped out of Monroe. One white man wrote to Williams from Syracuse, New York: "If it comes to violent defense against the attacks of the segregationists, there will be many of us with you, just as there were in the time of John Brown."[45] That same month, Williams confided to an interviewer: "What some people don't understand is that in the South we're fighting for our lives."[46]

For five years, Williams and his constituency had enforced a strained peace in Monroe. Williams's efforts antagonized local white supremacists, and when the NAACP decided to picket the town's swimming pool in June 1961, local white supremacists swung into action.[47] By pressuring for desegregation, Williams invoked the wrath of the Ku Klux Klan, which rallied at the pool in counter-protest. Looking for trouble, white ruffians milled about the picket line. When the crowd closed in on Williams and other protestors (mostly young students), an armed showdown ensued among the protestors, police, and crowd members. Williams brandished a .45-caliber automatic, waving it at both police and counter-protestors. He and the other protestors managed to escape unscathed. "Goddamn, goddamn," an elderly white man cried through his tears, "what is this goddamn country coming to that the niggers have got guns, the niggers are armed and the police can't even arrest them!"[48]

After the pool showdown, Williams received national and international support. Unlike earlier incidents, Williams's actions now began to receive coverage in the mainstream press. This fact, combined with the dissemination of his newsletter, made him a national celebrity, of sorts. Supporters wrote from California and Illinois; letters also poured in from faraway locales such as Scandinavia and the Netherlands.[49] Other supporters sent clothing for needy black persons in and around Monroe. As the result of a front-page story in the Baltimore *Afro-American*, which reported a meeting in Harlem that had raised $260.00 to purchase rifles for the embattled black populace of Monroe, Williams began to receive invitations from all over the United States to come help other Afro-American communities set up rifle clubs.[50]

Williams was quickly assuming a place within popular black folklore as a "bad nigger" who would tolerate no affronts from whites. For example, the poet Langston Hughes included Williams in a story published in July 1961 in the *Tri-State Defender*. In the story, Hughes's fictive character, Jesse B. Simple, recounts a dream in which he dies and goes to heaven, where he is told by Gabriel to use the rear entrance. "It's too bad I left my weapons down on earth," Simple says.

> I am not a Freedom Rider, neither a Sit-In Kid. The two cheeks I have to turn have done turned enough—they shall turn no more. You all better get out of my way and let me through this Golden Gate. . . . Maybe the Lord sent for me to clean up heaven. In which case, wait a minute. I will ghost back to earth and round up my boys, the Muslims, the Now Now, and the Buy Blacks—also Robert Williams from Monroe, North Carolina. I will ask them, "Are you willing to die for your rights in heaven as on earth?" If so, die now, make ghosts out of yourselves, and come with me.

Upon waking, Simple learns it was nothing but a dream and that he had not actually died. "It is a good thing," he concludes, "because had my dream been real, I would of tore up that Golden Gate! Plumb up! White folks can run hell, if they want to, but they better not start no stuff in the Glory Land."[51]

Circumstances in Monroe spiraled toward chaos, devolving when Freedom Riders came to town on August 21, 1961. Among them was James Forman, who would soon become executive director of SNCC. He and the other Freedom Riders sought to make a nonviolent stand on Williams's home turf. Williams claimed that the Freedom Riders weakened his own position in Monroe because of their "pacifist philosophy." He wrote: "Their turn-the-other-cheekism inspired the KKK to resort to the use of violence again."[52] Williams resented the racially one-sided nature of nonviolent philosophy. "White liberals who claim to abhor violence are pumping hundreds of thousands of dollars into Afro-American communities in a frantic effort to convert the restless black masses to pacifists," he wrote. "Nonviolent workshops are springing up throughout black communities. Not a single one has been established in racist white communities to curb the violence of the Ku Klux Klan."[53] He explained his position further, writing:

> There is an air that approximates latent racism and white chauvinism about these nonviolent moralists who cannot stand the thought of oppressed Afro-Americans violently defending themselves against white racist brutality, and yet being able to stand motionless and mute while black Americans are being raped, maimed, legally framed, murdered, starved, and driven into exile. What is more brutal? What is more violent?[54]

Unlike many other activists, Williams did not have a natural abhorrence of violence. He saw it as an analog of progress—indeed, of life itself.

> Social change is violence itself. You cannot have progress without friction and upheaval. For social change [to occur], two systems must clash. This must be a violent clash, because it's a struggle for survival for one and a struggle for liberation for the other. And always the powers in command are ruthless and unmerciful in defending their position and privileges.[55]

One telling incident, which occurred at the height of tensions in Monroe, dramatized the rift between proponents of self-defense and proponents of nonviolence. Mistaking an eight-year-old boy for Williams's son, three white men "stomped him" and "almost killed him," according to Williams. The following day, black high school students cornered some white toughs cruising in their neighborhood and attacked them. One student hurled a brick into the face of one of the whites, which prompted a white Freedom Rider named Thompson to intervene, shielding the white youth from the black youths. Williams later challenged Thompson, who chastised Williams and his followers for "dropping to their level" and being "brutes" like the white youths. Williams, furious about the attack on the little boy, responded:

> Thompson, let me tell you one thing . . . if you can't stand to see a white man hurt, if you can't stand to see white blood flow, you better get your suitcase and get out of here. . . . I'm going to tell you one thing: the next time you jump in front of a car to protect a white man who is attacking us, you know what we are going to do? . . . we going to shoot so many holes through you going to look like a screen wire. . . . [56]

Williams came under intense scrutiny by those in the civil rights movement who distrusted his angry rhetoric and his decree of self-defense. "That Rob Williams and his adherents are brave and admirable people, I have no doubt," assured one critic. "But I do doubt that they are revolutionaries. For the violent and destructive way in which they would counter their opponents . . . is none other than the violent and destructive way that the reactionaries of all ages have countered their opponents; and it has little or no chance of making better men either of themselves or their adversaries."[57] For him, and others who accused Williams of vigilantism, it was a question of means versus ends.

If what he advocated was vigilantism, Williams countered, then it was of a sort justified by the absence of protection for some segments of the American population, namely black southerners. "Self-defense is not a love of violence," he explained. "It is a love of justice."[58] He disagreed with the notion that any form of violence is immoral. He both "used and approved" nonviolent resistance as a tactic; however, he also believed that "a man cannot have human dignity if he allows himself to be abused."[59]

He later argued that the Monroe sit-ins "proved that self-defense and nonviolence could be successfully combined."[60] To support this argument, he pointed out that there had been less violence in the Monroe sit-ins than in any other sit-ins in the South and, indeed, Williams could substantiate this claim. In March 1960, the Monroe NAACP had attempted to integrate the lunch counters at Jones's and Secrest's drug stores. Secrest's agreed to the protestors' demands "without incident." Although the manager of Jones's had Williams arrested for trespassing, no violence occurred. Furthermore, while Williams was not openly armed at these events, he had made his "meet violence with violence" speech in May 1959 (almost an entire year before the March 1960 sit-ins), and local whites undoubtedly were aware that he advocated self-defense.[61]

Williams's philosophy was not complicated. He felt that nonviolence could be dogmatic, inflexible, and "mechanically deceptive."[62] He believed in a flexible approach to the black freedom struggle, one that utilized what worked, and events in Monroe proved to Williams that it was self-defense that worked. "I am not opposed to nonviolence per se," he wrote. "I am opposed to it only when it becomes an object of dogmatism. I am opposed to it when it denies the logic of flexibility."[63]

From the outset of his activism, Williams emphasized that his personal struggle was *against* white supremacy, not *for* integration. "The struggles of the Freedom Riders and the sit-in movements have concentrated on a single goal: the right to eat at a lunch counter, the right to sit anywhere on a bus," he noted. "These are important rights because their denial is a direct personal assault on a Negro's dignity." Such protests against segregation were "an important part of the overall Negro struggle," but useful only until "they shift attention to the basic evils" of racism and economic injustice. [64]

He likened racism to a disease, a mass psychosis treatable like any other mental illness. "I've read that one of the best treatments for some forms of mental illness is the shock treatment," he noted wryly, "and the shock treatment must come primarily from the Afro-American people themselves in conjunction with the white youth." He did not reject the aid of white liberals in the civil rights movement, but saw their monetary contributions as a massive effort to convert blacks to pacifism. "We realize that there must be a struggle within our own ranks to take the leadership away from the black Quislings who betray us," he wrote. "Then the white liberals who are dumping hundreds of thousands of dollars into our struggle in the South to convert us to pacifism will have to accept *our* understanding of the situation or drop their liberal pretensions." [65]

The real enemies, as far as Williams could tell, were poor whites, flaunting the one thing southern society allowed them: their superiority over blacks. "[M]ost of the people who were sympathetic toward us were either intellectuals, upper class or middle-class people," he recalled, "and the children, their children, but I did not know any workers, in fact any farmers in the South when I lived there who were sympathetic." [66] "Rednecks," as he saw them, were a lifelong source of annoyance for Williams.

In response to the charge that fighting back would bring only extermination to blacks in America, he replied that his race was already being exterminated. "It is being exterminated by economic strangulation, by mass unemployment, poor housing in ghettoes that breed disease and violence, by impotent education, by police brutality, kangaroo courts and inadequate medical attention that produces a higher-than-natural mortality rate. Every Afro-American is being short-changed out of a part of his life because of [such] conditions. . . ." [67]

Williams also thought of the freedom struggle as a kind of war. He conceptualized the movement in terms of net gain on the "battlefield," of strategic wins and losses. "We [black veterans] had been taught to fight and you expect casualties in war, you expect casualties in the Army, so pretty soon you start thinking in terms of casualties." As soldiers, they had learned that they could expect to become casualties, and this expectation "took away some of the fear" and led to "more resistance."[68]

By August 1961, Monroe resembled a vial of nitroglycerine, ready to explode at the slightest jog. The presence of the Freedom Riders galled local whites. These "outside agitators," comprised of northern-educated, white, college students (many of whom were Jewish) as well as "uppity Negroes," played on a number of stereotypes and led many white southerners to suspect a conspiracy to undercut the "southern way of life." Politeness turned to viciousness as townspeople heckled demonstrators. Violence escalated. Rioting broke out. Then, as serious conflict seemed unavoidable, a bizarre saga unfolded, causing Williams to flee Monroe and leave the country.

As night fell on Sunday, August 27, 1961, carloads of white toughs began pouring into Williams's neighborhood. Local black citizens armed themselves. A white couple from nearby Marshall drove within a block of Williams's house before they were stopped at gunpoint and escorted to Williams's residence. What happened next is unclear. Authorities charged that Williams kidnapped the couple, Mr. and Mrs. Bruce Stegall. Maintaining his innocence, Williams claimed that he ushered the couple into his house for their own protection during a firefight with the Klan, and in doing so saved their lives. Regardless, on Monday, the Union County Grand Jury indicted Williams for kidnapping. Police raided his home; however, he and his family escaped to Cuba by way of Canada.[69]

What happened in Monroe on August 27, 1961, was so distorted by official sources as well as by various witnesses that one person complained: "[T]he American public needs to be informed of the facts in the case, for so rarely in the history of U. S. journalism has such shameful treatment been given to a story."[70] A number of local blacks and Freedom Riders were subsequently arrested, including John Lowry and Mae Mallory, a mother from Harlem; the group became known as the Monroe Defendants. Outrage among those who sympathized with Williams led to the formation of the Committee to Aid the Monroe Defendants, an organization formed to provide legal counsel and to pay court expenses for those remaining in Monroe who needed aid. Conrad Lynn was the group's chief legal advisor. Dr. A. E. Perry, former vice-president of the Union County NAACP, chaired the committee, which counted Norman Mailer and W. E. B. DuBois among its ranks.

After Williams fled Monroe, the United States government targeted him for character assassination. FBI "wanted" posters, tacked in post offices around the country, portrayed Williams as a criminal and fugitive from justice. They described him as "heavily armed and dangerous" and diagnosed him as mad. Detailed (and inaccurate) descriptions of scars stereotyped Williams as a razor-fighting black man. The government did its best to publicly discredit Williams. Such vilification completed his evolution "from reformer to radical to revolutionary."[71]

In Cuba, Fidel Castro granted Williams and his family political asylum as "refugees from the United States," and the Cuban government became responsible for their welfare. They survived on a relatively small allowance of 300 to 400 pesos each month. The government also provided them with a house and car. Williams received this privileged treatment because he had met Castro the previous year when he had accompanied a group of black newspapermen to Cuba.[72] Officials welcomed him then and encouraged him to stay, but Williams wanted to go home. Never did he seriously entertain notions of expatriation or defection.

In 1962, Williams published *Negroes with Guns*, in which he gave his version of what had happened in Monroe and also outlined his philosophy of self-defense. Marc Shaeffer of NBC News arranged for the publication of *Negroes with Guns* with Marzani and Munsell. The book was later translated into French (*Des Nègres avec des fusils*) and published by François Maspero in 1966. *Muhammad Speaks*, the official publication of the Nation of Islam, called the book "powerful," "provocative," "inspiring," and "fascinating," in addition to "the most significant and prophetic book since *The Souls of Black Folk*."[73] Ahead of its time, the book was received quietly but grew to become an underground classic, particularly among black militants. Renewed interest in the book led to a second edition in 1973, published by Third World Press.

Williams's ideas resonated with the Nation of Islam, which C. Eric Lincoln characterized in 1961 as "America's fastest growing racist sect."[74] The "Black Muslims," as they were known, comprised a religious movement founded in Detroit in 1930 by the self-proclaimed prophet Wallace D. Fard, a.k.a. W. D. Fard Muhammad. Muhammad was succeeded as leader of the

Nation of Islam by The Honorable Elijah (Poole) Muhammad, who mixed the message of African pride with black separatism and hostility toward whites. The Black Muslims soon produced a spokesman whose words regarding self-defense rang in the ears of black and white Americans alike in a way that Robert Williams's pronouncements had not.

In the late 1950s, Williams's pro-self-defense position seemed incongruent with prevailing pro-nonviolence sentiments within the civil rights movement. However, by the early 1960s, the social and political climate of the South had changed, and Williams's "radical" ideas regarding self-defense did not seem as far-fetched to those Afro-American activists intoxicated by the successes of direct action. Activists had been beaten and bloodied, and nonviolence, for some, was beginning to lose its appeal. Younger activists, fresh to the struggle, seemed especially open to his ideas, and accounts of Williams's influence abound. For example, in 1961, after the murder of Herbert Lee, a young activist working for voter registration in McComb, Mississippi, local black citizens appealed to the Department of Justice and FBI with no results. Learning of what Williams had done in Monroe, they formed a "defense guard" and publicized its existence. They had no further trouble with voter registration. "That is the lesson of Monroe," claimed Conrad Lynn, Williams's attorney.[75] That same year, James Forman of SNCC was visiting Monroe the night Williams was accused of kidnapping. Williams made a tremendous impact on Forman, who would devote over fifty pages of his autobiography to Williams and the Monroe story.[76]

Williams's historical importance has become apparent over time. Williams's ideas made the militancy of Martin Luther King's SCLC and Roy Wilkins's NAACP seem moderate. To the civil rights movement, Williams contributed (in the eyes of most whites) an unpleasant alternative to the peaceable strategy of someone like King, and made King's plans and ideas seem more acceptable to the majority of Americans.[77] Furthermore, King's verbal sparring with Williams forced the SCLC minister to sharpen his own understanding of nonviolence and its role in the movement.

Williams was a well-known figure in the inner city, particularly in the latter 1960s when revolution seemed possible to many black nationalists. Entrepreneurs capitalized on Williams's stature (and contributed to it) by marketing merchandise embossed with his image. "Power Posters," a Philadelphia company, offered posters of Malcolm X, Stokely Carmichael,

H. Rap Brown, Muhammad Ali, and LeRoi Jones, but Williams topped the inventory list, and the firm's magazine advertisements featured a photograph not of these other celebrities, but of Williams, holding a cocked pistol.[78]

He foreshadowed the black radicals of the 1960s who answered his call to arms. Militants like Malcolm X, Huey Newton, and Eldridge Cleaver looked to the past for precedent and stumbled upon Williams as a man willing to defend his civil rights with force if necessary. Malcolm X noted that "Robert Williams became an exile from this country simply because he was trying to get out people to defend themselves against the Ku Klux Klan and other white supremacist elements."[79] On another occasion, he called Williams "a very good friend of mine" (though the two never met) who was "just a couple of years ahead of his time"; Williams, Malcolm X attested, "laid a good groundwork," and "will be given credit in history for the stand that he took prematurely."[80] Huey Newton reported that "*Negroes With Guns . . .* had a great influence on the kind of party we developed."[81] And Eldridge Cleaver confirmed Williams's impact on the Black Panthers. "Robert Williams and Malcolm X stand as two titans, even prophetic figures who heralded the coming of the gun, the day of the gun, and the resort to armed struggle by Afro-America . . . Williams has made just as much impact as Malcolm."[82]

If Williams "made just as much impact as Malcolm," he would seldom be found alongside Malcolm X in history textbooks. Both during and after the movement, national media attention tended to focus exclusively on Martin Luther King Jr. and the Southern Christian Leadership Conference as the sole determinants of black protest. Because white Americans preferred King's message of nonviolence to the exclusion of all other alternatives, instances of black self-defense during the civil rights movement were defined as "violent," and therefore aberrant, behavior. Historical records tended further to obfuscate those who did not conform to King's way of thinking. The most detailed historical records from the proceedings of courts, police departments, and various government agencies working to suppress black militancy tended to downplay "violent" protestors.

But Williams's influence was too great to go unnoticed. Despite being censored from the mainstream media, he left a paper trail around the globe, and many records of his life remain. His collected papers, for example, include a letter from a college student at the University of Redlands in

California. The student, C. Timothy Heaton, praised Williams's efforts and affirmed his tactics:

> You are right: violence should not be used for aggression, for this only gives the racists an excuse to beat the people down—but there is no reason why the people should not *defend* themselves against murderous mobs and Nazi-like officials. Fascists, white-supremac[ist] idiots, and "let-the-blood-spill, we-are-not-responsible" government agents will not be won to truth and justice with prayer—they must be shown that an aroused people will no longer tolerate injustice, and will no longer allow governments which ignore or promote it to force them into submission.[83]

As Heaton's letter illustrates, Williams won support at home and abroad, from whites and nonwhites alike. For example, in early 1972 ten thousand Japanese from different prefectures all over the Japanese mainland joined in a signature campaign to petition President Nixon for Williams's fair treatment upon returning to the U.S. By that time, Williams had become more celebrated overseas than at home: numerous, non-English periodicals, from Sweden to Tanzania, published front-page exposés about his plight. In the United States, outside Afro-American circles, Williams remained either relatively unknown or infamously reviled.

Those students of history who remember Williams and his activism in Monroe generally have tended to remember him "as a transitory phenomenon, a mere glitch in the chronology of those years—the exception to the rule."[84] More specialized monographs in recent years have been kinder to him, and a new wave of scholars, led by Timothy Tyson, have necessitated a reconsideration of Williams.[85] Tyson's excellent *Radio Free Dixie: Robert F. Williams and the Roots of Black Power* seems to have secured Williams's rightful place in the pantheon of twentieth-century civil rights leaders.[86]

Whatever Williams's place in prevailing histories, his contribution to the struggle for black equality is undeniable. His example inspired the formation of the Deacons for Defense and Justice in 1965, as well as a policy shift by SNCC from nonviolence to armed self-defense. He, along with Malcolm X, provided the inspiration for subsequent organizations such as the Black Panther Party and the League of Revolutionary Black Workers, in addition to the Revolutionary Action Movement, the Republic of New Africa, and countless other black militant groups.

Williams saw the quest for civil rights by his fellow black southerners as complementary to his own quixotic crusade against white supremacy. He believed civil liberties would come only after white racists had been compelled to see the error of their ways. His was a visceral struggle: a gritty, tooth-and-nail war waged in violent terms that violent whites could understand. Undoubtedly, he was enormously threatening to white supremacists because his own quest ballooned beyond the scope of the civil rights struggle of the 1950s and 1960s: he sought not simply equality, but also respect; not merely an end to segregation, but an end to racism. Most importantly, he seemed less concerned with civil and political rights than with fundamental human rights; consequently, he recognized "the right of self-preservation" as "the most basic of human rights."[87]

His ideas did not stem from his formal education.[88] Instead, they sprouted directly from his personal experience as a black man living in the American South. As an "organic intellectual," he was one of the most influential theoreticians the civil rights movement produced.[89] Unlike some of the other orators and writers commenting on race relations in the United States, his ideas had a plain, unpolished quality, originating in his daily trials in Monroe. Despite the wild trajectory of his life in exile, Robert Williams was not particularly unique in Afro-American history.[90] Certainly his courage and forward thinking merit special attention by historians and students of the civil rights movement, but, on one level, Williams was simply a man who stated the obvious: that black people should be able to defend themselves as white people could. That such an idea had revolutionary implications speaks much about the restrictive folkways of the South.

On September 5, 1961, King received a note from a J. W. Oakley, Sr., editor of The Centreville [Alabama] Press, which read, "I see were [sic] that bearded Monroe Negro is on the lam. Wishing to hear you were the same."[91] As "that bearded Monroe Negro" continued from abroad to enjoin his friends and neighbors to prepare to defend themselves, other Afro-Americans stood up for themselves by asserting their right to self-defense. Unlike Williams, no one publicized or celebrated their cases, and few people outside of their immediate areas would learn of their individual ordeals, but it was these personal moments of courage that inspired activists to continue their struggles.

Self-defense disrupted not only traditional patterns of white and black interaction in the South, but also how both white men and black men viewed black women. Importantly, self-defense took place within carefully prescribed gender roles. Local black women, such as Williams's wife Mabel, learned how to shoot, but Williams, by his own testimony, "kept them out of most of it." The women volunteered and "wanted to fight," but Williams and his male cadre insisted that they "stand by" in order to "render medical services" and to "help organize." The women prepared food and served as communicators to alert the community of impending threats.[92]

There is a deafening silence in *Negroes With Guns* that comes from the lack of a single, powerful voice: that of Mabel Williams, Robert's wife. It is clear that she was at his side throughout his ordeals, at home and abroad. It is clear that she, too, was ready to fight if necessary. To illustrate, Tim Tyson has featured a dramatic photograph in his biography of Robert Williams that depicts Mabel leveling a Walther P-38 9 mm pistol as her husband instructs her how to position the weapon. But Williams rarely, if ever, mentions her in his narrative. This absence might stem from the simple fact that Mabel was a woman, and self-defense, in her husband's view, was a man's prerogative. She did not belong in the story because she was peripheral: supporting cast to her husband's lead roles as defender of the family, protector of the community, and uplifter of the race.

Women did not fit into Williams's conception of self-defense as a male prerogative. To him, being a man required resorting to force, if circumstances required it. He did not expect women to resort to force, particularly when men were willing and able to do so for them. Indeed, his vision of manhood, like many other male Southerners involved in the movement, seemed to rely on a certain objectified vision of womanhood: virtuous, retiring, and dependent. Women needed men to defend them and men—in order to be men—needed to defend their women.

When women dared to suggest that they too had a right to self-defense, they were marginalized not only by white society but also by black men. They were ostracized, pushed to the fringe of civil rights activism as "radical elements."[93] It would seem that self-defense as a personal right was recognized regardless of gender, but that it became the domain of men once it became more organized and more politicized. In one of the glaring discrepancies of the struggle for black equality, the men involved in soliciting civil rights reform often ignored the rights of the women in their midst. As the movement evolved, this creeping sexism would become more and more apparent—and more onerous to the women involved.

But, of course, black women had need for self-defense, too. Whether they were men or women, young or old, middle-class or working-class, black people who were involved in the southern civil rights movement had need to protect themselves. The more important motivation behind fighting back was self-preservation, and despite the best efforts of well-meaning husbands and fathers and sons and brothers, women such as Mabel Williams asserted their right to defend themselves. In 1998, she reported:

> We knew how to use guns, but we never had to shoot anybody. We slept in shifts at home because of the telephone threats, the hate mail. People would come and sit with us. They'd take turns, sleep on the floor, sleep on the couch. And somebody would stand guard on the porch.
>
> Everybody in the neighborhood rose to the situation, *especially the old women.* . . . Even Mrs. Crowder, a neighbor a couple of doors below us, hid some guns in her house. She was a domestic, an older lady who had been in the community for years. All of these people were Christian, church-going people. But they were really fed up with the Klan intimidating them all these years.[94]

In such a context of guns and bravado, black men claimed self-defense as a man's responsibility and duty; figuratively, black women had to fight for position in this male-dominated space.

Ironically, it was a woman who came to model Williams's idealized requisites for black manhood. On a sweltering evening in early September 1962, twenty-one-year-old Rebecca Wilson, the maid of a physician, was staying in Dallas, Georgia at the house of her mother, Kate Philpot, with her ten younger brothers and sisters. All of the children but one were at home when seven men, wearing stocking masks, walked onto the porch. It was after 10:00 P.M.

Hearing footsteps, Wilson called through the door and asked what they wanted. The men replied that they wanted to "sell a little politics and leave you a card." She replied that she wasn't interested in what the men had to offer and waited for them to leave. When she did not hear them leave, she armed herself with a .22-caliber revolver. After waiting for a long while, she cautiously opened the door a crack to see if the men had left. One of the men immediately stuck a shotgun barrel through the space and fired. Mrs. Philpot screamed. The other children began crying and screaming. Wilson fired through the cracked door five times. "It was the idea of the masks, I guess," she later explained. "I was scared. I didn't know what I was shooting at. I just had my hand out the door."[95]

One of Wilson's shots instantly killed one of the men, Leroy Parks, with a bullet through the heart. Another, Gene Ables, was wounded in the forearm. With Parks dead and Ables wounded, the other men fled to their cars. The two youngest men, Billy Gamel and Jimmy Humphreys, ages eighteen and nineteen, later returned to pick up Parks's body and take it to the hospital. Jerome Clay, sheriff of Paulding County, arrested all of the men shortly afterward, including Franklin Parker, the son of the publisher of the local paper; Hoyt Prather, an automobile mechanic; and M. A. Nichols, an automobile plant worker. Parks, the man who was killed, worked for Billy Joe Jones, the county manager for Marvin Griffin's re-election campaign as governor of Georgia; Parks himself was a candidate for county representative. Ables, the wounded man, was clerk for the city of Dallas. The men were charged with attempted murder and violation of the state's anti-masking law, designed to curtail illegal activity by the Ku Klux Klan.

Mrs. Philpot closed up her house and moved her family to the home of relatives. Rebecca Wilson, who was taken into protective custody for a few days to protect against possible retaliation, later joined her husband in Indianapolis. She was not charged in the incident. It was a clear-cut case of self-defense.[96] The black press immediately praised Wilson who, according to the *Pittsburgh Courier*, "may have been using the right kind of medicine" when she "beat to the draw" the seven masked nightriders. "The fact that she was locked up along with six survivors was strictly in accordance with 'ye olde Southern custom'," the *Courier* reported, "but the further fact that an all-white coroner's jury set her free shows there is hope for the white South yet."[97]

This incident is most notable, not because of the men's actions, but because of Rebecca Wilson's response. In 1962, before Martin Luther King delivered his famous "I Have A Dream" speech at the March on Washington, before black southerners reaped the full-blown successes of civil rights agitation in the form of the Civil Rights Act of 1964 and Voting Rights Act of 1965, and long before the concept of Black Power engendered a new and healthy sense of impertinence among black Americans, Rebecca Wilson, like Robert Williams, fought back against white racists forcibly and swiftly. In the eyes of those accustomed to immediate deference, her use of a weapon to defend her mother's home must have seemed completely foreign. By staking a claim to life, she was asserting her civil rights.

Civil rights organizations felt the impact of the actions of individuals like Rebecca Wilson and the controversy surrounding Williams. By 1962, some members of CORE began to edge away from the nonviolent ideal. In one incident, two CORE field operatives working outside the South confessed in meetings with other CORE workers that "we don't talk about nonviolence anymore."[98] Wilfred Ussery, head of the San Francisco CORE chapter, told the local school board in September 1962, "The crucial point for the Negro is that . . . with respect to violence, he is not starting anything. . . ."[99] SNCC's fascination with nonviolence also waned. Many young members of SNCC seemed ready to break from nonviolence in the early 1960s, soon after the organization's inception. According to one SNCC activist, Curtis Hayes, SNCC stopped sponsoring regular workshops on nonviolent philosophy and techniques in 1961, although such workshops were held intermittently until 1964. Howard Zinn testified that SNCC began "looking the other way" as early as 1962 if black Mississippians, accustomed to carrying guns for self-defense as a "long-established custom," continued to do so in the presence of SNCC volunteers.[100] The period 1957–1962 marked the high tide of nonviolent direct action, with many nonviolent marches and protests and the desegregation of countless public accommodations in the South. At the same time, however, Robert Williams and other like-minded individuals continued the well-established tradition of black American armed self-defense.

We assert and affirm the right of self-defense, which is one of the most basic human rights known to mankind.

EMBOSSMENT, ORGANIZATION OF AFRO-AMERICAN UNITY MEMBERSHIP CARD

CHAPTER 4

WE ASSERT AND AFFIRM
Self-Defense Finds a Spokesman, 1963–1964

As Afro-Americans continued to defend themselves against white aggressors in everyday life, apart from civil rights protest, a new voice articulated the need for self-defense. Malcolm X, a minister and prominent spokesperson in the Nation of Islam, encouraged black people to defend themselves. As national media sources compared Malcolm X to King, the former reiterated the constitutional significance of self-defense for black Americans.

On the first day of school in 1963, Jasper Brown dropped off his children at the Bartlett-Yancey Elementary School in Yanceyville, North Carolina; they were four of sixteen black children enrolled at the formerly all-white school. Brown had been one of the original plaintiffs in the school's integration suit, begun in 1956. As he returned to his home in the Blanche community, a few miles away, several carloads of young whites harassed him. They jammed his car in front, in back, and alongside, boxing him in so he could not pass. Briefly eluding them, Brown drove directly to the office of Caswell County Sheriff Frank Daniel and asked for protection. The sheriff refused, telling him to "get off the street and go ahead on home." The youths continued to harass Brown, who pulled into a grocery store to telephone Sheriff Daniel again. Cursing Brown and threatening to kill him, the youths crowded into the store. Members of the state highway patrol chanced upon the scene and dispersed the crowd.[1]

Four friends volunteered to ride home with Brown. Yelling threats, racial slurs, and obscenities, the youths again surged around the car. In desperation, Brown wheeled into a stranger's driveway along the rural road. At the house, owned by a white man, Brown called the sheriff again and told him that the youths were blocking both exits of the semi-circular driveway. Sheriff Daniel promised to send someone to investigate. When, after a long period of waiting, no one showed up, the white homeowner called the sheriff again. Two deputies arrived. They cleared out the youths but refused to escort Brown the rest of the way home.

When the deputies left, the youths reappeared. As Brown sped toward his house, the youths hemmed in his automobile again. Eventually one cut in front of Brown's car and slammed on the brakes. Brown's car hit the rear bumper of the car in front as the two cars squealed to a halt. Two white youths jumped out of the front seat and started toward Brown. As he got out of his car, the other cars pulled up, and over a dozen angry youths advanced on him with curses and threats. Then the surprise came.

Brown pulled out a pistol and fired twice, hitting the two youths from the car in front. The others abandoned their cars and wounded friends and fled the scene on foot, running into the nearby woods and fields in all directions. Brown reloaded his pistol, got into his car, and drove back to town to the sheriff's office. Because the sheriff had refused him protection earlier, he chose instead to surrender to state highway patrolmen, who took him to an undisclosed jail outside Caswell County. He was freed on bond of three thousand dollars posted by Charles McDean, NAACP field secretary in Winston-Salem.

Similar conflicts were occurring all over the South. The following month, James Travis, a twenty-year-old SNCC field secretary, was shot by three white men while driving along a lonely highway outside of Greenwood,

Mississippi. Robert Moses, director of SNCC's Mississippi voter registration project, and Randolph Blackwell, field director of the Atlanta-based Voter Education Project, were riding with Travis when three white men in an untagged white Buick began following them. Moses reported that the three men fired into the car with pistols; bullets smashed both front windows. Travis, who was driving, shouted that he had been hit as Moses grabbed the wheel and brought the car to a halt. Travis was hospitalized in critical condition with a shoulder wound and a bullet lodged in his body. "We were all within inches of being killed," Moses reported. On April 24, William L. Moore, a white postman from Baltimore, was shot to death near Gadsden, Alabama, as he participated nonviolently in CORE activities.[2] In May, a black minister involved in an altercation with his estranged wife ensconced himself with a rifle behind an auto in his yard in Binghampton, Tennessee. Rev. Herbert V. Johnson exchanged shots with police and defiantly called out that he would "go down shooting" and "die with my boots on." As the *Tri-State Defender* reported, he "did just that."[3]

The most visible and striking example of an activist condoning self-defense was Gloria Richardson, a forty-year-old divorcee and mother of two who led the civil rights campaign in Cambridge, Maryland. Paula Giddings has described Richardson as "the first woman to be the unquestioned leader of a major movement——and one of the first major leaders to openly question nonviolence as a tactic."[4] In describing Richardson's leadership in Cambridge in 1963, Sandra Millner writes, "The woman who months before had been perceived by as an ardently somber middle-class Negro was by summer allegedly carrying a gun, challenging government troops, and in general acting in direct contradiction not only to civil rights ideology but to what was socially expected of someone of her age, gender, class, and race."[5]

In at least two regards, Richardson bucked the gender roles prescribed by the black men who claimed the civil rights movement as their own nonviolent crusade. First, she boldly led the Cambridge campaign in a way black women, restricted by the male-dominated world of national civil rights organizations, most often could not. Second, she acknowledged armed self-defense as an alternative to nonviolent direct action. "Self-defense may actually be a deterrent to further violence," Richardson asserted in an interview with *Ebony* magazine. "Hitherto, the government has moved into conflict situations only when matters approach the level of insurrection."[6]

In June, Medgar Evers, NAACP field secretary in Mississippi, was assassinated in the driveway of his home in Jackson. Like Richardson, Evers had also counseled self-defense; his death prompted one black journalist to suggest bodyguards for civil rights activists. "Who knows when someone, lurking in the cover of darkness, will peep through a telescopic sight and squeeze the trigger of a high-powered rifle and snuff out the life of another heroic fighter . . . in this 'land of the free and the home of the brave'?" asked Thaddeus T. Stokes. Noting that Daisy Bates (one of the nine students who desegregated Central High School in Little Rock in 1957) and her husband L. C. had survived in Arkansas by keeping guns and employing armed guards, Stokes posited, "If Negro Civil Rights leaders cannot receive protection from the city, state, or Federal government then they must rely upon their neighbors for protection."[7] Representative Adam Clayton Powell (D–New York) emphasized this growing impatience in a speech delivered at Richmond's Municipal Auditorium in September. Citing both Moore's and Evers's murders, Powell suggested that unless action were taken to stop such atrocities, black Americans should employ stronger measures to achieve equality.[8]

Nonviolence, when submitted to the litmus test of public opinion, was often considered to be less viable by black folks than by white folks. For example, *Newsweek*, with the help of Louis Harris and Associates, polled a nationwide sampling of Afro-Americans from all social levels, including one hundred black leaders. The interviewers, predominately black themselves, asked over two hundred-fifty questions, including the awkwardly phrased, "Do you personally feel Negroes today can win their rights without resorting to violence or do you think that it will have to be an eye for an eye and a tooth for a tooth?" Almost two-thirds of what the poll called the "rank and file" in the South, and exactly one-half outside the South, pinned their hopes on nonviolence; the rest were either uncertain or convinced that violence, in some form, was necessary. Nonviolent sentiment was far from unanimous. The pollsters concluded: "Throughout the civil-rights struggle the Negro leaders have been dedicated to nonviolence, but clearly a sizable number of their followers, roughly five million, are resigned to the possibility that they may have to fight their way to freedom."[9] Had he been polled, Malcolm X might have been counted among the five million.

The stark difference in beliefs between Malcolm X and Martin Luther King Jr. also encouraged the custom of conceptualizing the tactical strategy of the civil rights movement in terms of violence versus nonviolence. In the same way Booker T. Washington and W. E. B. DuBois represented two different approaches to the "uplift of the race" at the turn of the century, so too did Martin and Malcolm come to represent a two-pronged attack on the nation's racial dilemma. To many Americans, Malcolm X embodied a violent approach to civil-rights activism.

Malcolm X was born Malcolm Little, the son of a Baptist preacher in Omaha, Nebraska. He believed that Black Legionnaires, members of a white racist organization akin to the Ku Klux Klan, murdered his father when he was six years old. His mother went insane, and authorities subsequently placed him and his siblings in foster homes. He dropped out of school in Detroit after the eighth grade. Making his life on the street, he became a hustler, a thief, and a pimp. Convicted of burglary at the age of twenty-one, he went to prison, where he learned of the teachings of Elijah Muhammad, leader of the Nation of Islam. Muhammad preached an unorthodox mixture of Afrocentrism, nationalism, and eschatology, all of which combined to harness Malcolm's formidable intellect. His anger and eloquence quickly propelled him to the pulpit of Temple No. 7 in Harlem, where he became minister.[10]

Malcolm X spoke best in Harlem before black audiences; within the safety of his mosque, he blasted white people. He condemned white crimes against black people and lambasted the "blue-eyed, white devils" who had long tormented his people. The venom of his speeches attracted the attention of the media: in 1959, WNDT-TV, Channel 13 in New York, broadcast "The Hate that Hate Produced," a five-part report by Mike Wallace which brought the Black Muslims and Malcolm X to the attention of the general American public. Three years later, in April 1962, Muhammad dispatched Malcolm to the Nation of Islam (NOI mosque in Los Angeles, where police had shot seven Muslims; one of the victims, Ronald Stokes, died. Malcolm again captured the spotlight. At this time, rumors of Muhammad's sexual indiscretions were beginning to circulate, and Malcolm's faith in his leader was tested. But Malcolm never questioned Muhammad's insistence on the necessity of self-defense. In a 1963 speech before ten thousand followers in Philadelphia, Elijah Muhammad cited two scriptural sources for the practice of self-defense when he noted that the Koran instructs a Muslim to "fight with those who fight against you," and that "the law of God handed down to Moses" counsels "an eye for an eye." Nonviolence was not acceptable because "it plays right into the white man's 'trigger fingers'," and the Nation of Islam would no longer tolerate beatings, killings, "frame-ups," bombings, and mosque "invasions" without "striking back."[11]

A series of interviews and public appearances confirmed Malcolm's position as a public figure. Without becoming directly involved, he emerged as an outspoken critic of the civil rights movement and its leadership. After increasingly strained relations with Elijah Muhammad, he split with the Nation of Islam and made a pilgrimage to Mecca, where he underwent a religious conversion, recognizing the humanity of white folks. He founded the Organization of Afro-American Unity upon his return in June 1964. On February 21, 1965, three assassins shot Malcolm to death while he spoke at the Audubon Ballroom in Harlem. Elijah Muhammad quickly denied complicity in the murder; but, on March 11, 1966, the New York Supreme Court found three Black Muslims guilty of the crime. It was rumored that Louis Farakhan helped orchestrate the assassination.

In Malcolm's death, as in his life, comparisons to King were common. There were many obvious differences between the two men. One advocated integration, the other separation. One was Christian, the other Muslim. The biggest difference seemed to be that one lauded nonviolence and the other did not. It may have seemed quite natural to the media and the public to view the two men as halves of the same whole rather than as separate entities, but it led to an inaccurate dichotomization.

The teachings of Elijah Muhammad also reinforced such dichotomies. Muhammad's message was "couched in starkly fundamentalist terms, in extremes and contrasts—black versus white; sin versus righteousness; utter depravity versus pure holiness."[12] In the Nation of Islam, there were few gray areas. The Black Muslims' stern moral code and conservative appearance led many civil rights activists to conclude that they were fundamentalist and austere. For example, James Farmer observed: "The Muslims are all black and CORE is interracial. The Muslims are separationists and CORE is integrationist. The Muslims do not reject violence as a solution; CORE does."[13]

The press and the American public contributed to the same bifurcation. Either unwilling to disseminate the complexities of the movement or unable to or both, the media produced easily digestible information for those trying to understand what was happening on America's troubled racial front. It was much simpler for most Americans, black and white alike, to know that King was nonviolent and integrationist and that Malcolm was violent and segregationist. As a result, the public's impressions of each man became more true to a publicly manufactured image than to the ideas and personalities of the men themselves. The media also consistently cast Malcolm X in a posture of aggression. Although he never advocated wanton violence, it seemed that most folks—whites in particular, but many blacks, too—could understand him only in opposition to what they perceived as the pacifism of Martin Luther King Jr. This juxtaposition with King made Malcolm seem, to many white observers, a violent and unreasonable ogre.

For both activists, the question of violence boiled down to a question of ends and means. For Malcolm, self-defense was a matter of "plain, common sense."[14] For King, any form of violence was as much immoral as it was impractical. Violence was evil. The end is always pre-existent in the means; therefore, for King, violence could never serve a good end. King's deep commitment to the brotherhood of man clinched his adoption of nonviolence, but a certain degree of pragmatism and cold realism also drove King to nonviolence. As a numerical minority, violent revolution was an impossibility for black Americans in the United States. Numbers and material resources prohibited long-term violent rebellion by black Americans.[15] King was aware of these variables, as was Malcolm; therefore, there had to be another way. The key for Malcolm, as it was for Robert Williams and others, was self-defense.

The best descriptor of Malcolm X remains, not surprisingly, Malcolm X. No author has captured his essence better than the man himself.[16] Perhaps the combined strengths of his autobiography (written in collaboration with Alex Haley, author of *Roots*) and his collected speeches have hampered the creation of a definitive work about him. He was a pragmatic orator; that is, he said what worked at a given time for a given audience. Like many great extemporaneous speakers, he contradicted himself and, under close scrutiny, his speeches do exhibit a number of incongruencies. Nonetheless, considering the number of times he spoke, for the variety of different audiences both at home and abroad, his rhetoric was remarkably consistent. This consistency stemmed from his conviction in a number of core ideas that he preached again and again.[17]

First, he maintained that white people were the enemy. It is difficult to ignore this theme in his speeches and writings.[18] Second, he demonstrated that black people living in America faced systemic racism, built into the nation's institutions and political framework. Because the dominant culture had failed them, black people should withdraw from that culture and tend to their own needs. Third, he preached that Afro-Americans were beautiful, creative, and strong during a time when black people were just beginning to rediscover these qualities in themselves. Finally, and most importantly, he insisted not that blacks should take up arms against whites, but that an individual has the right to protect the integrity of his life, home, and property, using force if necessary.

All of Malcolm's ideas were rooted in a message of self-defense. Every speech and every sermon alluded, in some way, to the need for black people to protect themselves from a world aligned against them.[19] For example, in "Message to the Grass Roots," one of his best-known speeches, delivered in 1963, he equated redemptive suffering with Uncle Tom-ism. "The white man does the same thing to you [as a dentist] . . . when he wants to put knots on your head and take advantage of you and not have to be afraid of your fighting back," he declared. "To keep you from fighting back, he gets these old religious Uncle Toms to teach you and me, just like Novocain, to suffer peacefully. Don't stop suffering—just suffer peacefully." Suffering in any form was onerous, not redemptive. "There is nothing in our book, the Koran, that teaches us to suffer peacefully," he offered. The Koran teaches one to be intelligent, respectful, peaceable, and courteous; "but," he warned, "if someone puts his hand on you, send him to the cemetery." To Malcolm, such was the mark of "a good religion." In this way, Malcolm X used the appeal of self-defense to try to draw new converts to the Nation of Islam.[20]

Another speech, entitled "Communication and Reality," he delivered to the Domestic Peace Corps on December 12, 1964. This speech, purportedly about revolutions in Africa, quickly turned to self-defense. "Whatever weapon they [racists] use, that's the one I'll use," he said. "I go for talking the kind of language he talks." Racists could not understand nonviolence, which Malcolm believed beyond their schematic reference. "If a man is speaking French, you can talk German all night long, he won't know what you're talking about." Violence was a common tongue which all could understand. Reciprocity, he felt, was the key to combating racism.[21]

If the government wanted peace, he argued, then it should do its job in affording black people protection and equal opportunity. The onus of responsibility for peace should not fall upon black activists who did not start the violence in the first place. Defending oneself did not cause violence: it was simply a response to a pre-existing state of disorder. Malcolm worked to undermine the violent/nonviolent dichotomy perpetuated by the media by redefining self-defense as something other than violent behavior.

Because this is the situation, you and I have to preserve the right to do what is necessary to bring an end to that situation, and it doesn't mean that I advocate violence, but at the same time I am not against using violence in self-defense. I don't even call it violence when it's self-defense. I call it intelligence.

He explained the phrase "by any means necessary" as a measure of last resort. "Whenever someone is treating you in a criminal, illegal, or immoral way, why, you are well within your rights to use anything at your disposal to bring an end to that unjust, illegal, and immoral condition," he stated. He homed in on the racial double standard of self-defense, and on the difficulty in defining violence. "When it comes time for a black man to explode," he argued, "they call it violence, but white people can be exploding against black people all day long and it's never called violence." When the rest of the nation abandoned its violent ways, then black people could become nonviolent, too—but not before then. [22]

The rest of the nation proved slow to abandon its violent ways. Seeking to galvanize public opinion and prod the federal government to action, SCLC chose Birmingham in 1963 to highlight the clear record of brutality there, embodied by the city's public safety commissioner, Eugene "Bull" Connor. Connor's reputation for cruelty extended beyond the borders of Jefferson County, and King knew Connor would provide the spectacle of violence Pritchett had not. Officials such as Connor personified the city's reputation among Afro-Americans as violent, harsh, and repressive.

SCLC designed "Project C" (for "confrontation"), as it called its campaign in Birmingham, to cripple the city economically. Demonstrations, including an economic boycott, featured a full-scale assault on racist employment practices and segregated public accommodations. The drama that unfolded included marches, demonstrations, counter-demonstrations, jailings, beatings, and general chaos. The mayhem culminated May 3–7 when Connor instructed police with clubs and attack dogs and firemen with high-pressure water hoses, capable of stripping bark from trees, to charge demonstrators. The resulting carnage, televised before a national audience, prompted not only desegregation in Birmingham but also a wave of national sympathy and a rash of similar protests across the South. The civil rights movement climaxed on August 28, 1963, when a quarter million people participated in the March on Washington, where King delivered his famous "I Have a Dream" speech.

The euphoria from the victory in Birmingham was short-lived. Less than three weeks later, on September 15, 1963, Klansmen bombed the Sixteenth Street Baptist Church in Birmingham. The explosion killed four black girls. Many saw the bombing as an end to the nonviolent phase of the movement. As King prepared to deliver the eulogy at a joint funeral service for the little girls, novelist John Killens alluded that this tragedy marked the end of nonviolence in the movement. "Negroes must be prepared to protect themselves with guns," he said.[23]

Malcolm X agreed. He first went on record as a naysayer of nonviolent direct action in the spring of 1963, when he accused Dr. Martin Luther King Jr. of "disarming" black southerners in their struggle for rights. Two television interviews—one with Dr. Kenneth Clark, one with James Baldwin—confirmed his thoughts on nonviolence in the civil rights movement. "King is the best weapon that the white man, who wants to brutalize Negroes, has ever gotten in this country," he told Clark, "because he is setting up a situation where, when the white man wants to attack Negroes, they can't defend themselves."[24] Malcolm denounced King in the wake of the Birmingham protests, when many protestors were injured. "You can't take a black man who is being bitten by dogs and accuse him of advocating violence because he tries to defend himself from the bite of the dog."[25] The "dogs" to which he referred were both literal and metaphorical.

For Malcolm, as for many Americans, Birmingham in 1963 was a definitive juncture in the struggle for civil rights. The televised confrontations, water hoses, and German Shepherds elicited powerful reactions in those who saw them. For the general public, the drama of what transpired in Birmingham fixed Martin Luther King and the civil rights movement in the American consciousness. King himself realized in Birmingham that the nation needed new civil rights legislation. The meaning of Birmingham for Malcolm lay not in the mass marches or dime-store boycotts but in the ominous night of rioting on May 10 when city leaders and protestors reached an agreement to begin desegregation and to end demonstrations. The bombing of the Sixteenth Street Baptist Church on September 15 upset him terribly, and he referred to it often in his speeches and in conversation.[26] For example, in his famous speech "The Ballot or the Bullet," delivered on April 3, 1964, at Cory Methodist Church in Cleveland, Malcolm encouraged his audience to take up arms "any time you and I sit around and read where they bomb a church and murder in cold blood, not some grownups, but four little girls while they were praying to the same god the white man taught them to pray to. . . ." When journalists suggested his call for rifle clubs might lead to armed revolution, he responded, "What would you prefer? Civil war or more Birminghams?"[27] More than any other factor, what happened in Birmingham convinced Malcolm of the correctness of his position.

As in Montgomery, civil rights agitation in Birmingham raised the possibility of not only retaliation by black persons but also violent revolt by them. King exploited this fear to advance the movement. In a newspaper column in *New York Amsterdam News*, he cautioned that black people would remain nonviolent "only so long." His famous "Letter from Birmingham City Jail," written on scrap paper and smuggled out of the jail, similarly warned that without progress toward eradicating segregation, "a frightening racial nightmare" could arise from black Americans resorting to "black-nationalist ideologies."[28] King again redefined nonviolence as a surrogate for wanton violence, and in doing so, reaffirmed the either-or rationale of the violent/nonviolent dichotomy. Nonviolence originally represented an expression of theological commitment to peace, but King, in pleading for reconciliation and brotherhood in Birmingham, redefined it as an alternative to violence by black citizens against white aggressors.

The events in Birmingham—along with the assassination of NAACP field secretary Medgar Evers in Jackson, Mississippi on June 12, 1963—sparked debate regarding the role of self-defense in the struggle for black equality among civil rights activists in the Deep South. Indeed, self-defense became a focal point in Mississippi during the Summer Project of 1964 (Freedom Summer). Activists rankled at the prospect of being locked into King's plan for nonviolent resistance in any locale, under any circumstances. For example, Bob Zellner and Clarence Robinson, both members of SNCC, debated the virtues of self-defense at Greenwood's Friendship Church. "It has been proven time and time again," Robinson argued, "that when a man fights back he is not attacked. Now, I've never been the one to start a fight. But if someone is pushing me, I have to defend myself. You got to learn to stay flexible, to fight when you have to, but *only* when you have to." Zellner conceded Robinson's viewpoint by paraphrasing Gandhi: "If you can't be nonviolent, be violent rather than a coward." But he had also pledged himself to nonviolence, whatever that entailed. "The way I am," Zellner said, "I'd flatten anybody who came at me on the street. But when you're pledged to the discipline of a mass movement, you got to behave as you promised."[29] Gun-toting was pervasive in rural Mississippi communities, as evidenced by a memorandum Mary King, a SNCC organizer, wrote in August 1964, in regard to Hartman Turnbow, a local activist from Holmes County: "Mr. Hartman Turnbow represents the landed gentry of the movement. Holmes County is 70 percent Negro, and 70 percent of the land in this county is owned by Negroes. Coming south from Tchula, his house is across railroad tracks just before you turn left to the Mileston community center . . . *get directions or an escort as he may shoot.*"

It was SNCC's policy to conform to local custom and let local people steer organizing efforts in a given community; but, because many SNCC workers considered themselves to be "nonviolent," the issue of self-defense proved problematic in this regard. The central question facing SNCC, as Mary King explained in her autobiography, was: Should SNCC organizers follow a policy of nonviolence or have permission to arm themselves for self-defense when necessary?[30]

On a sweltering day in June 1964, the leadership cadre of SNCC—about two dozen core staff members, state directors, and field secretaries—gathered in the basement of Frazier's Lounge in Atlanta to discuss the Mississippi Summer Project. Seated around pitchers of iced tea, the discussants quickly turned to questions of self-defense and nonviolence.[31] Charlie Cobb, a Howard University graduate and son of a United Church of Christ minister, reported:

> Threats of violence have been made to five of our Negro staff in Greenwood. Two of them had guns given to them. One gun was placed in the office and two guns were placed in the Freedom House. Dick Frey, the only white member of our staff, is the only nonnative Mississippian against guns.

This information sparked an attempt to clarify SNCC's policy on nonviolence. Revealing the day-to-day difficulties in living out a commitment to nonviolence, Willie Peacock, a local youth from the Delta, told of asking a local man to fire on anyone who broke into the Freedom House. The man refused, and Peacock placed guns there "so that we could at least guard the Freedom House at night." He was convinced that whites in Greenwood "are more convinced than ever that they can kill a Negro and get away with it." Don Harris described the six shootings in eighteen months in southwest Georgia where he was organizing. "At a mass meeting two nights after the last shooting," he said, "we talked about nonviolence but the people walked out angry and frustrated." What right did he and the other staff members have, he wondered, to stop the local people from doing whatever they wanted to do? "You should decide," Frank Smith countered brusquely, "that if you go to Mississippi, you're going to get your ass whipped, go to jail, and get shot. You'll be functionally useless if you can't decide this. If you get hung up on your own personal safety, we're not going to get anything done." Courtland Cox agreed. "The question of arming ourselves is larger than Mississippi," he stated. "To the extent that we think about self-defense, we are immobilized." Such rationale allowed SNCC volunteers to function in the hostile climes of Mississippi.[32]

The debate raged on. Various members asked if it were appropriate for local people to defend organizers with guns. The group could not reach a consensus as individuals came to grips with the possibility of dying. Bob Moses weighed in. "Self-defense is so deeply ingrained in rural southern America that we as a small group can't affect it," he explained. "It's not contradictory for a farmer to say he's nonviolent and also to pledge to shoot a marauder's head off." The difference "is that we on staff have committed ourselves not to carry guns." Ella Baker concluded with an apparent endorsement of self-defense when she noted that an individual "would not be operating outside of SNCC" if he opted to "pick up the gun."

Such discussions reveal the pragmatic adaptations of the Student "Not-So-Nonviolent" Coordinating Committee during this period. Civil rights scholars have noted that almost every SNCC worker in the Deep South was carrying a firearm by the time of the Mississippi Summer Project (1964). To gauge how many SNCC workers were armed, Stokely Carmichael asked those who were carrying guns at an executive committee meeting in Holly Springs to place their weapons on the table. Most present did.[33]

Meanwhile, Malcolm was becoming increasingly interested in the civil rights movement. He was troubled by the struggle for civil rights in the South: specifically, he was troubled by integration, by acquiescence, and by the necessity of asking. Only when he could comprehend the movement as part of a larger struggle for human rights could he accept its aims. Those who knew him attest that Malcolm wanted to be involved in the civil rights movement. "He wanted to be involved with black people," said Ossie Davis, "whenever and wherever they were involved."[34] He monitored the doings of SNCC and CORE, visited the SCLC headquarters in Atlanta, and even showed up on the fringe of various protests and demonstrations. "He would just go and look," his lieutenant Charles Kenyatta said. "He wanted to do it so bad."[35]

Despite this yearning, he recognized the impossibility of his participation in the movement. Three reasons precluded his involvement. First, as Elijah Muhammad insisted and as Malcolm initially conceded, the Nation of Islam was not a civil rights organization: it was a religious movement. Muhammad insisted that Malcolm refrain from participating in protests not directly involving the NOI.[36] Second, Malcolm felt his views on nonviolence precluded him from being involved. The movement, which seemed to Malcolm to be under King's direction, was a self-described "nonviolent movement," and Malcolm was self-avowedly "not nonviolent."

Third, and perhaps most importantly, he saw his role as that of a critic. He worked better by offering a searing counterpoint to the comparatively mainstream viewpoints offered by King and others, and he knew that this was where his strength lay: as a commentator, rather than as a direct participant. He often referred to "them Uncle Toms," meaning the mainstays of the SCLC, NAACP, and Urban League: Martin Luther King, Roy Wilkins, and Whitney Young. In turn, the mainstream civil rights leadership ostracized Malcolm. Indeed, he existed on the periphery of the movement like dark storm clouds, building. His anger grew, and with it grew the impetus to effect change immediately.

Like King and Robert Williams, Martin Luther King and Malcolm X freely attacked one another without seeming to understand fully the other's position. While they met in person only once, they responded and challenged one another—sometimes by name, sometimes in veiled references—throughout their public lives. King was invariably more magnanimous with Malcolm than the other way around. Malcolm called nonviolence "foolish."[37] On different occasions, he referred to Dr. King as "an Uncle Tom" and "a chump not a champ." "Coffee with a cracker," he scoffed, "that's *success*?"[38] Malcolm X used King as a patsy to define his own militance.

Conversely, King used Malcolm to illustrate the alternative to legislative reform: chaos. Again, the dichotomy came into play, as King and Malcolm conformed to their media-crafted images. While Malcolm was still alive, King rarely acknowledged that there were multiple alternatives to legislative reform.[39] Instead, his rhetoric allowed only one alternative: death and destruction, courtesy of Malcolm X and his ilk. King would usually present the matter in terms of a choice: "We can deal with [the problem of second-class citizenship] now, or we can drive a seething humanity to a desperation it tried, asked, and hoped to avoid."[40] In his famous "Letter From Birmingham City Jail," he suggested that if white leaders failed to heed him, "millions of Negroes, out of frustration and despair" will "seek solace" in Malcolm X, a development that "will lead inevitably to a frightening racial nightmare."[41] While King helped to demonize Malcolm, what this exchange really proved was how self-fulfilling prophecies work: by treating Malcolm as a doomsayer, King in a sense forced him to become one.

King's and Malcolm's personalities dictated how they handled the issue of self-defense. King recognized that talking about self-defense needlessly agitated white audiences; therefore, he avoided doing so. Malcolm also recognized that talking about self-defense agitated white folks—which was exactly why he did it. In championing self-defense, Malcolm "proved" his detractors to have been right all along. He was a violent, dangerous man to those who threatened him.

Despite their differing opinions, both men recognized that their brands of activism were complementary, serving to shore up the other's weaknesses. King used Malcolm X to illustrate the alternative to his own proscriptions for racial justice, and Malcolm allowed King to use him this way as well. For example, Malcolm once told Coretta Scott King that he was not trying to make her husband's job more difficult, but rather was trying to show whites "what the alternative is."[42] King and X were not enemies, but cautious partners involved in bettering the lot of Afro-Americans.

One series of incidents, in particular, illustrates how Malcolm understood that he and King were part of the same struggle. Elijah Muhammad invited George Lincoln Rockwell and other members of the American Nazi Party to participate in a NOI convention in June 1961, to discuss the establishment of a black separatist state within the existing United States. Such an impossible alliance arose from the tacit understanding between both groups that black separatism was desirable: the Muslims wanted to segregate, and the Nazis were more than happy to oblige. Malcolm X rankled at the idea. Uncomfortable with such unlikely bedfellows, he privately complained to Muhammad about meeting with Rockwell; however, he presided at the conference after the latter feigned illness, as Muhammad often did to avoid public speaking engagements. Four years later, in 1965, Malcolm made public a telegram he had recently written to Rockwell, saying, "I am no longer held in check from fighting white supremacists by Elijah Muhammad's separatist Black Muslim movement," and warning "that if your present racist agitation against our people there in Alabama causes physical harm to Reverend King or any other black American, that you and your Ku Klux Klan friends will be met with maximum physical retaliation from those of us who . . . believe in asserting our right of self-defense—by any means necessary."[43]

Malcolm publicly defended King, in effect acknowledging King's successes in Alabama. He pledged to come to King's aid should Rockwell physically threaten him. This pledge reinforced Malcolm's role as understudy to King as principal player in the events unfolding in the South; but, conversely, it also testified to Malcolm's willingness to involve himself fully, in a manner of force, should the need arise. Furthermore, in pledging to defend King, Malcolm introduced the idea that self-defense was transferable; that is, if you are unwilling or unable to defend yourself, others more inclined or more capable might, in a manner of speaking, defend yourself for you. The Deacons for Defense and Justice would later build their organization on this concept, as would the Black Panthers.

The telegram also illustrates how even Malcolm, normally consistent in his understanding of self-defense and what that phrase meant, could blur the distinctions between true self-defense and aggressive, retaliatory violence. He used the phrase "maximum physical retaliation" in conjunction with his affirmation of "our right to self-defense—by any means necessary" and in doing so, equated the two. In the name of self-defense, he promised to destroy Rockwell should harm come to King.

Malcolm reveled in ambivalence and particularly enjoyed the consternation his metaphors and double-entendres caused among white audiences. Self-defense seemed like a synonym for revolution to many white southerners, and Malcolm did nothing to clarify his meaning to nervous white folks. His words induced fear, a powerful emotion. It was his way of carrying the war to the enemy.

Nor was he above suggesting retaliation. The way in which Malcolm spoke ambivalently, using metaphors to make his point, led him to cloud the distinction between self-defense and retaliation on more than one occasion. For example, he told an audience at the Audubon Ballroom on December 20, 1964:

> If I were to go home and find some blood on the leg of one of my little
> girls, and my wife told me that a snake bit the child, I'd go looking for the
> snake. And if I found the snake, I wouldn't necessarily take time to see if
> it had blood on its jaws. As far as I'm concerned the snake is the snake. So

if snakes don't want someone hunting snakes indiscriminately, I say that snakes should get together and clean out their snakey house. If snakes don't want people running around indiscriminately chopping off the heads of snakes, my advice would be to keep their house in order.

The message, as Malcolm intended, existed between the lines. If white people could not restrain violent racists, then all whites were at risk of random retribution. Malcolm cloaked the threat in metaphor, thereby protecting himself from charges of inciting violence. Referring to the men who killed Michael Schwerner, James Chaney, and Andrew Goodman in Philadelphia, Mississippi during the summer of 1964, he said, "Now those twenty-one snakes that killed those three brothers down there . . . those are snakes. And there is no law in any society on earth that would hold it against anyone for taking the heads of those snakes"; in fact, he suggested, "the whole world would honor you or honor anyone who did what the federal government refused to do. . . ." Malcolm excelled at these oblique suggestions.[44]

In this same speech, Malcolm suggested how white liberals, eager to prove their commitment to the cause, could help out. "When they tell me that they're liberal, I tell them, 'Great, go get me one of those snake heads.'" He believed that many white college students were sincere in their desire to help black Americans, but he felt that "encouraging our people to be nonviolent" was misguided. He induced liberals to act, not talk:

I'm telling you how to do it: You're a liberal; get you a sheet. And get you something up under that sheet that you know how to use, and walk right on in that camp of sheeted people with the rest of them. And show how liberal you are. I'll come back and shake your hand all day long.

If a white person were sincere in his commitment to aiding blacks, let him infiltrate a Ku Klux Klan meeting with a gun and start firing. Dressed as a Klansman, with a weapon secreted under his robes, a white person could do much to further the cause. He presented a similar scenario to Robert Penn Warren in 1965, saying: "If I see a white man who was willing to go to jail or throw himself in front of a car in behalf of the so-called Negro cause, the test that I would put to him, I'd ask him, 'Do you think Negroes—when Negroes are being attacked—should defend themselves even at the risk of having to kill the one who's attacking them?' If that white man told me, yes, I'd shake his hand." Actions, after all, spoke louder than words.[45]

While his views on integration, whites, and other issues evolved and changed over time, his opinions regarding self-defense remained static: they were a mainstay of his political theory and rhetoric. So intractable was his commitment to self-defense that he embossed it on the membership card of the political organization he founded after splitting from the Nation of Islam: the Organization of Afro-American Unity. The single declaration of purpose on the card did not mention justice or Pan-African solidarity. It simply read, "We assert and affirm the right of self-defense, which is one of the most basic human rights known to mankind."[46]

At no time after his conversion to Islam, until the days immediately before his death, did Malcolm carry a weapon of any sort; even then, he carried a non-lethal teargas pen. While he did possess a rifle and pistol for home defense,[47] the famous photograph of Malcolm peering out from behind a drawn curtain with a rifle in his hand is somewhat misleading. Different sources have heralded the photo, taken by Don Charles, as an example of the man's hatred and connivance to bring war to society. More accurately, it was a staged demonstration of his commitment to self-defense.[48]

On December 16, 1964, Alan Dershowitz introduced the featured guest speaker at the Harvard Law School Forum. The speaker, who had recently become the second most popular lecturer on college campuses (behind Presidential hopeful, Barry Goldwater), strode to the podium of a packed auditorium. Adjusting his eyeglasses, which gave him a learned, ascetic quality, the man leveled his gaze at the white audience. Tall, athletically built, and smartly dressed, he exuded strength and self-confidence. Without any notes, the lecturer spoke fluently and forcefully.

While the slated topic for discussion was "The African Revolution and Its Impact on the American Negro," "Brother Malcolm," as his fellow Black Muslims knew him, covered a number of issues in his speech. He explained his preference for the term "Afro-American" rather than "Negro." He explained his religious beliefs. He also explained why, to him, self-defense was such an essential part of the struggle for black equality. "The reason we never received the real thing ['education, housing, employment, everything'] is that we have not displayed any tendency to do the same for ourselves which other human beings do: to protect our humanity and project our humanity." White people would never "sit idly by" and tolerate "what we black men have been letting others do to us." Whites would not remain "passive, peaceful, and nonviolent." As soon as black people—black *men*, in particular—show that they "are willing to die just as quickly to protect our lives and property as whites have shown, they will "be recognized as human beings." It is "inhuman, absolutely subhuman," not to fight back. As part of a struggle for humanity—indeed, as part of a civil rights movement—how could one not defend himself? "[T]oday the black man in America has seen his mistake and is correcting it by lifting his struggle from the level of civil rights to the level of human rights."[49]

He summed up his speech by declaring that the Organization of Afro-American Unity believed that black people should no longer be victims. He wanted the Ku Klux Klan to know that "bloodshed is a two-way street . . . dying is a two-way street," and "killing is a two-way street." He concluded by evoking Shakespeare's Hamlet, who tried to decide whether it was no-bler "to suffer the slings and arrows of outrageous fortune," or whether it was nobler "to take up arms against a sea of troubles, and by opposing, end them." Malcolm felt that Hamlet's soliloquy answered itself: fretting about whether one should use slings and arrows could only bring suffer-ing.[50] Though many within the civil rights movement would disavow his involvement, Malcolm X helped set the tone of protest and dictated theory and tactics from the periphery. He advocated a kind of non-nonviolence, reflected in his praise of self-defense. But many people, particularly in the mid- to late 1960s, heard his words not as an exhortation of self-defense but as a coded invitation to participate in aggression toward whites. That which did not fit readily within the violent/nonviolent dichotomy, including Malcolm's insistence on self-protection, was lost to a bifurcated view of not only the civil rights struggle but also violence itself. Accordingly, a man like Jasper Brown, forced to protect himself, would seem (to many whites, at least) to be not so much an American exercising his constitutional right to self-defense as a crazy black man threatening white folks with a gun. The *groups* of black people who heeded Malcolm's advice by organizing to arm themselves for self-protection were even more notable. One such group was the Deacons for Defense and Justice.

[T]here were a lot of night-riders riding through the neighborhood. We stopped them. We put them out and gave them fair warning. . . . So the white man right away found out that a brand new Negro was born. We definitely couldn't swim and we was as close to the river as we could get so there was but one way to go.

CHARLES SIMS, BOGALUSA, LOUISIANA, 1965

CHAPTER 5

A BRAND NEW NEGRO
Self-Defense in Action, 1965–1966

The issue of self-defense continued to play an important role in the black freedom struggle after Malcolm X's murder. The Deacons for Defense and Justice, a self-defense advocacy group from Louisiana, combined Robert Williams's pragmatic, real-world approach to self-defense with Malcolm's insistence on the constitutional significance of self-defense for black Americans. The Deacons in turn began to organize collectively, and in doing so, they politicized self-defense within the civil rights movement.

On a muggy night in July 1965, a parade of cars driven by members of the Ku Klux Klan raced into the black neighborhood of Bogalusa, Louisiana, as they had done many times before. Leaning out of car windows, Klansmen taunted residents, hurled racial epithets, and insulted women while brandishing pistols and long guns. The Klansmen fired randomly into the homes of Bogalusa's black residents; then, unexpectedly, a fusillade of bullets met them in return. The unwelcome visitors sped out of the neighborhood. It was the Klan's first encounter with the Deacons for Defense and Justice.[1]

Shrouded in mystery, the Deacons defied definition, though several people have tried. Roy Reed, a correspondent for the *New York Times*, described them in 1965 as "the newest of the Negro civil rights organizations . . . an armed, semi-secret, loosely organized federation"; he also described them as "a tough-minded league of Negroes, formed to defend members of their race from white terrorism."[2] Howell Raines, another journalist, labeled them "the South's first organized black vigilantes." *Sepia* magazine called them "a sort of Black KKK."[3] Cleveland Sellers, a SNCC activist, effectively described them as "a group whose responsibility was to defend their communities or themselves against attack."[4] Charles Sims, president of the Bogalusa chapter, called his organization "a defense guard unit."[5] Most recently, Adam Fairclough has deemed them "a legend in the civil rights movement and an object of worried fascination to whites."[6] While all of these definitions help to fix the group's identity, the Deacons' raison d'être was self-protection; accordingly, any reasonable definition of the Deacons should emphasize their status as a self-defense advocacy group.

The origins of the Deacons trace to Jonesboro, Louisiana, in the summer of 1964, when young field workers for the Congress of Racial Equality (CORE) came to Jonesboro to organize desegregation efforts and voter registration; these efforts continued into the fall and following winter. When white toughs visited the CORE headquarters and threatened to return with reinforcements, word spread through the black neighborhood, known as "The Quarters." This neighborhood consisted, according to one observer, of "rows of unpainted frame houses with tin roofs, set closely together on poorly paved streets." Dozens of older black men carrying guns spontaneously assembled on the street and averted trouble.[7] One CORE volunteer, Fred Brooks, described the scene:

> We had a little trouble when we first got there [Jonesboro, Louisiana]—you
> know, people shooting at us, that type of thing. So after that, people started
> coming around, old people—fifty, sixty years old—started coming around
> with their guns and stuff at night, and they were really appreciative of what
> we were doing, and they would say, "Why don't y'all go on inside and go to

bed, and we'll stay out here and watch." They would stay out all night and watch. [8]

Following a KKK parade in which Klansmen drove through town with an escort of local police cars, the men—all veterans of the U.S. armed services, all solidly working-class—decided that if the white power structure would condone and abet such activity, then they must do something to help themselves. The next day, the men met to discuss how to protect their community. They purchased citizens-band radios and ammunition and began to patrol the black community at night. They created a formal command structure of elected officers to maximize efficiency. The men elected Percy Lee Bradford, a stockroom worker who also owned a taxicab, to serve as president of their new organization, and Henry Amos was elected vice-president. [9] "We pray a lot," Bradford explained in February 1965, "but we stay alert, too." [10]

The men, many of whom were religious, agreed on the name "Deacons" as a reflection of their background in the church. The name also represented their self-perception as servants of the community and defenders of the faith. Earnest Thomas, who pieced together a living for himself and his five children as a paper-mill worker, mason, handyman, and pool-hall hustler, began to organize full-time for the Deacons. [11] The group incorporated in March 1965 as a nonprofit corporation after increased Klan activity. The Federal Bureau of Investigation nervously monitored the comings and goings of the Deacons. A decoded copy of an FBI radio bulletin to the Director—dated January 6, 1965 and marked "Urgent"—advised that an organization "has been organized in Jackson Parish at Jonesboro, Louisiana, and that it has for its purposes much the same as those of the Congress of Racial Equality (CORE) but . . . is more militant than CORE and that it would be more inclined to use violence in dealing with any violent opposition encountered in civil rights matters." [12] A Justice Department bulletin to the FBI Director indicated the difficulty in characterizing the Deacons as "violent" or "nonviolent." One informant told the reporting agent that the Deacons were "a non-violent Negro movement" whose purpose was "to promote justice for the Negro"; however, the informant warned that the Deacons, unlike the CORE volunteers whom they otherwise emulated, would "defend themselves by use of force." [13]

The Deacons grew and expanded simultaneously in both Jonesboro and

Bogalusa, Louisiana. Though Jonesboro remained the official headquarters of the Deacons, the locus of power quickly shifted from Jonesboro to Bogalusa, where the Deacons garnered media attention and minor fame. To understand such activists, seemingly anomalous in a nonviolent movement, it is helpful to examine the environment and circumstances that created them. The Deacons reacted reflexively to the open hostility they encountered from violent whites in Louisiana. Their formation paralleled the buildup in Klan strength and activity in their area. The local press largely ignored the Deacons; but when they did pay attention, journalists often portrayed them as gun-slinging vigilantes: an image both misrepresentative and inaccurate. Taking a closer look at the climate of violence that surrounded the movement in Bogalusa, Louisiana, in the mid-1960s and how the Deacons developed within this milieu allows better understanding of their symbolism within the national civil rights movement.

Bogalusa, a small, inland town approximately two hours by car from Biloxi, Mississippi, boasted twenty-two thousand people in 1965. It was originally a sawmill town, which accounted for its location on the edge of the Pearl River swamps. However, in 1965, a paper mill operated by the Crown-Zellerbach Corporation dominated the town's economy and landscape, giving it an unmistakable appearance and odor. Otherwise, the town was unremarkable and indistinguishable from other Louisiana towns its size.[14] One visitor unflatteringly characterized Bogalusa as "a rarity among the small towns of the South in that it has no redeeming touch of grace, beauty, or elegance to surprise the eye or rest the spirit."[15] An article in the *Nation* called Bogalusa "Klantown, USA," and described it as having "possibly the largest Ku Klux Klan concentration per capita of any community in the South."[16] CORE officials estimated that the Klan had a membership of eight hundred in the city of Bogalusa alone, not counting membership in the surrounding Washington Parish.[17] Collaboration between the Klan and local officials was well known: one longtime resident speculated that the Klan headquarters "is at the fire station across from City Hall."[18]

The civil rights movement came to Bogalusa as it came to other small towns around the South: it arrived rather quietly in the form of local, grassroots activism, without the fanfare and bluster of nationally recognized organizations and the media attention they brought with them. Local blacks protested segregation and sought to integrate local facilities. They also criticized the lack of economic opportunities, police brutality, "separate-but-equal" public services and accommodations, and poor educational opportunities.

Their attention centered on the Crown-Zellerbach Corporation, which employed approximately four thousand persons, or roughly half of Bogalusa's total labor force. It was the major factor in the town's economy. Two unions represented the white employees and black employees, respectively; controversy swirled around charges of discrimination in local hiring and pay rates.[19] When Arkansas congressman Brooks Hays, a racial moderate, sought to share the experiences of other southern cities in dealing with racial problems, citizens of Bogalusa were warned not to attend the meeting. Six thousand handbills were distributed door to door, warning that the purpose of the Hays committee was "to convince you that you should help integration by sitting in church with the black man, hiring more of them in your businesses, serving and eating with them in your cafes, and allowing your children to sit by filthy, runny-nosed, ragged, ugly little niggers in your public schools." Those who attended the meetings would be "tagged as integrationists and . . . dealt with accordingly by the Knights of the Ku Klux Klan."[20]

This kind of vitriolic white supremacy lured CORE to Bogalusa in January 1965. The Ku Klux Klan tyrannized the area, and CORE, like other national civil rights organizations, relied on massive white resistance to advance its cause. White opposition galvanized protest, focused media attention, generated sympathy, and inadvertently propelled the movement toward success—but at a cost. The struggle for black equality in Bogalusa uprooted what little racial harmony existed there.

In a letter dated March 1, 1965, the CORE office in Baton Rouge posted a memo that announced thirty-three incidents, from bomb threats to beatings, in thirty-one days in Bogalusa. According to this memo,

the Crown plant is extremely segregated. There are segregated bathrooms, water fountains, and time clocks. These however are secondary to the jim crow locals which exist in the plant. There are two unions in the plant— International Pulp, Sulfite and Paper and the Paper Workers and Paper Makers Union. Being segregated into locals for whites and Negroes, these unions are bastions of segregation in the plant because each has its own line of progression. Each represents certain jobs, and since the white locals refuse to represent Negroes, they are restricted to a few categories. A Negro can progress only so far and then he becomes frozen to one job, because if he advances further he runs into the white jobs. Naturally these jobs are the lowest paying and the hardest physically.

In conjunction with Time, Inc., Crown owns another plant called the St. Francisville Paper Company, in St. Francisville, Louisiana. The conditions there are much worse. . . . [21]

Tension mounted as CORE stepped up its demonstration marches in the following month. Several hundred protestors, mostly local high school students, marched on April 9 to advocate equal educational opportunities in local integrated schools, among other issues. When marchers reached the downtown area, police ordered them to return to the local union hall after white spectators manhandled a white journalist and several marchers.

Black citizens sporadically picketed downtown businesses in Bogalusa as negotiators mediated the conflict. The United States Community Relations Service as well as businessmen listened to black protestors as negotiations lurched forward unpromisingly. The United Conservatives of Louisiana, akin to the White Citizens' Council, staged a rally in early May that attracted thousands and featured Sheriff Jim Clark of Selma, Alabama (though Clark withdrew at the request of the governor). City officials augmented the city's police force of thirty-four men with twelve deputized firemen and an equal number of county sheriff's deputies. The governor sent some three hundred highway patrolmen to the area, and the FBI also sent approximately thirty agents to the scene. Bogalusa geared up for a large-scale, violent confrontation. [22]

On May 23, Mayor Jesse H. Cutrer Jr. announced the repeal of all city segregation ordinances. He also promised that blacks would be hired by the police force and possibly other government agencies. "Everyone must recognize the fact that federal laws supercede city and state laws in the field of civil rights," he stated. "We must obey the law, no matter how bitter the taste." White reaction to Cutrer's proclamation ranged from lukewarm to openly hostile. Pressuring for follow-through, James Farmer of CORE cautiously praised the action. "The fight is not ended," Farmer prophetically warned. "The most difficult part is ahead." Local white citizens sought to remove Cutrer from office and moved for a recall election. White youths attacked a newspaper photographer sent to cover a pro-integration rally and destroyed his equipment. State and city police quelled street fights that broke out between blacks and whites in downtown Bogalusa. Police also arrested two white men for attempted arson outside the local Baptist church where James Farmer was to speak. The policemen expropriated a two-gallon can of gasoline from the suspects, as well as an unrepentant confession.[23]

The victory of desegregation turned out to be a Pyrrhic one. On June 2, newly-hired deputy sheriff O'Neal Moore was shot to death in his patrol car by a gunman in a passing pick-up truck in Varnado, outside of Bogalusa. He and his partner, Creed Rogers, who was wounded in the shooting, were two of Washington Parish's first Afro-American peacekeepers. Authorities arrested a white Bogalusa resident, Ernest Ray McElveen, and charged him with murder.[24]

It was this electrically-charged atmosphere of animosity and hair-trigger violence, fueled by white hatred and black frustration, which animated the Deacons. Until this point, the Deacons had been quietly making their presence known: watching events from a safe distance, formulating their policies, bolstering membership, and supplementing their growing arsenal of firearms. After announcing the repeal of city segregation ordinances, Mayor Cutrer warned in a veiled threat to the Deacons: "Anyone, white or Negro, who attempts to violate the rights of another or cause bodily harm will be promptly arrested, charged and prosecuted." After Moore's murder, several Deacons, in their first planned display of arms, guarded the homes of local black leaders.[25]

Moore's death prefaced the Deacons' rapid acceleration to the forefront of the movement in Bogalusa. Friends and family scheduled Moore's funeral for June 9, the following week, and James Farmer planned to speak at the service. He arrived at the New Orleans International Airport, where four state police detectives and four Deacons met him. The detectives warned Farmer of a Klan plot to assassinate him in Louisiana and offered to provide protection for him, though Charles Sims, who did not fully trust the detectives, insisted that Farmer ride with him. Sims, along with three other Deacons, chauffeured Farmer from New Orleans to Bogalusa—a distance of approximately sixty-five miles—with a pistol on the car seat beside him. Upon safe arrival, Farmer praised the Deacons. "CORE is nonviolent," said Farmer, "but we have no right to tell Negroes in Bogalusa or anywhere else that they do not have the right to defend their homes. It is a constitutional right." An estimated fifty Deacons attended Moore's funeral.[26]

The Deacons organized and spread with speed, silence, and secrecy. By early June, the group had organized in Homer and Tallulah, Louisiana, and had bridged the Mississippi River to Mississippi and Alabama. One of the most perplexing mysteries of the Deacons revolved around the question of membership. No one knew, and no one knows today, how many men joined the Deacons. Earnest Thomas, Jonesboro chapter vice-president and full-time organizer for the Deacons, claimed in June 1965 that the group had upwards of fifty chapters in various stages of organization in Louisiana, Mississippi, and Alabama, though he declined to disclose the number of members. Estimates ranged from five thousand to fifteen thousand, though these numbers were probably inflated. Thomas said that "with hard work" the organization could spread to every southern state in "six or seven months." Part of the Deacons' strategy was to conceal membership and blur actual numbers. "It would not make sense to tell you we got four hundred men here," Thomas said in June of the following year, "and let 'the man' bring eight hundred." The Deacons limited public knowledge of membership for tactical purposes: surprise, intimidation, and self-preservation. They cultivated the image of a fraternal, underground organization that permeated the entire South. Officially, only a handful of Deacons ever existed. Highly public members included Charles Sims, Earnest Thomas, Percy Lee Bradford, Bogalusa vice-president Royan Burris, and director of public relations Robert Hicks.[27]

The founding members of the Deacons were not young and spry. Younger activists in SNCC and CORE seemed struck by the Deacons' gray hair and grizzled visages. Earnest Thomas was thirty-two years old in 1965; one article described him as "hard-jawed" and "goateed."[28] The same article described the forty-two-year-old Charles Sims as "a stocky, graying man"; photos of Sims in 1965 depict a balding man with white hair at his temples.[29] Civil rights scholars often credit the young, impetuous activists in SNCC and CORE with radicalizing the civil rights movement in the mid-1960s. But as older activists willing to take up guns, the Deacons countered the ageist assumption that the younger, hotheaded activists exemplified by Stokely Carmichael were the ones pushing the movement in a more "militant" direction.

Under the aegis of their charter and by-laws, the Deacons reaffirmed the principles of American democracy and resembled other civic-minded agencies. Their charter, recognized under Louisiana state law, commissioned the group "to instruct, train, and teach citizens, and especially minority groups, in the principles of democracy." The group required each man to study and understand its by-laws before he could join. Each member took an oath, and pledged his life "to the defense of justice" and the defense of Negroes and civil rights workers wherever they required protection. Members paid ten dollars to join and two dollars each month thereafter.[30]

The organization provided ammunition that it purchased in bulk quantities discounted through a subsidy by the National Rifle Association (which, before its radical politicization in the 1960s, sponsored rifle-clubs and target-shooting contests across the nation); however, members provided their own guns. "Everybody owns his own piece," explained Earnest Thomas. Louisiana was known as the "Sportsman's Paradise," and as Charles Sims pointed out, "they do a lotta huntin' around there." Sims further explained that "having a weapon's nothing new. What bugged the people was something else—when they found out what was the program of the Deacons."[31] Of course, what made the Deacons novel was their use of guns to counteract white aggression. The national media later zeroed in on the Black Panther Party in Oakland, California, as the first blacks in America to arm themselves; but clearly, black Americans had always been armed, though perhaps not openly.[32]

When the Deacons first organized, they used what arms they had— primarily shotguns and a few handguns. Earnest Thomas sought to standardize weaponry for further savings and favored .30 M-1 carbines and .38 Special revolvers. Ultimately, how well they were armed is a matter of speculation and conjecture. Thomas surreptitiously hinted that the Deacons stashed grenades in Jonesboro, and that they had contacts in Houston and Chicago to acquire machine guns. Local police fretted that the Deacons possessed automatic weapons. Although Governor John J. McKeithen ordered the seizure of guns found in cars belonging to both Deacons and Klansmen, Louisiana state police recognized that confiscation of guns was illegal. Protected by the Second Amendment and the constitutional right to bear arms, the Deacons operated within the law. Of course, machine guns and hand grenades were a different matter: under the National Firearms Act of 1934 and the Federal Firearms Act of 1938, these items were illegal contraband, subject to seizure. For this reason, it seems unlikely that the Deacons would have owned them; they were attuned to the law and would have done nothing to jeopardize unnecessarily their organization or its mission.[33]

Importantly, the Deacons did not advocate using their guns for anything other than self-defense: they sought to use their guns defensively, not offensively. "A person knowingly exposes himself to white violence when he walks a picket line," Thomas explained, "but when he goes to bed at night he is entitled to rest without worry, and that is where the Deacons come in."[34] Sims assured anyone who would listen that the Deacons would not start a fight, but would fight back "in concert" if attacked by whites. "They [whites] bring the fight to us," Sims maintained. "We don't take it to them."[35] One reporter noted that the Deacons practiced "the kind of practical self-defense that Malcolm X advocated."[36] They used their guns solely for self-protection and for the protection of those working for the civil rights cause, many of whom were pacifists. Given their menacing public image, it might have surprised the public to learn that the Deacons reaffirmed the principle of nonviolent direct action. Many Deacons participated in nonviolent protest without weapons. Charles Sims felt that political and economic progress for blacks in America would be achieved through negotiations, not violence. When asked in an interview in August 1965 how activists could best advance the movement or achieve its aims most quickly without the use of nonviolence, Sims said, "I believe nonviolence is the only way."[37]

Sims ignited the Deacons' rise to prominence. His charisma and leadership anchored the organization, and his persona symbolized the Deacons' no-nonsense approach to the struggle for black equality. Unlike many other civil rights leaders, Sims did not hail from a middle-class background. He was a part-time insurance salesman and a tough, hard-nosed man with a previous police record that included assault and carrying a concealed weapon. According to legend, if his pistol jabbed him in the ribs when he sat down, Sims would nonchalantly toss it—along with his car keys and cigarettes—onto the nearest table with a clatter, often alarming anyone near. With disarming forwardness, Sims called prominent civil rights leaders (as well as white reporters) by their first names, calling well-known black author Louis Lomax "Louis," and CORE national president James Farmer "Jim." Revealing that he was not within the circle of accepted civil rights leadership, Sims mistakenly referred to SNCC's Julian Bond as "Julius," though he respectfully called King "Dr. King." Stiff-necked and brooding with a dark sense of humor, Sims did not take the civil rights movement or his role in it lightly.[38]

The Deacons signaled a new intolerance for both racist brutality and governmental indifference. The *New York Times* followed the Deacons with interest, but not to the satisfaction of one famous athlete-turned-newspaper columnist. "The *New York Times* may print 'all the news that's fit [to print]'," baseball legend Jackie Robinson wrote in the *Pittsburgh Courier*, "but it sure is late with this one. This column has been warning for many months—and so have our civil rights leaders—that Negroes are fed up being persecuted, bombed, burned out, flogged, and murdered while their Federal Government insists it is powerless to help." Robinson described the Deacons as men who "have guns, will travel with them and use them." He concluded by hoping that the Deacons' position would awaken the Justice Department into finding ways to protect black American citizens, and warned, "If it doesn't, the black people will damn sure defend themselves."[39] Elsewhere he wrote:

> As readers of this column are aware, we have an abiding respect and admiration for Dr. King. We can understand his disturbance about violence even if it is only preventive, defensive or retaliatory violence.
>
> On the other hand, we also have respect and admiration for—and a real empathy with—these men [the Deacons] and committed men of the South who have decided that the brutalities and killings of the Negro have gone unpunished too long.[40]

Robinson had warned, "time and time again," that if the government did not intervene, "the Negroes would finally say, ''Scuse me, Dr. King,' and stand up and fight back."[41]

Under Charles Sims's watchful eye, the civil rights movement in Bogalusa and the tension that accompanied it came to a head in July 1965. During a civil rights march on a downtown street on July 8, a flying bottle struck seventeen-year-old Hattie Mae Hill in the head, causing a gash. Leneva Tiebeman, a white nurse, rushed Hattie to a car driven by two Deacons, Henry Austan and Milton Johnson, who monitored the march from their automobile. White toughs hassled the girl and the nurse, who sought to take Hattie to a first-aid station in the black community. Miss Tiebeman hustled Hattie into the backseat of the car. When Austan and Johnson leaned from the car window, twenty-five-year-old Alton D. Crowe Jr. of nearby Pearl River struck them both repeatedly in the face. Austan shot Crowe in the chest and neck. Police yanked both Austan and Johnson from the car, cuffed them on the car's hood, and took the two men to an undisclosed locale for protection from angry whites, who shouted at policemen and attacked news photographers.[42]

That same night, two rallies occurred: one held by the Bogalusa Civic and Voters League, which coordinated black protest in Bogalusa, and one held by the National States Rights Party. The latter rally featured J. B. Stoner, an Atlanta attorney and outspoken racist who declared the "nigger" the "enemy" of his organization. "The nigger is not a human being," he told the crowd of two thousand men, women, and children. "He is somewhere between the white man and the ape." He observed that black people were taking white jobs. "Every time a nigger gets a job," he cautioned, "that's just one more job that you can't have." He urged whites to fire their black domestic help to speed black emigration from the South. Finally, Stoner played the trump card of southern phobias, saying, "You notice the niggers are singing, 'I Love Everybody.' They sure do love everybody, and especially our white women. What the nigger really wants is our white women."[43]

Over the next few days, pressure built, tension increased. Bigots and extremists prevailed as moderate voices hushed, fading into the background. Gunplay and sporadic street violence occurred between blacks and whites. Then, on July 10, Federal Judge Herbert W. Christenberry enjoined Bogalusa police from using threats or violence to prevent blacks from exercising their civil rights, ordered police to protect civil rights activists from harassment by whites, and refused to grant city officials a restraining order temporarily stopping demonstrations. City attorney John C. Martzell reaffirmed the right of the Bogalusa Civic and Voters League (BCVL) to march, "but if it does," he warned, "as conditions now exist in Bogalusa, it may result in gang warfare." Agreeing with Martzell, A. Z. Young, president of the BCVL, voluntarily called off a march scheduled for that day, but rescheduled it for the following one.[44]

Although they professed nonviolence, major civil rights organizations such as CORE refused to criticize the Deacons; to do so would have robbed them of the local support needed for their own agendas. James Farmer of CORE was able to accept the Deacons publicly by differentiating between the functions of the Deacons and his own organization. "CORE is in the rights business and the Deacons are in the protecting business," he determined. Farmer continued:

One thing is apparent in this year of our Lord 1965—Negroes in this nation are down to about their last ounce of patience. For all the hoopla and the speechmaking and legislation, very little has changed in the reality of Negro life in this country . . . rats still bite kids and citizens of Bogalusa still don't have the vote.

Now if you accept that as fact—then it's clear that violence may be on the horizon. And if violence is on the horizon, I would certainly prefer to see it channeled into a defense discipline than the random homicide and suicide of rioting.[45]

A. Z. Young and the BCVL welcomed protection from the Deacons. "I know the Klan would have already come in here and killed or whipped the leaders of the movement if it weren't for the Deacons," Young noted. "The Deacons give them something to think about."[46] Even some staff members of SCLC, known for its conservatism and strict adherence to nonviolence, carefully acknowledged what the Deacons were doing. "There is such a thing as the cup of endurance running over," said one of King's aides, who wished to be anonymous. "Dr King's position makes a distinction between defensive violence and aggressive violence. I think the Deacons come in the category of defensive violence." But he quickly added: "The goal of a nonviolent movement is to create a community where people can live in harmony and I don't think guns help that."[47]

Other organizations, desirous of peaceful integration, condemned the Deacons outright. "If the Deacons really catch hold," warned Paul Anthony, field director of the Southern Regional Council, a moderate biracial committee on race relations, "it could mean the end of nonviolence in some areas of the South. Potentially, this is an extremely serious development, which could cause a wave of violence with national repercussions." Ozell Sutton, associate director of another moderate group, the Arkansas Council on Human Relations, said: "Someday there's going to be a real bloodbath somewhere. I hate to say it, but by nature Negroes aren't any more nonviolent than anybody else."[48]

Segregationists shared the same sentiment. For example, W. J. Simmons, National Coordinator of the Citizens Councils of America, predicted: "The Deacons will move southern whites toward more violence, besides costing the civil rights movement a lot of liberal sympathy in the North." A local Klansman offered: "If violence has to settle this, then the sooner the better." With regard to the Deacons, he said, "I don't care how many guns that bunch of black Mau Maus has, they don't have the prerequisite—guts."[49]

On July 13, Governor John J. McKeithen, concerned with the damaging effect of demonstrations on the state's effort to attract northern industry to Louisiana, flew to Bogalusa to make a personal appeal for the cessation of protest activities for a thirty-day "cooling off period." Promising that demonstrations would be "stepped up," Bogalusa's black leaders rejected the plea, saying that the governor offered "nothing in return."[50] McKeithen washed his hands of the matter and lamented, "I think they have made a tragic mistake"; the presence of the Deacons, in his mind, would only "increase the possibility of violence."[51] United States Vice-President Hubert Humphrey and John Doar, head of the Civil Rights Division of the Justice Department, participated in the negotiations—to little avail—via telephone. With stop-gap reform and apparent stalemate, protest efforts in Bogalusa ironically succeeded in that they finally garnered complete attention from state and national officials.[52]

The following day, July 14, 1965, A. Z. Young swore a deposition in which he described conditions at the Crown-Zellerbach plant:

> The hiring practices of Crown-Zellerbach are discriminatory. Recruitment of women is limited exclusively to whites. The result of this is that equally qualified Negro women are forced to perform menial housekeeping work and babysitting for the working white women who earn many times what they pay the Negroes who do their housework for them. There are numerous qualified Negro women who want these jobs but cannot even get application forms.
>
> The promotion program in the several divisions of Crown-Zellerbach is designed and administered to keep Negroes out of the lines of progression except within very narrow limits. Negroes get jobs as porters and common laborers while white men who come in at similar levels soon bypass the Negroes and get better paying and more desirable jobs despite the fact that Negroes with long seniority are qualified. The lines of progression are fragmented so that Negroes are placed in spots from which advancement is in many cases severely limited and in most cases non-existent. In all cases the lines of progression result in the placement of Negroes in dead-end positions.

Young concluded by noting, "Crown-Zellerbach has contracts with the federal government,"[53] implying that the Johnson administration was complicit in these discriminatory practices.

As Young and the BCVL prepared for action in the courts, Sims and the

Deacons prepared for action in the streets and extended their reach. On August 2, both the Southern Christian Leadership Conference and the Deacons prepared to move into the Greensboro, Alabama area. Two weeks prior, a small delegation of Deacons from Bogalusa visited Eutaw, twenty miles northwest of Greensboro, to talk with local blacks about establishing a Deacons chapter there. Like SNCC and CORE, the Deacons sought to organize where the Ku Klux Klan was strong. Their move into Greensboro foreshadowed future conflict not only with the Klan, but also with Martin Luther King Jr.[54]

By August 1965, the Deacons had moved into Arkansas and Texas and had plans to organize in Georgia, North Carolina, and Florida. A group calling itself "The Committee to Aid the Deacons" formed in Austin, Texas.[55] In every instance, the formation of Deacon chapters resulted from parallel buildups in Klan strength and activity in those areas.[56] The organization mobilized later that month in Mississippi locales: Natchez, Greenville, Columbia, and Jackson, where Charles Sims led a ten-man delegation invited to discuss the possibility of organizing there. Sims told a crowd of three hundred black men at the Negro Masonic Hall on Lynch Street: "It is time for you men in Jackson to wake up and be men." Sims claimed he had been "shot five times and shot at about ten," and he was not afraid to come to Jackson.[57]

Gendered language often shaped the burgeoning debate over the place of guns in the movement, as well as the ongoing argument concerning self-defense, and Sims's rhetoric reflected this trend. The original chapter in Jonesboro included women in its ranks, and the founders briefly considered the possibility of "Deaconettes," a women's auxiliary. However, subsequent chapters of Deacons excluded women from their male-only clubs.[58] The Deacons were becoming, in many ways, an expression of manhood. "Everything we done," Sims said, "we walked like men."[59] Royan Burris, after repelling Klan invaders in Bogalusa, explained: "They finally found out that we really are men, and that we would do what we said, and that we meant what we said."[60] Such language often masked a deeper chauvinism within the civil rights movement as self-defense became a function of maleness. For example, Bishop Charles Eubank Tucker blessed marchers in 1966 and reassured, "Any Negro or white has the right to defend himself with arms. Any man who didn't ought to take off his pants and wear skirts."[61] The Deacons frequently employed this kind of wording. "It's time for black men," Earnest Thomas implored, "to start taking care of their black women and children."[62]

On another occasion, Charles Sims expressed himself in much cruder terms: "See, the southern white man is almost like Hitler in the South. He been dictating to the Negro people, 'Boy, this,' and 'Uncle, that,' and 'Granma, go here,' and people's been jumpin'. So he gets up one morning and discovers that 'boy' was a man, and that he can walk up and say something to 'boy' and 'boy' don't like what he say, he tell him to eat himself—you know?"[63]

Dr. Stephen E. Salenger of Los Angeles, a psychiatry resident who spent time in Jonesboro as a member of the Medical Committee for Human Rights, offered his own perspective on the Deacons' gendered expression. He said that he believed a white segregationist called a black man "boy" to disrespect and "de-sex" him, or at least to deny that the black man was a physical or sexual threat to his own supremacy. To combat this slander, Salenger claimed, the average Deacon flaunted the gun—a phallic symbol—to assert his own sexual competence and his contempt for the white man's power. This psychological evaluation of the Deacons might be highly questionable; however, the Deacons' assertion of their masculinity was not.[64]

Although local women were denied official positions in the organization, they nevertheless were proactive in protecting themselves. For example, rather than busying themselves with "wifely chitchat" at a tea party, the wives of Deacons discussed the threat of violence. "I'm going to get me a machine gun or some hand grenades," one claimed, as Robert Hicks, public relations director of the Deacons, offered a .30–30 Winchester for her inspection.[65] Private spaces defined women's spheres of influence with regard to self-defense, and how they behaved at home differed from how they behaved in public. For example, women such as Ora Bryant, Annie Reeves, Laura McGhee, Unita Blackwell, and others regularly participated in the defense of their homes; however, they rarely participated in community patrols.[66]

Outside of Louisiana, news of the Deacons' exploits traveled quickly and found a receptive audience. "It is fact that the Deacons of Defense will not be rejected by most Negro communities they visit," one reporter declared in September 1965, "and it is fact that to most Negroes, willingly or begrudgingly, the Deacons are not unwarranted."[67] However, if most black

Americans supported the Deacons in theory, then they failed to do so in practice. A fundraiser in New York City in October yielded little money. According to one reporter, "Apparently most of the audience wandered in to get out of the cold, bone-chilling Harlem air, because they emptied the church in a hurry when the leaders began asking for contributions."[68]

In an interview in November 1965, Henry Austan, a young member and organizer for the Deacons, explained how he understood the Deacons. "The Deacons are not just a gun-battling organization," he cautioned. "They are set up to participate in a wide-range of activity—from voter registration to transporting civil rights workers in safety into 'hot spots'." Born in New Orleans and raised in Baton Rouge, Austan found himself selling insurance in Bogalusa after leaving the Air Force ("We had a few disagreements," he explained); he joined the Deacons in March 1965 after several attempts on his life. Echoing one of Malcolm X's famous catch-phrases, he declared: "We are dedicated to freedom and we're willing to use any means necessary to obtain our freedom." His words announced a self-conscious, self-styled emulation of the NOI minister's admonition for black people to arm themselves for their own protection. Indeed, he continued: "Malcolm X is my idol. . . . [He] had not yet reached his peak [when he was killed], but I believe he was on the right road. The road I'm on is the one I think he was on."[69]

"Wherever they have organized," Austan boasted, "the Deacons have acted as a deterrent to Klan aggression and white hoodlum activity." He cited one incident in particular. When an eighteen-year-old girl from St. Louis was arrested along with other civil rights activists in Bogalusa, a crowd of white men assembled outside the jail yelling that they wanted to "rape the nigger bitch." Perhaps the sheriff could find no legal reason to detain her, or perhaps he was scared of the angry assemblage outside; perhaps even his sympathies lay with the lynchers. Regardless, he decided to release her while the crowd was there, in effect turning her over to the howling mob. She went straight to the nearest pay phone and called the Deacons, who were monitoring a nearby demonstration. Five of them rushed to her aid. When they arrived to confront the mob, according to Austan, "you could have heard a pin drop." She got in the car with the Deacons and drove away, unimpeded.[70]

Austan emphasized the dignity and respect to be gained in fighting back. "The Deacons have given the Negro throughout the nation an organization they can point to with dignity," he said. He saw little dignity in nonviolent direct action and even less "when a Negro woman is attacked." He felt certain that white aggressors "have little respect for the nonviolent."[71]

Austan also offered a different view of violence itself by comparing the civil rights movement to the war in Vietnam: "If violence is right in Vietnam, then surely violence is right in Mississippi. If violence can be a righteous tool for the white man then surely it can be just as righteous for the black man. If violence can be used to murder defenseless women and children in Vietnam, then certainly it can be used in Louisiana to defend Negroes' lives and property."[72]

By comparing the morally compromised killing fields of Vietnam to the embattled South, he sought to show the righteousness of the Deacons' position: if the government could use violence in an arguably unjust cause, why could southern Afro-Americans not use it in a just one? By questioning the notion that violence is by nature problematic, he sought to legitimate the Deacon's "violent" solution to the aggression they encountered in Bogalusa. Most people living in the United States in the 1960s shared a certain, commonsensical understanding that violence was somehow "bad"; however, Austan tried to show that force, in the guise of self-defense, could be a tempting solution to individual and group predicaments. For him, it was a means of suppressing even greater violence and a method of righting great wrongs. This notion of suppressing violence through the use of force held more and more appeal to activists as the list of egregious acts against them piled up.[73]

Charles Sims traveled to draw attention to Bogalusa, to raise money, and to seek help, but in typically desultory fashion, he lambasted his friends along with his enemies. Speaking at a meeting of the Boston chapter of CORE in March 1966, he criticized the "filthy, dirty streets I see whenever I visit Roxbury." He asked, "How can Negro leaders expect the people to respect and follow them if they can't even see and get rid of an obvious need such as the filth on the streets such as Blue Hill Avenue?" He encouraged black Bostonians to truck garbage to city hall in order to get the mayor's attention. "It amazes me that up here in the North, where you all don't face the kind of crackers we have to face, you let this kind of thing go on," he chided.[74] As reported by a local black newspaper, Sims continued his tirade later that week while speaking with Julian Bond at a Cultural Revival Meeting at Roxbury's Freedom House.[75] His admonition worked: after Sims returned to Louisiana, black Roxbury citizens formed a community group called Attack, which coordinated a clean-up campaign culminating in the dumping of garbage on the steps of Boston's city hall. Sims returned to his support base in Boston in May to make a concerted effort to raise bail money for three Bogalusa Deacons arrested after a shootout on May 13. According to Sims, Bruce Bain, a CORE field worker, and two Deacons, Leyton Griffin and Fletcher Anderson, were leaving the Acme Café in downtown Bogalusa when they were attacked by a group of eight white men. One of the Deacons drew his gun, which caused the men to retreat. The three black men got into their car and drove away; as they were driving down the main street of town, shots were fired through their rear window. The following morning the three men were arrested at their homes on charges of attempted murder. Their bail was set at twenty-five thousand dollars each. "So far, we in the Deacons have been strictly defensive in our activities, but we are getting very tired of this kind of stuff going on," Sims said. "Incidents of this type will force us to retaliate."[76] The Deacons found great favor in Boston, where local residents created the Greater Boston Friends of the Deacons, chaired by Hugh Gilkerson, but it is unclear how much money the group raised there.

Violence leapt the border into neighboring Mississippi in June 1966. Civil rights leaders flocked to the Meredith March Against Fear after James Meredith (who had desegregated the University of Mississippi in 1962) was shot and wounded from ambush on the highway. The march from Memphis to Jackson—a solo crusade begun by Meredith on June 5 as a display of defiance against white oppression—gained momentum when Dr. King of the Southern Christian Leadership Conference, Floyd McKissick and James Farmer of CORE, Stokely Carmichael of the Student Nonviolent Coordinating Committee, and others picked up the march where Meredith was gunned down (near Como) and spearheaded the demonstration as it pressed deeper into Mississippi. The Deacons participated, too, but only after much debate and tumult. It was there in Mississippi, during the Meredith March Against Fear, that the Deacons exploded onto the national scene.[77]

Charles Sims and his Deacons played a pivotal role in the Meredith March (also known as the Greenwood March), which stands as a watershed of the national civil rights movement and the flashpoint for the ongoing debate concerning the place of violence within the movement. Because of the Deacons' controversial image and use of guns, civil rights leaders disagreed as to whether or not the Deacons should participate in the Meredith

March. SNCC opted to continue Meredith's march across Mississippi. According to Cleveland Sellers, a SNCC activist, Stokely Carmichael argued that the march should "de-emphasize white participation, that it should be used to highlight the need for independent black political units, and that the Deacons . . . be permitted to join the march." Roy Wilkins and Whitney Young were "adamantly opposed" to Carmichael. "They wanted to send out a nationwide call to whites; they insisted that the Deacons be excluded and they demanded that [SNCC] issue a statement proclaiming . . . allegiance to nonviolence." Martin Luther King Jr. held the deciding vote. While he favored mass white participation and nonviolence, he was committed to the maintenance of a united front. King sided with Carmichael. Wilkins and Young withdrew their support and did not participate in the march.[78]

Sellers's account of the debate seems reliable, though historians have disagreed over what transpired, particularly over King's involvement in the discussion. King apparently attempted to dissuade the Deacons from making a show of force at the march. Representatives of SNCC and CORE concurred with the Deacons, but King "pressed on":

> He was not saying that Negroes shouldn't protect themselves and their
> houses when attacked. Yet self-defense was not the point here. The point
> was whether they should carry guns in an organized demonstration. To
> do so would only confuse and obscure the moral issues, and it would not
> expose Mississippi injustice. If Negroes came marching through the state
> brandishing .38s and rifles, they were bound to precipitate a calamitous
> confrontation. Whites from the governor down would use it as an excuse to
> start shooting Negroes at random.[79]

Carmichael and Floyd McKissick disagreed with King. McKissick asserted that "nonviolence had outlived its usefulness in this racist country" and that "Negroes ought to break the legs off the Statue of Liberty and 'throw her into the Mississippi'."[80]

Biographer David J. Garrow's account directly contradicts those of Sellers and Oates. Garrow has contended that King remained "largely silent throughout the long and contentious discussion." Carmichael antagonized Roy Wilkins and Whitney Young, yet King kept quiet:

> King's silence gave assistance to Carmichael's goal of dissuading the NAACP
> and the National Urban League from taking part. . . . [B]y remaining

silent King allowed SNCC's divisive desires to run their course. Carmichael interpreted King's silence as either intentional or unintentional support for SNCC. "When we were acting really impolite . . . King made no move at all. He kept quiet."

If King indeed did remain silent during the discussion and did not "plead" for nonviolence and the exclusion of the Deacons, how might his close-mouthed reaction be interpreted? King's silence could be seen as tacit approval of the Deacons and what they represented. Sellers said, "Everyone realized that without [the Deacons], our lives would have been much less secure." Perhaps "everyone," including King, appreciated the Deacons' protection and recognized their participation as complementary, rather than antithetical, to the larger movement.[81]

Charles Sims's own testimony holds the key to unlocking the mystery surrounding the Deacon debates and King's enigmatic behavior. Sims claimed "a lot of things happened on the Meredith march that was never told." For example, he described the funeral of Armstead Phipps, an elderly participant who collapsed and died of a heart attack during the protest, "marchin' for his freedom." King was asked to preach at his funeral "way up in the Delta." King agreed to go to the service, but he would not go unless Sims "carried him."

> And he knowed the only way for me to carry him in the Delta, I had to carry him with my gun and my mens, not his. He can let his men trail along at the tail end, but in front and behind, it was gon' be me. And that was the only way he'd go. So, when the chips were down, I won't say the man woulda picked up a gun, but I'll say this, he didn't run one away, 'cause I was with the man.[82]

Sims had spurned King just a year before. When asking civil rights leaders to come to Bogalusa in 1965, Sims said, "I want everybody here except Martin Luther King. If he came and they gun him, I couldn't protect him, because he don't believe in me." Sims apparently changed his opinion of King after the two men discussed self-defense and the goals of the movement. A year later, during the Meredith March, Sims told King, "Now you do yo' thing and I'm gonna back you up in doin' yo' thing, cause this is my job." Sims admitted that he respected and admired King as a "brilliant" man. According to Sims, King recognized a place for the Deacons within the movement. Both of them, he felt, saw the complementary nature of civil rights activism and armed self-defense by blacks.[83]

During the march, the Deacons provided protection for the marchers by serving as "bodyguards." They stopped suspicious whites loitering near the march route and demanded that they state their business. They walked the ridges of hills adjacent to the road. Earnest Thomas observed the march from his car (complete with a windshield sticker that read "Friends of the Deacons"). Thomas and the Deacons guarded the campsites at night with rifles, pistols, and shotguns, and provided armed escorts for marchers who traveled at night to the airport in Memphis.[84] Reverend Theodore Seamans, pastor of Woodbridge Methodist Church in Woodbridge, New Jersey, saw weapons in the Deacons' cars. He spoke for many when he said, "I was astounded and made my views known. The movement is no place for guns."[85]

Trading shots, whites and blacks skirmished later that month in Philadelphia, Mississippi, where three young civil rights activists—James Chaney, Michael Schwerner, and Andrew Goodman—had been slain exactly two years before, on June 21. There is no evidence to suggest that the black gunmen were Deacons. The Deacons came under fire figuratively later that day when King lashed out at the Deacons in a speech in Yazoo City. In a thinly veiled reproof directed toward the Deacons, King admonished those who used the same methods of violence as "our oppressor"; he did so to reassure the public of the movement's commitment to nonviolence. Also that same day, a recovered James Meredith announced that he would rejoin the march in Canton and evaded the question of whether or not he would carry a gun. Cocksure and maverick as ever, Meredith disavowed the Deacons, saying, "I don't know them. I don't know that they have any capabilities. I don't favor any group. I don't favor the Deacons."[86]

During the Meredith March, Stokely Carmichael introduced the phrase "Black Power" in a speech in Greenwood, Mississippi. The day after the Greenwood rally, SNCC printed up leaflets and placards with the Black Power slogan at the SNCC print shop in Atlanta.[87] Historians have noted Greenwood as a divisive turning point in the movement during which the concept of Black Power split the radical and moderate factions within the movement. While the introduction of Black Power did drive a wedge between some younger and older activists, it united others. Cleveland Sellers noted that although King was forced by "political circumstances" to distance himself and SCLC from Black Power, the Meredith March confirmed King as a "staunch ally" of SNCC and a "true brother."[88]

Sims wavered on the subject of Black Power. Initially he sought to define the phrase broadly. Noting that the phrase "had resulted from a need for southern Negroes to have some say in determining our affairs," he surmised that the press had "misinterpreted" the expression:

When Rev. Martin Luther King led the Montgomery Bus Boycott in 1957, that was nothing more than a display of Black Power. When Negroes in the South work in voter registration campaigns, that's nothing more than a display of Black Power. When Negroes press for passage of federal civil rights and voting rights bills, they're using their Black Power to get those bills through Congress. To say that we're in favor of increasing our Black Power does not mean that we won't use white help we can get to aid us in our fight. Black Power is not racist any more than Irish power is racist. As I understand it, the Irish practically own Boston. They use their strength in numbers to get themselves elected and to hire other Irishmen once they get in. Well, that's exactly what we intend to do in the South.[89]

Notably, Sims would later denunciate Black Power and the multivalent ideas for which it stood. "The slogan Black Power didn't do a damn thing but hurt the movement," he told Howell Raines. "I don't wanna live under Black Power. I don't wanna live under white power. I want equal power, and that's what I push." He saw not only the mentality of black supremacy but also the phrase "Black Power" itself as divisive. "How can you work with a son of a bitch that every time you look up he's thowin' up his fist talkin' 'bout Black Power? . . . Put too much power in any one son of a bitch's hands, it's too much." He continued:

[T]he cats that was hollerin' Black Power, I was protectin' and guardin' they damn ass. I don't see nothin' they was doin' to even be talkin' 'bout no Black Power. The Black Power, we had it. In them thirty rounds of ammunition on a man's shoulder, we had the Black Power.

To Sims, Stokely Carmichael's brand of Black Power was only rhetoric; *real* "Black Power" grew from vigilant self-protection.[90]

Robert Rester, the city attorney of Bogalusa, called for a grand jury investigation of both the Deacons and the BCVL to determine "whether they have possibly violated any state laws pertaining to possession of firearms," but the investigation apparently had little impact on the group.[91] Henry Austan, as public relations director for the Deacons, spoke in Boston in January 1967, when he noted how irrelevant the civil rights movement had become:

> The civil rights movement is no longer relative to the questions that black people in this country are facing. . . . The civil rights movement was originally a protest addressed to the power structure by the bourgeoisie, it was never addressed to the power structure by the people in the streets, blacks in the ghetto, the ones who are trapped, the ones who really have a problem. . . . The people in the ghettos who are now saying give me something to eat, give me a place to stay, give me a job . . . things that America is incapable of giving at the moment.[92]

Blasting the Voting Rights Act of 1965, he observed, "OK, now you legally have the right to vote, we have legally had the right to vote for one hundred years, but there is still the problem of registering to vote, and after you register there is the problem of living long enough to vote." He further explained the affiliation of the Deacons with other organizations when he said, "I think our primary role in Roxbury would be to help disseminate information, distribute leaflets, etcetera. But you must remember that the Deacon membership overlaps into other organizations, so whoever is a Deacon here is working in another organization and only when he is really needed as a Deacon does he work as a Deacon." The group enjoyed tight connections with several civil rights organizations, particularly the young activists of CORE. "One thing we felt extremely proud of in the South," he concluded, "is when black kids would come and they would see the Deacons and they would say, 'This is what I want to be'—for once they were seeing black men stand up and be men."[93]

As quickly as they soared to notoriety, the Deacons faded from fame. After the Meredith March, they all but disappeared from the national media. The Deacons made one last major news splash in September 1967 before they slipped into obscurity. The local NAACP led a march in Woodville, Mississippi to protest Negro teachers who did not favor blacks running in Democratic primaries. At the march, police disarmed Deacons who were present.[94]

Curiously, as the Deacons faded from the scene, the Federal Bureau of Investigation, with characteristic untimeliness, targeted the organization to be "disrupted" and "neutralized," along with SNCC, SCLC, CORE, the Revolutionary Action Movement (RAM), and the Nation of Islam. Director J. Edgar Hoover addressed a memo headed "Personal Attention to All Offices" on August 25, 1967 concerning what he termed "Black Nationalist Hate Groups." The Deacons were later downgraded as a primary target, displaced by the other groups because of the national scope of these organizations and their "most violent and radical" orientations.[95]

Contrary to FBI sources, the Deacons tried to avoid provoking a clash of arms, though their opponents argued that by arming themselves in the first place, the Deacons instigated conflict in an already explosive situation. It is debatable whether or not possessing weapons served as a catalyst for violence. Sims and his cohorts felt that having weapons at hand effectively deterred violence. Discussing armed self-defense and exhibiting a proclivity to fight back seemed to fuel progress in the struggle for black equality in Bogalusa. Sims found that merely showing a weapon could often avert violence. "The showing of a weapon stops many things," he said. "Everybody want to live and nobody want to die."[96] Simply being seen with Sims was insurance enough for many local blacks. "I'm one of the few peoples who is really known as a Deacon and anybody that I associate with, they [whites] just take for granted they are Deacons," Sims explained. "I show up, then ten, twelve more mens show up, whether they Deacons or not, they branded." In this case, being "branded" as a Deacon meant freedom from molestation by whites.[97]

A fine line existed, and still exists, between self-defense and aggressive violence. In hot spots such as Bogalusa, legitimate self-defense against an aggressor could switch quickly to something more retaliatory. The Deacons could have slipped across the precipice of legitimacy at any time, crossing into the morally questionable realm of aggressive violence. Where the two planes intersected was not always clear, as Charles Sims illustrated:

> See, we had made up our mind on one thing. I know where just about every honkie here live. If he'd attacked any my mens, he couldn't go to his house and sleep no more, 'cause if he do, I don't know what woulda happened to him. I won't say we'da killed him. I got more sense than to use those words, but I'm not sure what would have happened.[98]

Sims came perilously close to promising retributive violence, but did not. Undoubtedly, the threat existed, whether he verbally expressed it or not. The Deacons seemed aware of their precarious position and took pains to avoid the labels "aggressive" or "violent." They stressed that whatever force they used was defensive, rather than offensive. They did not see their advocacy of self-protection as "violence," per se.[99]

The Deacons' rapid disappearance raises important questions: What led to the demise of the organization? Did government repression play a role? Perhaps the group dissipated as the character of the movement became more "violent" and more militant. In other words, it is possible that the movement outgrew the Deacons. Perhaps as the goals of the larger civil rights movement incorporated the ideals of the Deacons, the group no longer had a place; no longer needed for protective purposes, the Deacons became obsolete. In the mid-to-late 1960s, fewer and fewer activists had qualms about self-defense or about picking up a gun to further the aims of the movement; the Deacons helped bring about this trend.[100] It is also possible that the Deacons recoiled from public view because of ideological differences with other activists, exemplified by King's repudiation of the group and their own disillusionment with Black Power advocates. The focus of the FBI, the national media, and the general public shifted to the West Coast at this time, when the Black Panthers began to garner attention.

Sims claimed that the Deacons had chapters all across the country. COIN-TELPRO FBI files do not confirm organization on a national level; however, they do indicate chapters in places such as Washington, D.C. and Chicago.[101] The FBI carefully monitored black militant groups in major U.S. cities from 1967 on, and the Bureau records present some evidence of "cell" activity in different cities. An FBI memorandum dated July 12, 1966, confirmed that Earnest Thomas, as "Regional Vice-President and Northern Director of the DDJ," was traveling around the United States. Thomas claimed to have set up Deacons chapters, "on a militant basis," in several cities. However, the memorandum also noted that Thomas was acting "strictly on his own behalf," without official sanction from other Deacons; furthermore, it noted:

> The DDJ headquarters in Jonesboro has reportedly never received any
> requests for charters from anywhere outside of the state of Louisiana and
> they could not issue charters outside of the state if they were so requested.[102]

The Deacons' leadership insisted on the pervasiveness of the group. For example, an interviewer asked Robert Hicks in 1969 if the Deacons were still in existence, and how long they might continue. Hicks replied, "Well,

I think this will probably be as long as black people are oppressed and the white man is still trying to use force to keep the black man down. . . . The Deacons are still in existence today . . . still on call if anything would happen to a black person in the community."[103] Speculation regarding the disappearance of the Deacons points to the possibility that the organization did not disappear outright, but merely became translucent, incarnate in the black struggle for equality. Secrecy and indeterminate membership pertaining to the Deacons fortify this theory. Sims ominously surmised, "If push hadda come to shove, we were well covered."[104]

Essential in understanding their origins, defining the Deacons becomes essential in determining their fate as well. "Anytime a Negro and a white man have any kind of round up and the Negro decide he going to fight him back," Sims once said, "he's a Deacon."[105] The Bogalusa president further complicated defining the organization by extending its membership to all those who stood up to "the man."[106] The Deacons became, in an abstract sense, a mindset, a broad concept of empowerment and self-protection.

As the nine days' wonder of the civil rights movement, the Deacons waxed and waned in a strikingly short period of time, but their impact was considerable. They punctured the double standard of self-defense in America. They homed in on the lesser amounts of protection offered blacks by southern polity and made a conscious effort to change the discrepancy. "I think the Louisiana state law says a man can carry a weapon in his car as long as it is not concealed," said Sims. "We found out in Bogalusa that that law meant for the white man, it didn't mean for the colored. Any time a colored man was caught with a weapon in his car, they jailed him for carrying a concealed weapon. So we carried them to court."[107] Sims noted that police only interfered when empowered black men and women asserted their civil rights. For example, the police in Philadelphia, Mississippi made no move to interfere in black-white clashes "until half a dozen Negroes began to fight back."[108] Sims also observed, "in the southern states, the police have never done their job when the white and the Negro are involved—unless the Negro's getting the best of the white man."[109] James Farmer summed it up best when he explained: "Understand, the Deacons don't replace legal law enforcement—there is no such thing as legal law enforcement in much of the South that will protect a Negro citizen."[110] The law eventually helped the Deacons, who helped themselves in a situation where inclusive law and order had broken down.

Farmer's interest in the Deacons was more than rhetorical. The Deacons' stand on self-defense profoundly influenced many CORE operatives, and caused a deep rift within the organization. CORE's "Rules for Action" included the assertion: "He [a CORE member] will meet the anger of any individual or group in the spirit of good will and creative reconciliation: he will submit to assault and will not retaliate in kind either by act or word."[111] But as the movement evolved, CORE edged away from the nonviolent ideal and co-opted the Deacons' philosophy of self-defense. A CORE worker in Ferriday, Louisiana, stated in 1965 that self-defense in protection of one's home and person was "taken for granted," and most of CORE's headquarters in dangerous areas of Louisiana and Mississippi had weapons on the premises to protect against attack.[112]

The debate between armed, southern field workers and long-time pacifists split CORE, which almost rescinded its official policy on nonviolence at its national convention in 1965. The push for rescinding CORE's commitment to nonviolence was so strong that it was defeated only by the intervention of Deacon leader Earnest Thomas, who surprisingly urged CORE members to maintain their traditional adherence to nonviolence. Farmer also helped to kill the issue by carefully distinguishing between nonviolent direct action in demonstrations and the constitutional right to self-defense.[113] Still, CORE's Northeast Region resolved that "CORE accepts the concept of self-defense by the Deacons, and believes that the use of guns by CORE workers on a southern project is a personal decision, with the approval of that project's and the Regional directors."[114]

Similarly, the Deacons influenced a younger generation of activists, drawn to the promise of sweeping change and immediate results. Geronimo Pratt, for example, saw nothing new about the Deacons. He traced a "straight line" from the Deacons all the way back to Marcus Garvey's Legionnaires, a "military protectorate" organized in the 1920s to combat the Ku Klux Klan. Pratt understood the Deacons, like the Legionnaires, to be operating in "simple self-defense" against "burning churches" and "preaching hate." The Deacons inspired Pratt to a life of activism. After learning of the shootings of O'neal Moore and Creed Rogers in Washington Parish, north of his hometown of Morgan City, Louisiana, he "was ready to take on the whole KKK single-handed." The testimony in Pratt's biography, *Last Man Standing*, indicates that he chose the Army over going to college in order to receive the military training—"munitions, perimeter defense, sandbagging, riflery, hand-to-hand combat, stuff like that"—that the older generation of Deacons learned in World War II and the Korean War. Such training prepared Pratt for his active leadership role in the Black Panther Party in Los Angeles. "We had to develop a new generation of black warriors or the Klan was gonna overwhelm us," he claimed. "They were *already* overwhelming us."[115] Fred Brooks admitted, "I think we learned a lot from the Deacons. . . . By adopting their philosophy of protecting yourself instead of being nonviolent toward someone who is trying to take violence upon you has allowed people to live where ordinarily they'd probably be killed."[116] In this way, the Deacons influenced a younger generation of activists and impacted an area well beyond Louisiana.

Charles Sims and the Deacons seemed acutely conscious of their role in history. Sims felt that standing up to white supremacists by defending their homes and by participating in rallies signaled the birth of "a brand new Negro." He explained, "We told [the southern white man] that a brand new Negro was born. The one he'd been pushin' around, he didn't exist anymore. . . . We definitely couldn't swim, and we was as close to the river as we could get so there was but one way to go."[117]

In 1965, there was no such legal concept as collective self-defense, but it did exist in reality, as the Deacons demonstrated; that is, collective self-defense, in the guise of citizens' patrols, represented a *de facto* expression of black self-determination. The very act of defending themselves and protecting their interests transformed ordinary men like Charles Sims, Robert Hicks, and Henry Austan into activists, as self-defense was becoming a vehicle for civil rights reform. As one scholar has explained, the Deacons "made Bogalusa one of the places in the South where armed self-defense supplemented tactical nonviolent direct action in the civil rights movement. . . . Their discipline and dedication inspired the community, their very existence made black people in Bogalusa think more of themselves as people who could not be pushed around."[118] Defending the Quarters in Bogalusa seemed to be the only recourse for the Deacons, confronted with police personnel who were often indifferent to their plight and sometimes complicit in injustices directed against them.

The Deacons personified self-defense in the civil rights movement; they also marked the development of strategies for communities, as well as individuals. As part of a concerted, organized effort on the part of local citizens to challenge Klan ascendancy, the Deacons signified a new era in southern race relations in which Afro-Americans developed increasingly more organized, collective forms of armed self-defense. Their development of collective self-defense as armed resistance marked the beginning of the politicization of self-defense within Afro-American history; this trend would reach its zenith with the actions of another group, the Black Panther Party for Self-Defense. As means supplanted end, what had begun as a necessary complement to civil rights protest—i.e., self-defense by activists threatened with violence—was becoming a vehicle of reform itself. But before that would occur, something happened on the West Coast of the United States that would shock the nation and shake the civil rights movement to its core. Less than a month after the Deacons chased Klansmen out of the Quarters in Bogalusa, Watts burned.

Burn baby, burn!

MAGNIFICENT MONTAGUE, RADIO DJ, LOS ANGELES, 1965

CHAPTER 6

CODE 1199, OFFICER NEEDS HELP

Rioting as Self-Defense in Watts, 1965

Often explained as a spasmodic event, a convulsion of discontent, Watts has come to symbolize, more than any other similar occurrence of the 1960s, the uncontrolled and uncontrollable violence of the urban poor, a voiceless and powerless subset of American society. However, there is much evidence to suggest that what happened in Watts was itself a kind of collective self-defense, not entirely unlike what the Deacons did in Bogalusa and what the Black Panthers would attempt to do in Oakland.

There is still a great deal of controversy over the best way to characterize the events in Watts, Detroit, Newark, and other cities in the 1960s. Many politically conscious activists insist on calling the incidents "uprisings" or "rebellions," while others, emphasizing the lawlessness of the events, insist on calling them "riots." This controversy has often split along racial lines, with Afro-Americans favoring the former and white Americans preferring the latter. How one labels such events reveals as much about the labeler's assumptions and preconceptions as it does about the events themselves, and different terms carry categorically specialized meanings. For example, "pogrom" connotes official consent, often accompanied by state and police participation. "Riot" connotes chaos and/or unrestrained destruction. "Uprising" connotes spontaneity, often coming from the lower classes of society. "Rebellion" implies political consciousness. "Revolution," "revolt," and "insurrection" are synonymous terms meaning the violent overthrow of existing governmental forms. The last five terms usually refer to casting off some form of oppression. For a number of reasons, not the least of which is a refusal to recognize such seemingly random violence as selective and deliberate, "riot" continues to be the default designation for such events in the 1960s, including what happened in Watts. However, the appellation "conflagration" may be preferable with regard to Watts for at least two reasons: it is a neutral term not already laden with politically charged meanings, and it captures the central role of fire in the destruction.

The so-called riots of the 1960s marked a turning point in the civil rights movement and in Afro-American history in general. In the first half of the twentieth century, the United States experienced racially motivated riots at the rate of about one per year, with varying degrees of severity. Most were small in scope and concentrated during World Wars I and II. But during the "long hot summers" of the mid- to late-1960s, widespread racial violence became almost routine in America's urban enclaves. During these years there were, by one account, 239 riots serious enough for local law enforcement agencies to call upon outside assistance.[1] Signaling a shift toward a more destructive kind of protest by the nation's poor peoples of color, and toward an intolerance of violence as a mode of expression by the nation's white middle and upper classes, the riots heralded a new rift between blacks and whites after a brief period of promise.

The riots also symbolized a change in the nature of racial violence itself. Before the 1960s, a "race riot" customarily meant a group of whites wantonly killing and destroying property in a local black community. The tenor and tone of race riots in the 1960s were dramatically different from their nineteenth- and early twentieth-century counterparts. Instead of lynchings and other attacks in which Afro-Americans were the sole victims, angry black city dwellers in the 1960s were attacking whites and destroying white property in the ghettoes. White Americans were generally surprised by the outbreak and the ferocity of these events, the most notable of which occurred in 1965 in an impoverished, ethnically diverse section of south-central Los Angeles known as Watts.

Like other riots that would follow, the Watts conflagration was sparked by a routine traffic stop. Marquette Frye, a black motorist, was pulled over, along with his stepbrother, for speeding and erratic driving the night of August 11, 1965. Trying to lighten the situation and perhaps humor the officer into a light reprimand, Frye verbally sparred with the white policeman, Officer Lee Minikus of the California Highway Patrol (CHP). The two joked, smiled, and kidded one another as a friendly crowd gathered, curious about what was happening. After a series of sobriety tests, the officer decided to arrest Frye for speeding and drunk driving. Officer Robert Lewis, Minikus's partner, arrived with a patrol car and a tow truck at about the same time as Frye's mother, Rena Frye, reached the scene. When confronted by his mother, Frye insisted he was not drunk, but she smelled liquor on his breath and encouraged her son to go with the policemen. Frye's mood shifted abruptly: he became defiant and belligerent, insisting that he would not be arrested. The officers, prepared for such a contingency, responded with the usual procedures for dealing with a recalcitrant suspect, but the scene quickly deteriorated: Lewis radioed "code 1199," which means "Officer Needs Help." As Officers Minikus and Lewis attempted to cuff Frye, other officers arrived; one produced a shotgun and used it to shove onlookers away from the scene. Chief William H. Parker of the Los Angeles Police Department testified: "In response to an 'Officer Needs Help' call broadcast at 7:18 P.M., the first LAPD officers found ten California Highway Patrolmen, with the Fryes in custody, facing a hostile crowd of from 300 to 500 Negroes."[2]

What happened next is unclear, but blows were exchanged as officers used batons to subdue Frye and his stepbrother. Mrs. Frye, involved in the altercation, was also arrested. More onlookers and more officers were pouring into the area as the crowd became openly hostile toward the policemen. Someone spat upon one of the policemen; the police grabbed the culprit, a young woman named Joyce Ann Gaines. Gaines, who worked at a local barbershop, was wearing a smock that resembled a maternity dress. As police whisked her into a patrol car, word quickly spread that the officers had manhandled a pregnant mother. It was enough to touch off a full-scale "riot" or, more accurately, a series of riots in different localized spots over the course of several days.

Bill Stout, a CBS reporter, described the scene for a television audience:

> Small army of policemen, most of them carrying shotguns; National Guardsmen riding jeeps with .30-caliber machine guns. Bodies of several Negroes who have been shot already in this battle, stretched out beside the curb. Acres and acres of broken glass, burned, gutted and looted stores, junk heaps. Now this hunt is like something out of a bad war movie, a western perhaps: policemen on the rooftops, in the streets.[3]

Pleas for peace fell on deaf ears. When Martin Luther King Jr. visited Los Angeles on August 18, he was heckled and jeered by Watts residents at a neighborhood meeting. "You all know my philosophy, you all know that I believe firmly in nonviolence," he implored. "So maybe some of you don't quite agree with this. I want you to be willing to say that." An unidentified man in the audience replied, "Sure we like to be nonviolent, but we up here in Los Angeles will not turn that other cheek." His reply met cheers from the audience.[4] Comedian and social activist Dick Gregory, also pleading for peace, was shot in the leg by a rioter on the street.[5]

When the flames had died and the smoke had cleared, at least thirty-four persons were dead. Thirty-one persons had been fatally shot by law enforcement officers, National Guardsmen, and "persons unknown" during the rioting; one sheriff's deputy, one policeman, and one fireman were also killed. There may have been additional deaths, uncounted by official statistics. The number of people involved is muddy: studies indicate that at least 31,000 black people actively participated, and double this number—between 64,000 and 72,000 persons—may have been involved as close spectators. Sixteen thousand National Guardsmen, Los Angeles Police Department officers, California Highway Patrolmen, and other law enforcement personnel participated. There were 1032 reported injuries, including 90 police officers, 136 firemen, 23 government personnel, and 773 civilians; 118 of the injuries were from gunshot wounds. More than six hundred buildings were damaged by burning and looting; of this number, more than two hundred were totally destroyed by fire. Total property damage was estimated at around forty million dollars. Most of those killed were black, while most of the property damage accrued to white-owned businesses: markets, liquor stores, pawnshops, and stores specializing in furniture, appliances, and clothing.[6]

Almost as soon as the rioting had ceased, speculations about its origins ignited a different kind of firestorm. The search for the factors that sparked the riot caused in-fighting among government agencies and officials. Journalists and reporters sought to blame politicians for the rioting, and politicians sought to blame each other. Los Angeles mayor Sam Yorty and California Governor Edmund G. Brown, political rivals for the Democratic nomination in the 1966 California gubernatorial race, took turns blaming each other for the incident. Critics heaped the most blame on Los Angeles Police Chief William H. Parker. As head of the opprobrious Los Angeles Police Department (LAPD), Parker embraced a combat-oriented approach to police work that escalated tensions between black Angelenos and law enforcement personnel, and his prejudicial beliefs won few nonwhite admirers. "One person threw a rock," he noted in explaining how the riot started, "and then, like monkeys in a zoo, others started throwing rocks." On another occasion, when the rioting was subsiding, Parker stated, "We're on top and they are on the bottom." Whom he meant by "we" and "they" is unclear, but Parker's insensitive comments during and after the riots enraged blacks across the nation. He too cast blame, accusing the California Highway Patrol of improperly handling the situation. In what seemed to be an attempt to divert unwanted attention from himself and the LAPD, Chief Parker told a national audience on NBC's "Meet the Press" that the CHP lacked the training and experience to handle such arrests; if the LAPD had made the arrests on August 11, he concluded, the rioting would have been averted.[7]

Governor Brown appointed a commission to investigate the riots. Faced with explaining the violence, Brown appointed John A. McCone, a former CIA director and staunch conservative, to offset his own liberal and sympathetic attitudes toward Afro-Americans. In its report, released later that same year, the McCone Commission described the events of August 1965:

The rioting in Los Angeles in the late, hot summer of 1965 took six days to run its full grievous course. . . . In the ugliest interval, which lasted from Thursday through Saturday, perhaps as many as 10,000 Negroes took to the streets in marauding bands. They looted stores, set fires, beat up white passersby whom they hauled from stopped cars, many of which were turned upsidedown and burned, exchanged shots with law enforcement officers, and stoned and shot at firemen. The rioters seemed to have been caught up in an insensate rage of destruction.[8]

Members of the McCone Commission scratched their heads, wondering why the riot happened when it did, and why it happened in Los Angeles, and answers were not forthcoming. Los Angeles, by most accounts, was a nice place to live, free of the urban blight common in America's proto-typical black enclave, Harlem. The streets were wide and clean, with trees and parks and playgrounds. The McCone Report noted that a "statistical portrait" drawn in 1964 by the Urban League, which rated American cities in terms of "ten basic aspects of Negro life"—such as housing, employment, and income—ranked L.A. first among the sixty-eight cities that were examined. If Los Angeles had been in the South, then its racial woes might have been more easily fathomable by McCone and his team, but it was not; unlike southern cities, L.A. did not suffer from segregation. Black Angelenos could come and go as they pleased, sit where they wanted, shop where they chose, and vote for the candidate of their choice. The McCone Commission surmised: "The opportunity to succeed [in Los Angeles] is probably unequaled in any other major American city."[9]

Indeed, the problems of Watts were not readily noticeable to the casual observer. The streets of south-central Los Angeles were not dark; the buildings were neither rat-infested, northern tenements nor dilapidated southern schoolhouses, but Watts was rotting from the inside out, and its distress lay camouflaged beneath a proud façade of neatly manicured lawns and flower gardens. Observers and participants helped the McCone Commission to see past the neighborhood's veneer of middle-class normality; after providing a detailed description of the destruction, it used the remainder of its report to discuss the "serious deterioration" of living conditions and facilities in the affected area, particularly as related to employment, education, transportation, business, welfare, health, and housing. As Mary Ann Forniss, boarding-house keeper and mother of five, explained, "Watts is a pretty bad old neighborhood. It is not a neighborhood where people would love to be too well. . . . We have too many broken down, bad houses, and unkempt homes. . . ."[10] Still, the Commissioners could not comprehend why the riots happened, clinging to the idea that the kind of behavior engendered in civil unrest was necessarily irrational, self-defeating, immoderate, senseless, formless, malign, incoherent, destructive, and somehow different from the normal group processes of society. The Commission assessed: "What happened was an explosion—a formless, quite senseless, all but hopeless violent protest—engaged in by a few but bringing great distress to all." The McCone Commission blandly concluded that there was a "need for leadership" from "Negro leaders" to ameliorate conditions in Watts. Amazingly, the Commission did not recommend an adjustment in police behavior in the ghetto, but rather prescribed a "correction of misunderstandings involving law enforcement."[11]

Receptions of the McCone Commission's findings by black Americans and liberal whites were lukewarm at best. Critics charged that the Commission's brief 101-page report was generally unsympathetic and overly focused on criminal activity. "We are sorely disappointed by the McCone Commission Report," stated one group. "It prescribes aspirin where surgery is required."[12] Most white Americans, however, seemed content with the Commission's findings. They sympathized little with what they saw as a savage and frightening outburst by out-of-control Afro-Americans. The typical response was expressed in *Anarchy Los Angeles*, a privately published exposé that characterized the Watts conflagration not as an "insurrection" but as "hoodlumism" informed by "fun" and "recreation." A sensational and unsympathetic explanation of mob violence, *Anarchy Los Angeles* proffered: "As time passes, the element of 'monkey see, monkey do' becomes a big factor at work. People yell, smash, loot, and burn with no thought as to why they are doing it." It included an offensive description of the happenings in Watts that mirrored British characterizations of the Mau Mau rebellion in East Africa: "Faces shown in the red glow, teeth glistened, and voices chanted 'Burn, baby, burn'. . . ." The patronizingly racist portrayal omitted only the sound of beating drums in its Conradian description of fiery ritual, shiny faces, glinting teeth, and native chanting.[13]

Conventional explanations of the Watts conflagration, typified by the McCone Commission's report, were—and continue to be—patently similar, blending together into a single, popular, causal theory. For years the people of south-central Los Angeles had experienced discrimination, poverty, and dire frustration. No one, including their affluent neighbors to the north, east, and west, paid much attention to the inadequate housing, limited economic opportunity, and substandard living conditions so common in the inner city. A paucity of jobs led residents to do menial tasks when and where they could find employment. While making substantial strides toward political equality, the civil rights movement in the South had raised hopes and expectations without providing any real gains for black folks living in cities such as Los Angeles, outside the South. Feelings of resentment and futility ran high. Amidst a heightening atmosphere of militancy, as evidenced by the growing influence of the Black Muslims and various cultural nationalists who advocated black self-determination mixed with anti-white sentiment, it took only a spark to ignite the powder keg of racial animosity that was Watts.[14]

There are two major problems with this conventional explanation. First, it focuses on surrounding social conditions, rather than on reasons given by participants and observers themselves. An overview of sociological factors—including employment, health services, housing, education, welfare, child care, and recreation—all facilitate a complete understanding of the standard of living in America's ghettos, but they do not explain what motivated Watts inhabitants to act with violence when they did. Clearly, the McCone Commission's appraisal was insufficient in so far as it largely neglected the attitudes that propelled participants to act.

These explanations instead turn quickly to the underlying sociological factors—poverty, crime, drugs, despair, and inopportunity—which made life in the ghetto unbearable. Therefore, much of the popular interpretation of riots has revolved around an understanding of the desperate situation of those persons living in urban ghettos. But rioting was not exclusively a problem of poverty. Statistics related to those arrested during the Watts riot are helpful in making this point. According to one study, two-thirds of the men arrested and convicted were employed, and as many as one-third were earning a respectable three hundred dollars per month, or more. Thus, considerations other than financial distress may have drawn rioters into participation.[15]

In explaining the causes of the riots, residents, in conjunction with inquisitive social scientists, collectively formulated a kind of laundry list of all that was wrong with Watts, and they found plenty. For example, Mervyn M. Dynally, Assemblyman for the 53rd District in Los Angeles County, cited the following causes when interviewed after the conflagration: (1) "bad police-community relations," (2) "lack of community interest" in business matters, (3) "high rate of school drop-outs," (4) "poor communication with governmental agencies and poor identification with political boundaries," (5) "lack of adequate low-cost housing in the district," (6) "breakdown of the family unit," (7) "lack of educational opportunity," and (8) "high rate of families with dependent children" (as if there were any other kind of children). Dynally's analysis is only one of a score of inclusive attempts to articulate the entire range of factors contributing to the riots.[16]

This blanket attempt to exhaust all the possible social conditions that might have contributed to feelings of resentment or displeasure on the part of Watts residents gave the people of Watts a much-needed opportunity to air their grievances; however, it also had an obscuring effect. Instead of clarifying the cause or causes of the riots, the underlying prompts became murkier, clouded in a complicated skein of interwoven contributors. Subsequent attempts to capture the complexity of the riots, rather than ferreting out a predominant cause, complicated the issue because the explanations drifted further and further from the immediate circumstances of the Watts conflagration.[17]

Second, the conventional explanation, while succinct and a propos, also fails to address one key element in the riot: Marquette Frye's arrest. The intricate sociological surveys and studies of Watts tend, as a body, to ignore Frye's arrest and perceptions of that event. It was this event that sparked the rioting which, depending on how one viewed the events of August 11–18, either evolved into a kind of political protest or degenerated into a smash-and-grab free-for-all. What was it about Frye's arrest, in particular, that triggered the ire of thousands of black residents of south-central Los Angeles? Arrests of this sort took place daily in Watts; as two scholars have noted: "The rioting in Los Angeles followed from a routine arrest, one of many made every day in every part of the city." Another analysis characterizes Frye's incarceration as a "commonplace drunk-driving arrest."[18] Was the effect of these constant confrontations between white officers and black suspects cumulative, resulting in swelling frustration, or did other factors come into play? Indeed, analyses of the Watts riot tend to acknowledge the routine nature of arrests of black suspects by white officers without explaining how *Frye's* arrest—as opposed to all of the other arrests like his—generated a firestorm of violent response.

Occam's Razor, or law of parsimony, may be most helpful in reestablishing the most immediate causes of the event. This law of reasoning suggests that one should not increase, beyond what is necessary, the number of entities required to explain any phenomenon; in other words, the simplest explanation is often the best. By focusing on the circumstances surrounding the arrest of Marquette Frye, one might ascertain why Watts exploded when it did; indeed, doing so suggests that the Watts riot was caused not by internal factors of deprivation and neglect, but by an external factor, a foreign presence—namely, the heavy-handed, violent intrusion of the police that inspired Watts residents to respond in kind, violently. Interviews of participants and witnesses suggest that participants were not instigating a riot so much as they were responding to an invasive white presence in their community: law enforcement personnel. In other words, the Watts conflagration may have been not so much a "riot" but a defensive reaction: a collective expression of self-defense.

A sampling of surveys conducted after the conflagration provides unique insight into the minds of those who rioted. To investigators from the McCone Commission who conducted post-riot surveys and interviews, witnesses and participants offered a panoply of explanations regarding what caused the riots. Some interviewees offered no explanations, some said that people were "out of control," some cited the Frye case specifically, and others blamed social conditions such as poverty and unemployment; however, most respondents included some reference to the LAPD and its rough ways in dealing with black suspects. Witnesses and participants both repeatedly cited police presence and misbehavior in the ghetto as a primary cause for the rioting; in fact, a majority of those black arrestees who were interviewed after the conflagration cited the Los Angeles Police Department as a primary factor in causing the riots. For example, when asked what he thought of "protection provided by" and "relations with community of" the LAPD, Emile Burns replied, "Bad." When asked, "What do you think caused the riots?" Burns replied that "police brutality was the cause of resentment by people." Rosie Ellis, when asked what she believed caused the riots, replied, "Policemen, some very hateful, but some nice." Louis Edward Watkins said that "over-policing" was the cause, but felt it would not have been a problem if police had been courteous to black residents. Lovella Brumsley cited "police brutality" as the number-one cause of the riots, as did George Carter and Jimmie James Baker. (When asked if he participated in the riot, Carter regretfully replied, "No, but I should have.") Henry D. Atkins said the riot happened "because of the actions of police officers mistreating Negroes over a long period of time. . . . Negroes just got tired of it." Booker T. Allison stated that the riots were caused by "police injustices to Negroes over a number of years."[19]

Physical abuse, verbal mistreatment, and improper procedure by police were common complaints from interviewed arrestees. Johnnie Carter described the LAPD officers as "brutal, uncouth, and rugged." Willie Shorty testified that one officer clubbed him with a "riot gun" and repeatedly used the word "nigger," asking, "You niggers think you are going to take over this town like Mississippi?" He described the incident as "a field day for the LAPD," and heard one officer say, "I haven't shot a nigger since yesterday"; the officer added, "We like a little excitement once in a while. . . . We get a chance to shoot our guns." Interestingly, many interviewees cite favorable impressions of the Los Angeles County Sheriff's Department, the California Highway Patrol, and especially the National Guard, who restored order and, according to one arrestee, provided "good protection during the riot." Clarence Richards's testimony suggests that he valued the efforts of restoring order not only from the chaos of "hoodlums" but also from the punishing and sometimes murderous tactics of the LAPD officers, who damaged Richards's right hand when they applied handcuffs too tightly around his wrists.[20]

The violent actions of law enforcement personnel in the Frye arrest seemed to be direct determinants of what the police termed "riotous behavior." Richard Brice, a Watts store owner, testified: "The officer took his club and kept jamming it into his [Frye's] stomach. When that happened, all the people standing around got mad. I got mad. . . . Everybody got excited and started shouting. . . . His [the policeman's] action was breeding violence."[21] Mrs. Ovelmar Bradley, mother of seven, noted that things quieted down after the initial incident on Avalon, but then twenty-five or thirty police cars screamed into the area with sirens whining. "If the police hadn't come in like that," she noted, "people wouldn't all have come running out of their houses to see what was going on."[22] Peter Smith, a bread salesman and Watts resident, stated: "It was easily observable that the wrath of the crowd was focused on police."[23] A reporter noted: "The McCone Commission dug thoroughly into this event [Frye's arrest]. It found no basis for criticizing the conduct or judgment of officers on the scene. But no one questions that this was the incident, nothing more, the spark that lighted the fuse."[24]

After "touring" the Watts area on Sunday morning, August 18, and talking with residents, Governor Brown reported: "I got some complaints about police brutality. I found a general condition of dislike for Chief Parker, I would say it was almost unanimous among the people I spoke with, that they felt the police did not understand the problem of the Negro." The people with whom he spoke "had more confidence in the [National] Guard than they did in the police department." Brown had heard a rumor that Chief Parker had taken fifty thousand dollars allotted for community relations and "used it to buy riot helmets," adding "but I'm not in a position to judge that."[25] Bradford Crittenden, Administrator of Public Safety for the State of California and California Highway Patrol Commissioner, offered that "newly arrived Negro residents seem to resent the police uniform, whether it be the C.H.P., the Sheriff, or the LAPD"; however, interviews of those arrested indicate that whatever animosity black persons felt was mainly directed toward the LAPD.[26] Indeed, the actions of the LAPD, in particular, seemed to provoke a defensive response from black residents of Watts. When Adrian Dove, a representative of the California Department of Industrial Relations, entered the curfew area, residents informed him that "this was not a war against all whites" but rather "a continued war against the LAPD and Chief Parker."[27] Billy Mills, a city councilman, questioned the LAPD's brutality in quelling the rioting, and warned that citizens might need to take "protective measures" against the LAPD.[28]

Accordingly, the Watts conflagration may be understood as self-defense: a reflexive act of self-protection that evolved into an effort to rid the area of an invasive white presence, the most visible manifestation of which was the LAPD. The violence was responsive and reactive: an 18-year-old girl who admitted to throwing bricks told a white reporter, "Why not do it to you guys? You're doing it to us."[29] Many post-riot interviews confirm a xenophobic blend of anti-white sentiment and resentment of outsiders. "How can authorities living out of our area come in here and know how to solve our problems?" asked an anonymous middle-aged housewife living in the curfew area. "I will not take a Molotov cocktail but I am as mad as [those who did] are."[30] A twenty-year-old man identified only as "Joe" told an interviewer:

> I didn't realize what they [participants] were doing when the looting began.
> I didn't understand the object of the looting. At first it just began with
> people breaking windows and taking nothing. Then I realized the object of
> the looting: it was to move all the whites out of Watts. We don't want white
> people in Watts.[31]

Joe went on to declare, in a defiant assertion of self-defense: "As long as the whites keep trying to brutalize my people, I'll have to be out there trying to stop them."[32] Bill Stout reported: "The mobs might groan and curse in disappointment when a white got away and then cheer like a football crowd when a car went up in flames." Another black interviewee simply said: "People's getting tired of being pushed around by you white people. That's all."[33]

Wendell Collins, first vice chairman of the Los Angeles CORE chapter, seemed to recognize that it was the abrasive police presence that continued to cause resentment within the curfew area. He explained that his strategy for "calming down the riots" was to walk up and down 103rd Street to publicize a meeting at Will Rogers Park "to see if we can get the police out of the neighborhood." The antagonism toward police, the most visible white presence in Watts, spilled over into a generalized hatred of whites. "So we went to 55th and Main and stationed ourselves there and all the cars coming through that had white people, we turned them around. We said, 'Don't go in there. You will be killed. Just turn around.' Most of them did."[34] Collins advanced an interesting theory regarding the function of police in the ghetto:

> [T]he role of the police in modern American society in the Negro community is to break the Negro boy-child between the age of puberty and manhood; to accustom him to live in an inferior position in society. . . . They do this by accustoming him repeatedly to assaults on his person and his personality; to letting him know that, in the final analysis, he has no rights; that the white community is bound to have his respect.[35]

Collins expressed how many black Americans perceived police work to be biased, antagonistic, and one-dimensional with regard to Afro-American men. His testimony would also seem to affirm the psychological value of self-defense in establishing self-worth.

Racism penetrated all levels of California law enforcement, and the level of anti-black sentiment among high-level officials was often astounding and impolitic. Their own testimonies were salted with prejudiced statements, and the very exhibits they submitted to the McCone Commission to support their testimonies often contained insensitive, inflammatory remarks. Bradford Crittenden, Commissioner of the California Highway Patrol, submitted a confidential, in-house memo from his own office that read:

Especially in these areas [Watts and Willowbrook], we always find a problem if the person being pursued reaches his home and other members of the
family are present. They [blacks] do not understand that our enforcement
action is also to save the life of the person being cited or to save him from
injury. They only see in their childish minds that we are taking a member
of their family and are probably suspicious of the treatment police officers
generally give to this member of the family.[36]

Not to be outdone, Chief Parker told reporters on September 25, 1965:

The riot was finally put down and still now the questions are being asked
and the propaganda is being poured out that would indicate that perhaps
the police are something less than good; and this could again stir up these
antagonisms, and I think that's probably what happened in this incident
Tuesday night—that the police have been so demeaned by some of the
propagandists that, again, you're dealing with people [Afro-Americans] that
can't fully discern for themselves, and they sort of feel that they've got a
license or a pass to attack the police.[37]

It would come as little surprise if this sentiment affected the way law enforcement personnel dealt with black citizens as it trickled down to CHP
and LAPD officers, some of whom allegedly referred to their police batons
as "nigger knockers."[38]

In light of such testimony, it becomes much easier to understand how
participants were able to rationalize, and even politicize, unlawful behavior such as looting, sniping, or arson, and to understand why residents of
south-central Los Angeles would respond violently en masse to what most
accounts described as a "routine traffic stop." One active participant in the
Watts riot, "Joe," explained afterwards: "I went out there the first night
because it was my neighborhood and I wanted to see what was happening
to my neighborhood. In my neighborhood, the people know one another.
A person can't let other people come in and brutalize his neighbors, and
that's what those cops were doing."[39]

Self-defense was clearly a key motivator in the behavior of many Watts
rioters, and a number of participants expressed themselves using the rhetoric of self-defense. Paul A. Baker, an arrestee, suggested that the riots were a
"carryover of police treatment in the South into deprived areas of Los Angeles." He explained that this treatment "caused persons *to fight back* since they

felt that harassment and brutality had been left when leaving the South."[40] When asked in a post-riot interview if he had seen any "snipers," Patrick Lee Henry reported that he had seen riflemen atop the Figueroa Hotel at the intersection of Figueroa and Santa Barbara. He suggested that they were shooting "because of innocent people being shot and *in self-defense* a number of persons began using weapons rather than to be shot without provocation."[41] Ralph Reese, another participant, characterized the event as a battle in which residents of Watts had to defend themselves against armed attack by the Los Angeles Police Department and the National Guard.[42]

Jean Turner, aka Ika Ballard, surmised that people rioted because it was "the only way they knew *to fight back.*"[43] In light of such testimony, the brick or chunk of concrete in the hands of a rioter may have been less a tool of insensate destruction and more the armament of the dispossessed. "It is getting to the point where the Negro man does not mind facing a gun with a rock in his hand," claimed Charles Hardie, a World War II veteran and resident of Watts. "A lot of people are wishing it will happen again," said J.B., a janitor and Watts resident. "Next time, we'll have guns. We'll be able *to fight back.*"[44]

Clearly many of those who participated in the Watts conflagration exhibited awareness of groups and individuals who advocated self-defense, and this awareness cross-pollinated a growing political consciousness. Participants referred to the Deacons for Defense and Justice, active in promoting self-defense for blacks in Bogalusa, Louisiana. When California Highway Patrolman instructed the crowd at Avalon and 116th to disperse during the initial incident at Frye's arrest, crowd members replied with profanity and shouts of "Let's get them cops. . . . Bogalusa—this is the end for you, white man." The following day rioters, pursuing firemen while hurling bricks and hunks of concrete, shouted, "That's for Bogalusa. . . . That's for Selma."[45] Another commentator noted: "With the right type of leadership and the right type of planning, you wouldn't have these many killings in Watts. . . . If the Deacons had been started out there, the way these people had been fighting, it would be revolution in California."[46] It was this sort of political consciousness, centered on the question of self-defense, that would give rise to the Black Panther Party for Self-Defense.[47]

Opinionated and blunt, Chief Parker maintained that "the police department didn't cause the Watts riot." Attempting to divert unwanted attention from himself and his department, Parker blamed the riot wholly on the

California Highway Patrol's handling of the Frye arrest, noting that the CHP "failed and neglected to move their prisoners out of the area with dispatch, lingering needlessly with 'the mob'." He also blamed "widespread support of civil disobedience as a tool for social and economic progress" and media coverage as twin factors in causing the riots, as well as hoodlums, criminals, black nationalists, and those "under the stress of unemployment and economic despair." He opposed calling in the National Guard, which "is in effect a military occupation" that "presents an undesirable picture from the community standpoint." Undergoing intense scrutiny after the riot, Parker said he felt like a scapegoat, a "symbol target"; he claimed that charges of police brutality were part of a "big lie technique" to smear him and his department, and he complained that "our poor little uneducated policemen" were unfairly subjected to undue criticism.[48]

Chief Parker resented the notion that his officers policed black people differently than white people, and he felt that his officers enforced the law equitably; he also felt that no group warranted special treatment. "I don't think that any element of this community has the right to demand that the police department accommodate totally to that element without any effort on their part for a bilateral accommodation," he exclaimed. The result would be "a dead department that rides around and sees nothing more than it has to see." Parker was—in his mind, at least—trying to police L.A. judiciously, but he faced criticism from all fronts. For example, the chief disapproved of sending black officers exclusively into Watts, preferring instead to disperse them over the force where they would "be given the same opportunities as any other office of the department." Black officers "shouldn't all be herded in one division," which would be tantamount to "ghettoizing the Negro officer." Criticized for this view, the chief mused, "The things we have been urged to do suddenly become the wrong things. They were right yesterday, they are wrong today."[49]

Chief Parker was correct in noting that the Watts riot could not be romanticized. Even under the broadest definition possible, it is difficult to justify much of what went on during the riots as self-defense. Much of what happened seems to have been smash-and-grab looting, but when viewed solely as a collection of criminal acts, the contextual meaning of the Watts violence is lost. As one writer has explained, "There are no excuses for pillaging and murder, nor are there valid reasons for turning our hearts and minds—as busy as they may be—from the despair that causes riots."[50] To call the violence "meaningless" or random or mob-like, as much contemporary coverage did, is to minimize the motivations of those involved.

On August 15, Officer Robert Lewis gave the call on his radio that he needed assistance (code 1199: "Officer Needs Help"), and indeed, officers did need help in subduing a recalcitrant arrestee and keeping a hostile crowd at bay. But the phrase suggests another meaning too. The Watts riot signaled that officers of the LAPD needed a different kind of help: help in interfacing with a foreign and increasingly alienated black subculture; help in understanding the complicated changes in race relations wrought by the civil rights movement; help in recognizing that diplomacy and tact could effectively police an area where force and severity could not; and help in keeping their own brutally racist tendencies in check. Those living in the inner city were energized but frustrated by what they saw happening in the South: energized by the progress being made on the front lines of racial equality, frustrated by lack of progress in their own lives. The LAPD faced an increasingly militant and hostile inner city, and those at its helm condoned and encouraged the kind of draconian measures with which its officers seemed most comfortable. Residents of Watts knew firsthand of the LAPD's notoriously violent racism, and it is not unreasonable to suggest that the LAPD forced the beleaguered community into a posture of self-protection. Many of the residents evidently felt that self-defense was their last recourse in dealing with a hostile and relentless police department.

Likewise, it would be overly simple to argue that the Watts riot stemmed from a single cause. For example, if Watts marked the racialization of disorder, it also marked a new class consciousness in racial violence. In fact, the Watts uprising was as much a reaction against the black elite, symbolized by middle-class civil rights leaders, as it was a spontaneous rebellion against white authority: Martin Luther King Jr.'s frosty reception by Watts residents exemplifies this development. Those who rebelled were poor and impoverished and increasingly impatient with being poor and impoverished, and issues of poverty, unemployment, welfare, health services, housing, education, child care, recreation, and economic opportunity cannot be overlooked in assessing why Watts burned. However, there is compelling evidence to suggest that police officers (in addition to white developers and businessmen) were encroaching on the one space in Los Angeles where many Afro-Americans felt safe; that white law enforcement personnel were bullying black residents in their own neighborhoods; that black Angelenos perceived that their community was being besieged by outside forces; and that Watts residents perceived that they were being assailed by a white majority insensitive, if not indifferent, to their particular circumstances in Watts. These perceptions may have contributed to a growing willingness to defend themselves forcefully—even against the formidable LAPD.

Accordingly, what motivated one Watts resident to take his own life in a highly symbolic and absurdly poignant gesture might be interpreted as the ultimate expression of self-defense.[51] In *Burn, Baby, Burn!: The Los Angeles Race Riot, August 1965*, Jerry Cohen and William Murphy tell the story of Charles Fizer, a successful recording star fallen on hard times. Fizer's group, the Olympics, had sold over a million copies of the hit record "Hully Gully" in the early '60s, but he himself had difficulty translating his talent as a singer into commercial success. Turning to drugs and street life, he became embittered and angry, blaming racism for his problems. After serving six months at hard labor on a county prison farm after being arrested with illegal barbiturates, Fizer was released on Thursday, August 12, into a riot in progress and a black community at war with predominately white soldiers and law enforcement personnel. Visiting a girlfriend and planning to return home before the 8:00 P.M. curfew, Fizer borrowed his uncle's 1955 Buick. An hour after the curfew deadline, he was still cruising the streets of his riot-torn community. After stopping short of a National Guard roadblock at 102nd and Beach Streets, Fizer inexplicably floored the car's accelerator. The Guardsmen shouted a warning as the Buick barreled toward the barricade. They fired warning shots into the air and, when Fizer failed to yield, riddled the automobile with bullets. The car abruptly swerved and crashed short of the barricade. It was unclear to the Guardsmen why the driver did not heed their order to stop.[52] Fizer's actions may be interpreted as a suicidal act of defiance, comparable to those of Robert Charles in 1900. Like Charles, who gunned down a number of New Orleans policemen in the wake of the Sam Hose lynching, Fizer lashed out in a time of crisis at the most intrusive symbol of white authority in his life: the National Guard. While Charles used a Winchester lever-action rifle as his weapon of choice, Fizer used a Buick. Huey Newton might have called Fizer's death, as he would later title his own autobiography, "revolutionary suicide."

Blood to the horse's brow, and woe to those who can't swim!

CAPTION, *BLACK PANTHER* NEWSLETTER, 1969

CHAPTER 7

BLOOD TO THE HORSE'S BROW

Self-Defense Used and Abused, 1966–1968

Like the Deacons for Defense and Justice, the Black Panther Party (BPP) began as a self-defense advocacy group. As a pugnacious expression of Black Power and as a reflection of the radical activism of the latter sixties, the Panthers quickly evolved into a revolutionary vanguard, leading "the Movement"—the hybridized amalgam of civil rights reform, anti-war protest, class struggle, anti-racism, anti-capitalism, and countercultural stylings— toward Marxism, direct challenge of middle-class values, and a confrontational showdown with the nation's police forces. By its second full year of existence, what had begun as self-defense advocacy in the tradition of Robert

Williams, Malcolm X, and the Deacons had rapidly evolved into a warlike challenge to the American system itself.

To understand Huey Newton, Bobby Seale, and the organization they founded in 1966, it helps to examine the Lowndes County [Alabama] Freedom Organization (LCFO), its adjunct political party, the Black Panther Party, and the concept of Black Power. Stokely Carmichael and other activists in the Student Nonviolent Coordinating Committee not only promoted Black Power but also publicized and popularized the Black Panther name and logo in Alabama in 1965 and 1966. The people of Lowndes County, who with SNCC were the progenitors of the Alabama-based Black Panther Party, provided Newton and Seale with a model of Black Power in action.

Lowndes County lies in the heart of Alabama's so-called Black Belt, a region with fertile black soil that produces bountiful crops and where, not so coincidentally, many of the state's black inhabitants live. In 1966, that land was producing cotton, corn, and profits—little of which went to the black folks who worked it. Most white people living in the area suffered from the same staggering poverty as local black citizens. However, a handful of whites lived, as one observer remarked, like "a class of feudal flies in amber, fixed in a permanent state of moral decay and financial advantage." In 1966, there were four times as many blacks as whites in Lowndes (twelve thousand blacks and three thousand whites), but eighty-nine white families owned 90 percent of the land. Most blacks were sharecroppers or tenants; a few owned small plots of land, and fewer still owned small farms. Half of the black women who worked did so as maids in Montgomery, more than twenty miles distant, for about $4 a day. The median family income for blacks was $935; for whites, it was $4,440. The median education level for blacks was slightly more than five years of schooling, significantly less than local whites, although 80 percent of blacks and whites alike were functionally illiterate. The schools and other facilities for blacks were inferior to those for whites.[1]

Hungry for change, black citizens in Lowndes County created a political party, the Lowndes County Freedom Organization (LCFO), that was called at the time "one of the most broadly democratic political parties in the country." The party was created with the help of SNCC, whose aid black citizens solicited as preferable to that of the Southern Christian Leadership Conference.[2] SNCC was "the only organization that came into the county and began to move around that issue: getting people registered to vote and developing something for themselves," according to John Jackson, a Lowndes County resident who became state project director of SNCC in Alabama.[3] The first SNCC workers active in Lowndes included Robert Mants, Stokely Carmichael, Judy Richardson, Willie Vaughn, and Scottie B. Smith.

Specific incidents of violence in 1965 horrified the black people of Lowndes County but reinforced their determination to see justice. Viola Liuzzo, a white woman from Detroit and mother of five children, was shuttling marchers from Montgomery to Selma when she was shot to death in her car. Jonathan Daniels, a twenty-six-year-old white seminary student, was gunned down in Hayneville on August 20, 1965.[4] Rather than deterring further civil rights activities, the murders of Liuzzo and Daniels inspired black citizens of Lowndes to organize more effectively to achieve their goals.

To mobilize voters, John Hulett, Jesse Favors, and other local black citizens founded the Lowndes County Christian Movement for Human Rights, which was quickly eclipsed by its political parallel, the LCFO. The LCFO began organizing in October 1965; eight months later, in May 1966, they were ready to enter the political arena. Their immediate aim was to control local government through the election of seven county officials in November 1966; after that goal was achieved, the LCFO aimed to "take over the courthouse" in subsequent elections. To achieve these revolutionary goals, the LCFO and SNCC began a massive voter registration drive. Black folks living in the county knew that any kind of political activity in Lowndes, where the Republican Party did not even exist, would mean trouble for them. But inspired by gains made in the nearby cities of Montgomery and Selma, many participated anyway. What they attempted was "black power" at its most basic level.

Black Power later became a controversial abstraction in the North and in the minds of those who intellectualized the movement, but in places like Lowndes County, it was fairly simple and straightforward. The right to vote was now the law of the land under the Voting Rights Act of 1965, but for many black folks the struggle was just beginning. Lowndes illustrated the power of the vote because so much was at stake there: jobs, land, education, their very lives. Andrew Jones knew that becoming registered meant becoming a citizen. "I went out and let people know," he said, "they wouldn't be free until they were registered."[5]

On May 3, 1966, nine hundred people attended the LCFO's nominating convention; this group nominated seven of their ranks to run in the county's general election for the offices of sheriff, coroner, tax assessor, and tax collector, in addition to three positions on the board of education. Sidney Logan ran for the office of sheriff; Frank Miles ran for tax collector. Alice Moore, candidate for tax assessor, promised that if she were elected she would "tax the rich and feed the poor"; she felt that poor blacks and whites reaped no benefits from their tax money.[6]

The seven candidates were to run under the Black Panther Party banner, which symbolized the empowerment of those involved. As John Hulett said, "He [the panther] never bothers anything, but when you start pushing him, he moves backwards, backwards, and backwards into his corner, and then he comes out to destroy everything that's before him." Hulett's description of a panther's behavior mirrored conventional justifications of self-defense, which presume that the defendant has no other means of escape from the assailant. Practically, the symbol of the panther served to identify candidates for those voters who could not read and write, but who could pull the lever in the voting booth: ballots actually had representations of black panthers imprinted on them next to the names of appropriate candidates.

The nominating convention did not go unchallenged. The county sheriff refused to let the LCFO use the courthouse for their gathering, and he deputized 550 white men to carry out his order. John Hulett, LCFO chairman, said that the blacks would come armed, too. At the last minute, Attorney General Richmond Flowers, in conjunction with the U.S. Department of Justice, worked out a compromise to avoid bloodshed, and Hulett agreed to hold the convention at a nearby church.

On Monday, November 7, 1966, the night before the historic election, seven hundred black folks gathered at the Mt. Mariah Baptist Church to receive final instructions on what to do on election day. Campaign signs, emblazoned with the snarling cat, read: "VOTE NOV. 8TH / PULL THE LEVER FOR THE BLACK PANTHER AND GO HOME." On November 8, armed black guards stood near the polls, ready for trouble.

Not one of the LCFO candidates were elected. SNCC workers suspected that white landowners had forced their black tenants to vote against the LCFO. However, the failed campaign was not without effects. Bob Mants, a local SNCC worker, claimed (somewhat erroneously) that the LCFO altered the nature of state politics by forcing some southern Democrats, such as George Wallace, to run later as independent candidates; the campaign also brought about a "cohesiveness," according to Mants, among black folks "throughout the Alabama Black Belt."[7]

As a key player in SNCC efforts in Lowndes County, Stokely Carmichael had combined novel ideas with "old-time religion" to encourage the people of Lowndes to organize. Carmichael had left the county in May 1966 after he was elected national chairman of SNCC, and he took with him a new understanding of what was important in the struggle for black equality. Lowndes showed him the political power of the vote, but it also showed him the possibilities of political power backed by a show of force. He had known such power in the hands of whites, but Lowndes County was the first place he had ever seen black folks supplement political organizing with armed resistance. John Jackson credited Lowndes with transforming Carmichael's views on nonviolence. "When he [Carmichael] was staying here," remembered Jackson, "my father had guns and that's why white people didn't mess with him when he was here."[8] The spectacle of armed black men going to the polls was not wasted on Carmichael, who began to think about the implications of power, and about what "power" really meant.

Less than a month after Carmichael left Lowndes County to replace John Lewis as chairman of SNCC, James Meredith was shot on June 6, 1966, the second day of his 220-mile "March Against Fear": a quixotic, solo hike from Memphis, Tennessee to Jackson, Mississippi intended to inspire black southerners to register to vote. Wounded by a white sniper, Meredith was unable to continue. However, Carmichael, Dr. King, Floyd McKissick of CORE, and other activists opted to continue the march. As the newly dubbed "Meredith March" progressed over the next three weeks, Carmichael and another SNCC activist, Willie Ricks, began to promote the slogan "Black Power" to express a growing feeling of racial pride and self-sufficiency; it was Carmichael's use of the phrase at a rally toward the end of the march that electrified the media and popularized the phrase.

When Carmichael and Ricks introduced (or, more accurately, resurrected) the phrase "Black Power," they alarmed white folks.[9] Carmichael tapped the same reservoir of white fear that Robert Williams had tapped, and just as they had misunderstood Williams and armed self-defense, white Americans largely misunderstood Carmichael and the concept of Black Power. For most black folks, the appeal of Black Power lay in its excitement and energy, not its threat. Linda Bryant Hall, a young activist, noted that Carmichael "came with the same kind of energy Malcolm X came with. That's what we liked, not that we wanted to overthrow our government . . . and not that we wanted to do anything violent."[10] But as the notion of Black Power expanded and took on a life of its own, some black activists used its ominous overtones as a loosely veiled threat to whites.[11]

Stokely Carmichael challenged proponents of nonviolent direct action with the rhetoric of power; they responded in turn. He argued: "We cannot be expected any longer to march and have our heads broken in order to say to whites: 'Come on, you're nice guys.' For you are not nice guys. We have found you out. We had to work for power, because this country does not function by morality, love and nonviolence, but by power."[12] SCLC activist Andrew Young replied: "In a pluralistic society, to have real power you have to deny it. And if you go around claiming power, the whole society turns on you and crushes you."[13]

Conceptions of Black Power were hazy at best, and the phrase clearly meant different things to different people.[14] The press attached implications of violence to the phrase. As a result, many whites saw Black Power as an ugly expression of hatred and violence, or as a ploy to grab white power and resources and use them against whites. Carmichael observed, "To most whites, Black Power seems to mean that the Mau Mau are coming to the suburbs at night."[15] But to him, Black Power entailed, at its most basic level, self-defense:

> From our viewpoint, rampaging white mobs and white nightriders must be made to understand that their days of free head-whipping are over. Black people should and must fight back. Nothing more quickly repels someone bent on destroying you than the unequivocal message: "O.K., fool, make your move, and run the same risk I run—of dying."[16]

To Carmichael, the Deacons for Defense and Justice provided a model of Black Power. "The Deacons and all other blacks who resort to self-defense represent a simple answer to a simple question: what man would not defend his family and home from attack?"[17] Similarly, a member of Maulana Karenga's organization, US, explained, "When somebody asked us, 'Well what is this thing called Black Power?' . . . [we would respond by saying] the three ends of Black Power are self-determination, self-respect, and self-defense."[18]

To Afro-Americans as a whole, Black Power was indispensable, as one scholar has observed, in so far as "pride in being black proved invaluable in aiding blacks to discard the disabling self-hatred inculcated by white culture."[19] Most importantly, Black Power was an Afro-American expression of political and social empowerment, rather than an ideology of racial supremacy. It is worth noting that, for most activists, being pro-black did not mean being anti-white. Carmichael advised SNCC sympathizers wary of Black Power that they had to understand that the Afro-American wanted "to build something of his own, something that he builds with his own hands. And that is *not* anti-white. When you build your own house, it doesn't mean you tear down the house across the street."[20]

A variety of other interpretations of Black Power would later sprout up. For example, King wrote in *Where Do We Go From Here?* (1967):

> One of the greatest paradoxes of the Black Power movement is that it talks unceasingly about not imitating the values of white society, but in advocating violence it is imitating the worst, the most brutal and the most uncivilized value of American life . . . Violence has been the inseparable twin of materialism, the hallmark of its grandeur and misery. This is one thing about modern civilization that I do not care to imitate.[21]

John Oliver Killens, a novelist, articulated Black Power in language not unlike that of Charles Sims, president of the Deacons for Defense and Justice. "If you [whites] practice violence against me," Killens wrote, "I mean to give back to you in kind. . . . Maybe this will help whip some sense into your head[s]."[22] Others disagreed, turning this notion of reciprocal violence on its head. Ed Vaughn, bookstore owner and member of Detroit's Forum Movement, applied an interesting perspective of Black Power to rioting in 1967. "It wasn't Black Power that caused the rebellion," Vaughn observed. "It was the *lack* of power that caused the rebellions around the country. People did not see any hope for themselves."[23]

Undoubtedly, notions of black self-determination, self-sufficiency, and self-protection lay at the heart of Black Power ideology. Accordingly, after the Watts conflagration of 1965, local black citizens in Los Angeles formed a Community Action Patrol to monitor police conduct during arrests. The following year, two students at Oakland City College (now Merritt College) carried the idea slightly further by instituting armed patrols in Oakland, California. Swept up in the rising tide of militancy encouraged by

Black Power ideology, Huey Newton enlisted the help of an older class-mate, Bobby Seale, to create a new organization in Oakland. The two class-mates had been involved in various groups such as the local chapter of the Revolutionary Action Movement (RAM) and the Soul Students Advisory Council. They bounced from organization to organization as they searched for a cadre of people to energize and inspire them. They could not find one, and so they started their own, calling it the Black Panther Party for Self-Defense. Co-opting the name and image of the LCFO's political wing, Newton and Seale created their own Black Panther Party in Oakland. In fact, before Newton's organization in Oakland became known as *the* Black Panther Party, many organizations inspired by the Lowndes County group adopted the name "Black Panther," but the Oakland group quickly eclipsed them.[24] While the Black Panther Party was not a civil rights organization, per se, the Panthers employed direct action in the finest tradition of the southern freedom struggle, and they labored to improve standards of living for Oakland's black citizens.

Claiming North Oakland's mean streets as their home turf, the found-ing members of the Black Panthers not only witnessed the abuse of police privileges there but also perceived that law enforcement personnel were in-fringing upon their own right to self-protection. As a result, the Panthers effectively became a law unto themselves, stretching the concept of collec-tive self-defense to its legal and jurisdictional extremes. They acted not as vigilantes, supplementing an overworked police authority, but as surrogates, replacing the officially sanctioned Oakland Police Department; in fact, they defined themselves in opposition to the police. Their actions raised the question of whether rights ordinarily and justly belonging to individual cit-izens may be extended to a racial group as a whole, and whether in law, as in fact, there exists such a thing as collective self-defense. As guardians of the community, ostensibly armed for purposes of self-defense, the Panthers operated as a paramilitary army under the direction of an appointed minister of defense. In their early years, the Panthers claimed that they did not arm as a group but as individuals, exercising their constitutional right to bear arms. However, as their ideology evolved, they claimed to be an oppressed colony with the United States, to which they owed no allegiance.

Before the Panthers were community activists, political spokesmen, or revolutionaries, they were advocates of self-defense. This emphasis on self-defense shaped their political platform, the way they were perceived by the media, and the response they received from government agencies, especially the police. Although guns became sine qua non to the Panthers' image, initially they were simply a function of the members' personal needs for self-protection. It is important to note that Newton and Seale originally sold copies of Chairman Mao Tse Tung's "Little Red Book" not because they were interested in disseminating communist propaganda, but because they were trying to raise money to purchase guns. Seale later jokingly confessed, "We hadn't even read the thing. . . . We must have sold the thing for two or three months before we even opened it up."[25] Clearly, understanding the priority the Panthers placed on armed self-defense predicates full understanding of the Black Panther Party itself.

Working within the established tradition of armed, Afro-American self-defense, Huey P. Newton and Bobby Seale consciously followed the precedent set by Robert Williams and the Deacons for Defense and Justice. "*Negroes with Guns* by Robert Williams had a great influence on the kind of party we developed," explained Huey Newton. "We also had some literature about the Deacons for Defense and Justice in Louisiana. . . . One of their leaders had come through the Bay Area on a speaking and fund-raising tour, and we liked what he said."[26] Seale claimed to have learned of Robert Williams in 1962.[27] What the Panthers did—brandishing weapons in public—seemed unprecedented to those who knew nothing of Williams or the Deacons and who, with the selective memory characteristic of Americans, remembered little of the David Walkers and Henry Highland Garnets of the nineteenth century. But the Panthers were not really saying anything new. In their belief in self-defense, the Panthers were much more evolutionary than revolutionary.[28]

The founding members of the Black Panther Party also heeded Malcolm X, who encouraged black people to arm themselves to thwart racist police brutality. Bobby Seale envisioned "a black community group" of some kind "to teach brothers like Malcolm X said"; that is, "to righteously defend themselves from racists."[29] Seale later recalled his friend, Isaac, who was anxious about Seale's yelling at a policeman. "What you did back there, hollering at that cop," Isaac worried. "They'll put us in jail. They'll kill us." Seale responded by cursing and flipping through the pages of a pamphlet "trying to find where Malcolm said every man had a right to keep a shotgun in his home."[30] Newton considered Malcolm's influence "ever-present" in the existence of the BPP, and considered the Panthers "a living testament to his life work."[31] He also emphasized the parallels between the Panthers and the Nation of Islam. "Our program we structured after the Black Muslim program," Newton explained, "minus the religion."[32]

Self-defense was the cornerstone of the Panthers' manifesto, the Ten Point Program, written by Newton and Seale, which enumerated the Panthers' beliefs and goals. The Ten Point Program constituted the warp and woof of the BPP. As a living constitution, it shaped the Panthers' daily actions. To highlight blacks' inferior social and economic status and to emphasize self-defense, the Ten-Point Program drew heavily on the rhetoric of the Declaration of Independence, the United States Constitution, and Bill of Rights. The seventh point read:

> We want an immediate end to POLICE BRUTALITY and MURDER of Black people. We believe we can end police brutality in our Black community by organizing Black self-defense groups that are dedicated to defending our Black community from racist police oppression and brutality. The Second Amendment to the Constitution of the United States gives a right to bear arms. We therefore believe that all Black people should arm themselves for self-defense.

It was this point that always seemed to receive the largest applause from audiences.[33] The Panthers based their armed patrols on the legality of the Second Amendment. "We don't use our guns, we have never used our guns to go into the white community to shoot up white people," Seale later explained. "We only defend ourselves against anybody—be they black, blue, green, or red—who attacks us unjustly and tries to murder us and kill us for implementing our programs."[34]

The right to bear arms was a constitutional right; like the Fourteenth Amendment, it became reflective, through the Panthers' actions, of Afro-Americans' battle to determine their identity as Americans. When the Panthers provided security at a conference to commemorate Malcolm X in San Francisco on February 21, 1967, Newton integrated self-defense with politics. The conference was planned by the "other Panther group," the Black Panther Party of Northern California, which asked Newton and his group to provide armed protection for the guest of honor, Betty Shabazz, Malcolm's widow. When asked if he would like to speak on the occasion, Newton answered affirmatively. He was told he could lecture on the history of self-defense. "I'll be talking about politics," Newton responded. "Do you want to speak on self-defense or politics?" they queried. "It doesn't make any difference, they're both one and the same," he replied. "If I'm talking about self-defense, I'm talking about politics; if I'm talking about politics, I'm talking about self-defense. You can't separate them." Newton became frustrated with the "paper Panthers" who could not understand this tenet of revolution.[35]

Similarly, by marching on the state capitol in Sacramento to protest the Mulford Act on May 2, 1967, the Panthers politicized the issue of self-defense for blacks in America. The bill in question was written by Donald Mulford, a California Republican state legislator from Piedmont, and it specifically targeted the Panthers. It prohibited carrying loaded firearms in public places and was designed to disarm the Panthers in their provocative showdowns with Oakland cops. In a display of protest, nineteen Panthers walked into the capitol in Sacramento with their guns and read a statement to a shocked throng of assemblymen, photographers, cameramen, and reporters. The nation was electrified. All eyes were focused on the Panthers' guns.[36]

Capitalizing on this focus, Newton engendered a cult-like respect for firearms as key to black liberation. "Guns Baby Guns," a poem by Newton in an early issue of the *Black Panther* newsletter, conveyed this fetish in a lyrical way:

Army 45 will stop all jive
Buckshots will down the cops
P38 will open Prison gates
Carbine will stop a war machine
357 will win us our heaven
And if you don't believe in lead
You are already dead[37]

Apart from their functionality, guns were a critical element in the Panthers' rhetoric, representing both a recruiting device and an exclamation point at the end of any declaration of their political agenda. Elaine Brown used an interesting choice of words when she explained this function of the Panthers' weaponry in her autobiography. "Guns were the natural *accessory* of the new black militants," she wrote, "who were determined to claim their manhood 'by any means necessary.'"[38] Indeed, the Panthers used firearms to accessorize their wardrobes. Guns, like leather jackets and black berets, were an essential part of the Panther uniform, which conveyed strength, power, and unity. Bobby Seale described an instance in 1966 when he and Newton carried guns into a party. One of the partygoers curiously asked the two men why they were armed. "These guns represent a new black organization, brother," Newton replied.[39] Their weaponry was not only an empowering accoutrement but also a billboard to advertise the Panthers and their ideas.

The Panthers did not carry their weapons everywhere, and at times they were conspicuously unarmed.

> We don't take guns with us to implement these programs [e.g., the Free Breakfast program], but we understand and know from our own history that we're going to be attacked, and that we have to be able to defend ourselves. They're going to attack us viciously and fascisticly [sic] and try to say it was all justifiable homicide, in the same manner they've always attacked black people in the black communities.[40]

Newton and Seale both had justification for their fears. Their personal histories seem to bear out their claims of police harassment and brutality. As youths, both were repeatedly incarcerated and, according to their autobiographies, menaced by police. The two men perceived a serious threat from police not only to their personal survival but also to the survival of the race, and they armed themselves accordingly.[41] The seventh point in the Ten-Point Program specifically addressed police brutality and the "murder of black people" by police. For Newton and Seale, the police were the enforcement agency of a racist power structure that sought to subjugate, if not exterminate, Afro-Americans. They justified their own resort to arms as a result of violence initiated by police.[42] Like Robert Williams, the Panthers approached self-defense pragmatically. Their conception of self-protection had less to do with books and theory than with the immediate, personal danger posed by the Oakland Police Department, notorious for its brutality and highly questionable methods in dealing with the city's black ghettos.[43] Undoubtedly, their use of guns stemmed from a very real need to protect themselves.

In defining the Panthers, Newton addressed the growing trend of cultural nationalism, with which he flirted and ultimately rejected. Cultural nationalism involved turning traditionally racist understandings of black inferiority upside-down by celebrating blackness in a new sense of spiritual and cultural awareness. Such awareness was symbolically represented in "afro" or natural hairstyles, traditional African dress made of kente cloth, and the adoption of African names. Newton rejected cultural nationalism for four main reasons. First, it failed to recognize the specific historical circumstances that differentiated Afro-Americans and Africans. Second, it detracted from the task at hand: namely, bringing about revolution. Third, it was theoretically deficient. As he explained: "We have to realize our black heritage in order to give us strength to move on and progress. But as far as returning to the old African culture, it's unnecessary and it's not advantageous in many respects. We believe that *culture itself will not liberate us*. We're going to need some stronger stuff."[44] Fourth, Newton believed that it was impossible to resolve the problems of black people under the structure of American capitalism. Newton's disenchantment with cultural nationalism led him to rebuke the Black Panther Party of Northern California, a group of cultural nationalists in San Francisco.

The same factors that might have given Newton and Seale a proclivity toward criminal activity instead made them social activists. As lower-class kids growing up in Oakland, they were blocked from conventional middle-class opportunities by the burdens of poverty and urban decay. They lived poor in close proximity to the wealthy neighborhoods of the Berkeley and Oakland hills, as well as Piedmont, an affluent community. They obeyed the rules of street life, which put them in conflict with the dominant culture. Finally, they lacked the means to attain the goals of mainstream society.

Newton and Seale also displayed a propensity towards violence that stemmed from their upbringings and rationalized self-defense. David Hilliard, Chief of Staff of the Black Panther Party and Huey's childhood friend, explained his growing up in Mobile, Alabama and later Oakland:

Quick, powerful hands are something to respect; and there is nothing strange about people being beaten, cut, even killed. Violence is an accepted condition of life. If you go to the store or clubs you run the risk of a fight. On Friday nights, and whenever there's a family argument, and especially when people start pouring their alcohol, you can be fairly certain that somebody's going to do something before too long. There's going to be some shit, as the saying goes. Violence is the norm; because of this, violence is part of my personality, part of my value system. I grow up expecting it, always on the alert, never relaxed, never lowering my vigilance.[45]

Hilliard shared this culture of violence with other Panthers, like Seale and Newton, who grew up poor and black in the city. Violence, particularly self-defense, came quite naturally to them. Hilliard's family encouraged him, as a boy, to act violently; on one occasion, his mother bought a handgun for him at a local pawnshop and encouraged him to hunt down his tormentor, another schoolboy. After another altercation with a white boy, she told her son, "I don't care what color that boy was. If he hit you first you had a right to fight him. In fact, if you *hadn't* hit him, I would have hit you." His father felt the same way, expecting his children to stand up for their self-respect. "[I]f you got hit, you'd better hit back. That was the rule we grew up with." Hilliard's parents punished him physically, whipping him with a leather belt or the thin branches of a peach tree ("switches"). He carried a knife for protection; his sister carried a Coke bottle ("to coldcock any guy"), and his brother's girlfriend had "a razor soaked in garlic and lemon juice." "For us," he explained, "fighting's like words: a way to work things out. We fight to make friends, get rid of our frustration and boredom, assert our identities. Fighting is a creative outlet." Violence was everywhere in Hilliard's world. "Everything that surrounds me," he wrote, "encourages me to believe in the rule of force."[46]

Newton's understanding and justifications of self-defense, like David Hilliard's, grew out of the marginal and sometimes violent settings of his adolescence: street corners, parties, local clubs, and bars. For example, he explained:

> [Y]ou may go to a party and step on someone's shoes and apologize, and if the person accepts the apology, then nothing happens. If you hear something like "An apology won't shine my shoes," then you know he is really saying, "I'm going to fight you." So you defend yourself, and in that case striking first would be a defensive act, not an offensive one. You are trying to get an advantage over an opponent who has already declared war.[47]

As a way of understanding the world, violence made sense to most of the Panthers. Seale conceived of two kinds of violence: that kind "perpetrated against our people by the fascist aggression of the power structure," and self-defense, "a form of violence used to defend ourselves from the unjust violence inflicted upon us."[48] Newton added several other forms of violence, too:

We also wanted to show that the other kinds of violence poor people suffer—unemployment, poor housing, inferior education, lack of public facilities, the inequity of the draft—were part of the same fabric. If we could organize people against police brutality . . . we might move them toward eliminating related forms of oppression. The system, in fact, destroys us through neglect much more often than by the police revolver. The gun is only the coup de grâce, the enforcer. To wipe out the conditions lead- ing to the coup de grâce—that was our goal. The gun and the murder it represented would then fade away.[49]

Newton viewed violence as a condition of human relationships. He argued that starving people is a kind of violence, robbing them of their dignity and self-respect is violence, denying them their political rights or discriminat- ing against them is violence. Such a definition inflated any conventional understanding of the term "violence," generally considered to mean bring- ing force, or the threat of force, against a person to effect something against his or her will; however, by defining violence in such terms, Newton would be able to justify his own violent tendencies as being not only in the best interest of oppressed people, but also completely justified. Violence, in any shade or form, necessitated defense from that violence.

At times, the two founding members disavowed violent conflict. "We aren't hungry for violence," Seale declared in *Seize the Time*. "Violence is ugly. Guns are ugly." But he and Newton felt that the police left them little peaceful alternative. They felt that the government persecuted the Black Panther Party specifically because the Panthers' community programs "ex- posed" the government as hypocritical and prejudiced.[50]

The Party's stand on self-defense was a logical extension of its founders' personal experiences into the political realm; however, individual Panthers' understandings of self-defense were often different from legal, ethical, and moral norms embraced by the majority culture.

If the black panther symbolized fighting back when cornered to some Panthers, then to others it symbolized attacking. One Party member ad- mired how the panther "moves quickly and quietly, how it strikes before anyone realizes what has happened."[51] His understanding of self-defense, and of the panther, resembled the logic of the preemptive strike. Don Cox assented:

[F]or us to talk about survival we must talk about self-defense against this brutality and murder that is defined by the racist power structure as justifiable homicide. So when a self-defense group moves against this oppressive system, by executing a pig by any means, sniping, stabbing, bombing, etc., in defense against 400 years of racist brutality and murder this can only be defined correctly as self-defense . . . all self-defense groups must strike blows against the slavemaster until we have secured our survival as a people and if this takes shooting every pig and blowing up every pig sty then let's get on up.[52]

Black Panther Party members did not necessarily share Newton's original vision of an essentially defensive organization. "We'd been in the Army, we were armed," explained Panther Landon Williams. "We'd read Nat Turner. We said, look—maybe it is just a black-white thing, and so what we gotta do is just take as many of 'em with us as we can. And so we armed up."[53] Huey Newton himself would later declare: "We're not a self-defense group in the limited fashion that you usually think of self-defense groups."[54]

Within these broad parameters, self-defense evolved into an offensive weapon. "To show them [bigger guys] I was as 'bad' as they were," Newton told of his youth, "I would fight at the drop of a hat. As soon as I saw a dude rearing up, I struck him before he struck me, but only when there was going to be a fight anyway." He struck first "because a fight usually did not last very long," and because "nine times out of ten the winner was the one who got in his first lick."[55] Don Cox, a Panther field marshal, declared, "It's time to intensify the struggle. We must broaden our self-defense tactics and *counterattack*." David Hilliard concurred: "We know that the only way to stop these ＿＿＿ is by picking up the guns and killing those ＿＿＿ before they get a chance to kill us."[56]

The Panthers' self-perception as revolutionaries may have helped to complicate the legitimacy of their claim to self-defense. The group blended self-defense—immediate, counter-violence to stop an attack—and revolution, defined as a sudden political overthrow or seizure of power. "Revolutionary strategy for Black people in America begins with the defensive movement of picking up the Gun, as the condition for ending the pigs' reign of terror by the Gun," announced one article in the *Black Panther*. "Black people picking up the gun for self-defense is the only basis in America for a revolutionary offensive against Imperialist state power."[57] To the average white citizen, the contradictions in this statement might have appeared glaring: "revolution" is hardly a "defensive movement," and "picking up the gun for self-defense" cannot logically be a "revolutionary offensive," if offense and defense are diametrically opposed. But the BPP leadership viewed themselves as oppressed persons who were therefore immune from the constraints of normal citizens. Oppressed people have the right to protect themselves from the state, and "protection" in this case was broadly defined: oppressed peoples have a right to kill their tyrants, just as slaves have a right to kill their masters.

Newton, Seale, and Eldridge Cleaver, minister of information of the Black Panther Party, had all studied Frantz Fanon[58] as well as Mikhail Aleksandrovich Bakunin, a contemporary of Karl Marx who advocated "the science of destruction" in his *Catechism of the Revolutionist*. This publication was a textbook for would-be anarchists and one of a number of pieces that various student groups plagiarized, published, and circulated in pamphlet form in the 1960s and 1970s. Revolutionists, Bakunin instructed, must forgo conventionality and devote themselves to "mechanics, physics, chemistry, and possibly medicine," in so far as they contribute to their sole interest: "the revolution." The revolutionist, "merciless toward the state," should delight solely in "inexorable destruction." He may befriend only those who "prove themselves by their actions" to be revolutionists like himself. "He is to consider himself as capital," Bakunin wrote, "fated to be spent for the triumph of the revolutionary cause"; however, "he has no right personally and alone to dispose of that capital, without the consent of the aggregate of the fully initiated." Bakunin encouraged those involved in the struggle to "join hands" with outlaws and bandits, "the only genuine revolutionists." In a preface to the pamphlet, Cleaver called the *Catechism* "one of the most important formulations of principles in the entire history of revolution." However, Bakunin, whose notions of violence were direct and immoderate, had little to say about self-defense.[59] The only way for the Panthers to incorporate theorists such as Bakunin into their own ideology, which exonerated violence in the name of self-protection, was to widen their definition of self-defense.

If poverty and malnutrition and unemployment and judicial inequity were "violent," then these things, by the revolutionaries' logic, could be reciprocally fought with violence. As one militant argued, "We have been assaulted by our environment."[60] This position neutralized any counter-arguments that violence was unjustifiable. Under these criteria, it was impossible for black militants to act aggressively: liberation "by any means necessary" was merely a defensive recourse. The history of the struggle for black equality put contemporary appeals for self-defense in their proper context. "You see, we've been backed into a corner for the last four hundred years," one Panther explained, "so anything we do now is defensive."[61] This sentiment represented a dangerous kind of moral relativism to many whites. To those white liberals who valued the racially progressive gains of the early 1960s, it signified a black nihilism born of deprivation and resentment; to less sympathetic whites, it confirmed their suspicions of racism in reverse. The fear engendered by such rhetoric alienated any whites who might have been otherwise sympathetic to the plight of poor blacks living in centers of urban decay.

But to many—indeed perhaps most—Black Panthers, it made little sense to characterize their actions against police officers as just or unjust, given the larger context of police conduct in American black communities. The long, unbroken, and well-documented record of police brutality justified a violent response. To them, it was a matter of reaping what had been sown. Every Panther had first-hand experience, or knew someone personally who had been unfairly targeted because he or she was black; many knew neighbors, friends, or family members who had been brutalized because they were not white and because the police felt they could get away with such treatment. Given these experiences, it was easy for many Panthers to talk about violence against the police unremorsefully.

Newton understood that, as a black man living under laws foisted upon him by a hostile state, any violence he perpetrated was not aggressive but plausibly defensive; it was this logic that pushed the Panthers' defensive violence into the realm of offensive violence. David Hilliard further explained Huey Newton's implementation of offensive violence. "Fear is what makes him [Newton] fight so desperately," he explained, "be so severe and extreme. He always *imagines* that what he does to you, you're going to do to him. So he beats you to it."[62] The March 23, 1968, issue of the *Black Panther* made Newton's position clear, in capital letters, by addressing the police:

HALT IN THE NAME OF HUMANITY! YOU SHALL MAKE NO MORE WAR ON
UNARMED PEOPLE. YOU WILL NOT KILL ANOTHER BLACK PERSON AND WALK
THE STREETS OF THE BLACK COMMUNITY TO GLOAT ABOUT IT AND SNEER

AT THE DEFENSELESS RELATIVES OF YOUR VICTIMS. FROM NOW ON, WHEN YOU MURDER A BLACK PERSON IN THIS BABYLON OF BABYLONS, YOU MAY AS WELL GIVE IT UP BECAUSE WE WILL GET YOUR ASS AND GOD CAN'T HIDE YOU.[63]

As evidenced by this essay, the Panthers sometimes redefined conventional notions of self-defense to include retaliation and revenge.

Simultaneously, the Black Panthers shouldered the burden of defending the black community of Oakland, and in doing so they transformed self-defense from a personal prerogative to a civic duty. With the ascendance of the Panthers, self-defense was no longer an individual act, but rather a collective measure of survival. Typically, civilians defending themselves and their families are exercising what is at best a personal privilege serving only the particular interests of those defended, not those of the community at large. But as the Panthers understood it, self-protection *was* defense of the community. Without apparent consciousness of any difference, Panther rhetoric addressed community defense as if it were only individual self-protection writ large. To illustrate, a cartoon by Emory Douglas depicted a Godzilla-sized black panther chasing a giant, white rat (wearing Uncle Sam's top hat) out of a black neighborhood as flames engulf the surrounding buildings. "DEFEND THE GHETTO," the caption boldly entreats.[64] When antagonistic white police officers in Oakland failed to assume the primary responsibility of law enforcement—protection of the community—only black citizens, such as the Panthers, could assume this responsibility.

The Panthers' conceptualization of self-defense had a political dimension as well. Newton explained:

To be political, you must have a political consequence when you do not receive your desires—otherwise you are nonpolitical.

When Black people send a representative, he is somewhat absurd because he represents no political power. He does not represent land power because we do not own any land. He does not represent economic or industrial power because Black people do not own the means of production. The only way he can become political is to represent what is commonly called a military power—which the BLACK PANTHER PARTY FOR SELF-DEFENSE calls Self-Defense Power. Black people can develop Self-Defense Power by arming themselves from house to house, block to block, community to community, throughout the nation. Then we will choose a political representative and he will state to the power structure the desire of the Black masses. If the desires are met, the power structure will receive a political consequence.[65]

The "political consequence" to which Newton referred was force, or what he called "Self-Defense Power," which offered blacks political leverage. In this way, the Black Panther Party politicized the issue of self-defense at the same time it made self-defense a matter for public, not private, concern.

Politicizing self-defense again raised the issue of violence in the struggle for black equality, and it repelled the white middle class. The Panthers' aggressive rhetoric, specifically, gained them little sympathy in the public eye. Certain slogans, such as "Off the pig" and "Guns baby guns," did little to ingratiate them to the white public, and the use of coarse language also offended many whites. David Hilliard alarmed and frightened many when he announced that the Panthers would "kill Richard Nixon" if he "stood in the way of our freedom."[66]

The Deacons for Defense and Justice sailed between the Scylla of self-defense and the Charybdis of aggressive violence and emerged unscathed; however, the Black Panthers were not so lucky. The Panthers ultimately succumbed to the same brand of offensive self-defense they lauded. Their concept of self-defense was "seen by many as a thinly disguised exhortation to take pot shots at cops."[67] The local law enforcement community, with abundant assistance from the Federal Bureau of Investigation, responded to this personal threat from the Panthers with extreme prejudice. They cracked down on the Black Panther Party with a vehemence reserved only for the most dangerous enemies of the public: cop-killers.

After Newton allegedly shot and killed patrolman John Frey of the Oakland Police Department in 1967, local, state, and federal law enforcement agencies marked the Panthers for extinction.[68] Police arrested Newton on October 28, 1967, for Frey's murder. They arrested Seale for possession of illegal weapons on February 25, 1968, after a raid on his home. Police killed Bobby Hutton, teenage treasurer of the Black Panther Party, on April 6, 1968; Eldridge Cleaver was wounded in the same firefight. Expressing her condolence, Betty Shabazz, widow of Malcolm X, wrote in a Western Union telegram to Hutton's family, "The question is not will it be non-violence versus violence but whether a human being can practice his God-given right of self-defense."[69] In August 1968, the LAPD raided Panther headquarters in Los Angeles; this action resulted in many arrests and purging from *within* the Party by Panthers hunting for police informants. That same month, police firebombed the office in Newark and skirmished with Panthers in Detroit. In the most notorious example, on December 4, 1969, police raided an apartment in Chicago where they killed Mark Clark and shot Fred Hampton to death in his bed. Police systematically harassed, arrested, and killed off the Panthers in a coordinated, nationwide effort managed by the Federal Bureau of Investigation.[70]

The pressure from law enforcement agencies proved more than the Party could bear, and the final years of the Black Panther Party became quite bleak. "The Party engaged in fratricide," explained Landon Williams. "The army turned on itself. . . . That's what killed the Black Panther Party."[71] There was much infighting. Party leaders purged the rank-and-file for police informants. Undisciplined Panthers resorted to extortion and other strong-arm tactics to fund their activities. Allegations of murder and contract assassinations swept the black community. Like gangsters, some Panthers ran wild, terrorizing the community; consequently, the Party alienated many residents of Oakland.[72]

In the early 1970s, Huey Newton succumbed to drugs, paranoid delusions, and increased reliance on criminal activity to subsidize the Black Panther Party. He turned on those closest to him, expelling David Hilliard, beating Elaine Brown, and brutalizing Bobby Seale. He expunged Party members with increasing frequency for trifling reasons; others he "disciplined" by pistol-whipping. He ordered beatings and worse, such as "mud holing" (gangland-style, group stomping). Newton pistol-whipped his tailor, Preston Callins, spattering the ceiling of his Lake Merritt penthouse with blood. In 1974, he was arrested for killing a seventeen-year-old prostitute, Kathleen Smith; he was later acquitted, though an eyewitness identified him as the murderer. The "revolution" that unfolded in Oakland in the 1970s was hardly the stuff of '60s activism, but it was swift and violent: "blood to the horse's brow, and woe to those who can't swim."

As the Party moved away from its original mission of self-defense, Newton attempted to shore up the organization with theory. He explained his vision of the Panthers in an essay entitled "The Original Vision of the Black Panther Party," published as a thin pamphlet in 1973. "The original vision of the Black Panther Party," he explained, "was to serve the needs of the oppressed people in our communities and defend them against their oppressors." In this document, Newton presented the Ten Point Program as an expression of revolution, which is itself a process; therefore, he explained, he had designed the Program as an evolutionary document that would change and adapt to the people's needs, rather than as a manifesto.[73]

The rhetoric of the pamphlet, like that of many Panther speeches, was wooden and doctrinal. It referred to oppressed black persons in typically Marxist terminology as the "lumpenproletariat," and decried taxes, war, ethnocentric education, malnutrition, poverty, and sickle cell anemia, among a host of other ills plaguing blacks in Oakland. But it also revealed much about how Newton wanted the Panthers to be remembered. He noted that democracy in America "means nothing more than the domination of the majority over the minority"; upsetting this power balance was an appropriate response for any minority. In response to such activism, Newton wrote that he and Seale "expected repression" from the government, and accordingly they prepared to meet force with force.[74]

Newton delineated the causes of the evils afflicting Afro-Americans. Since all institutions were aligned against him, a black man has a right to arm himself for self-defense. He believed that no ruling class ever surrendered its privileges voluntarily and urged organization for planning and carrying out rebellion. White supremacists would not capitulate except by force. "The Black Panther Party," he wrote, "was born in a period of stress when Black people were moving away from the philosophy and strategy of nonviolent action toward sterner actions" and "stronger stuff." Openly displaying weapons and talking about "the necessity of the community to arm itself for its own self-defense" was, according to Newton, "above-ground action" that identified the Black Panther Party as a progressive political movement, not an underground terrorist organization. The gun itself was not political power, but a preliminary step towards it.[75]

The positive deeds of the Panthers—including the Free Breakfast Programs, Free Health Clinics, Clothing and Shoe Programs, and Buses-to-Prisons Program—were often overshadowed by their violent rhetoric, and by the early 1970s, the scurrilous deeds of some Panthers had eclipsed whatever good the group had accomplished in Oakland. By November 26, 1973, the FBI had ascertained that the Black Panther Party was "a thing of the past" and reported that Huey Newton is "now attempting to create an organization-type of movement in the area to control, among other things, dope pushers, prostitutes, and private social clubs."[76]

But as some defenders have observed, to focus on any "bad seeds" within the organization, or to highlight the criminal tendencies of some members (which unquestionably existed), would be to reduce the Black Panther Party to its worst element. The drugs and alcohol, along with the law-breaking and violence, were only part of the story: the historical legacy of the Black Panther Party lies not in these errant behaviors but in the group's willingness to confront unjust authority. Carl Miller, a reader of the *East Bay Express*, reacted to news of Huey Newton's 1989 murder by a drug dealer in a letter to the editor:

> Sure the Huey Newton some riffraff shot was probably a murderer, thief, alcoholic, and drug addict. . . . But the man we remember was much more than just another thug. We remember the Huey Newton who stood up strong and black, who faced down the pigs and scared shit out of racists whose worst nightmare seemed about to come true. . . . We knew in our heart of hearts that they [the Black Panthers] never really had a chance. And that the tactic of armed resistance was contradictory, at best counter-productive, and for sure downright dangerous. But oh what a rush Huey gave us. . . . The Huey we remember was a tonic that at the time our community sorely needed. . . ."[77]

Indeed, the Black Panthers' greatest achievement may have been instilling fear into those who had been fearless: that is, they created a situation in which criminally violent police officers shared in the fear that black people endured every day in places like Oakland.

As Huey's brother, Melvin Newton, noted, the Black Panther Party was about "ideals." It was about "a social movement." It was about "social change."[78] Had the Panthers found a way to commingle their revolutionary goals with the historically acceptable (indeed, even admirable) American practice of self-defense, then the group may have accomplished even more than they did. The original name of the Panthers—the "Black Panther Party for Self-Defense"—was clunky and cumbersome, but it captured the spirit of the organization. The Panthers began, like Robert Williams and the Deacons for Defense and Justice, as self-defense advocates; however, the group rapidly became the vanguard of a social revolution, moving away from the *goal* of self-defense (that is, immediate self-protection) at the same time that they justified their actions using the *rhetoric* of self-defense. In becoming a revolutionary vanguard, the Black Panthers ceased staving off attacks and began formulating their own attacks. Coincidentally, the name change to "Black Panther Party" signified more than a change of appellation. It marked a symbolic shift toward a new phase of the black freedom movement.[79] It was a change that most people—including the Panthers—were ill prepared to face.

In the late 1960s, confrontations between black militants and police officers became a feud verging on open warfare. Policemen and militants shared the blame for escalated violence. The police sometimes unfairly targeted political activists; the activists, for their part, sometimes pinned all of their hostility and frustration on hapless policemen just trying to perform what they understood to be their duties. Studies of the police showed that their attitudes and behaviors toward black persons differed greatly from their attitudes and behaviors toward other whites. Similar studies showed that Afro-Americans tended to perceive the police as hostile, prejudiced, and corrupt.[80]

Racial prejudice blended with a skewed sense of duty in some law enforcement officers to create a strain of policemen ill-equipped for duty in black communities. These policemen often saw black persons as people who wanted something for nothing, as a lesser race, as "the enemy," or as the dupes of a foreign power determined to eradicate the "American way of life." There were "good guys," they reasoned, and there were "bad guys": they, as policemen authorized to protect and serve the public, were clearly "good guys." Because of the power vested in them by the state, some police officers assumed that they could do no wrong. Implicit in this assumption was the diffused notion that a person who "stepped out of line" deserved the worst of any encounter—if only to re-establish a proper respect for the law. Policemen trusted this attitude because of the latitude it granted them in dealing with suspects. Above all, policemen respected authority and expected others to do so.

Furthermore, white society generally condoned the rough tactics of the police in the ghetto because whites felt policemen were acting in the best interest of the community. Drug use and crime needed to be eradicated, and these activities proliferated in the nation's slums. Many whites even carried this logic to an oversimplified and spurious extreme: white policemen dealt with an inordinate number of criminals who were black; therefore, many black people must be "bad guys."

But black residents living in these areas rejected the notion that they were more felonious than other Americans. They saw the police presence in their neighborhoods as selective and invasive. By 1968, policemen were no longer (if they had ever been at all) a neutral symbol of law and order in black communities. Activists such as the Panthers had exposed the actions of some policemen to be excessive and discriminatory. What little respect the typical ghetto dweller had for white cops ebbed in the riots of the mid- to late 1960s.[81]

In Newark, New Jersey, on the other side of the country from the Black Panthers' national headquarters, LeRoi Jones gave voice to this mistrust of law enforcement officers in his one-act play, *Arm Yourself or Harm Yourself: A Message of Self-Defense to Black Men*. The play, published as a pamphlet in the late 1960s, dramatized the new mentality of self-defense in a concise, easily digestible form meant for widespread distribution.

The front cover of the play depicts a helmet-wearing policeman shooting an unarmed black man in the back; the back cover depicts two policemen, revolvers drawn, saying "Open up, or we'll shoot!" They stand at the door of a black man, who clutches a small boy and replies, "I haven't done anything! Leave me alone!" The dialogue consists of a conversation between two men, one of whom is trying to convince the other of the merits of self-defense:

First Brother: Kill us off like crazy-ass animals. Nothin' but us on the ground getting stomped and beat and shot down. Cain't do nuthin. Cain't do nuthin. . . . I'm sick of this muthafuckin shit. . . .

Second Brother: You ain't sick as I am, man [takes out his piece, pulls back the hammer]. Ain't no devil on this planet gonna put his bloody claws on me, brother. Not no more, my man . . . not no more.

First Brother: Man, what you talkin' bout??

Second Brother: I'm talking *fire*. Can you dig it? *Fire* of Allaahhhh! And protecting my family and surviving past these soulless savages. Surviving, man.[82]

The second brother berates the first brother for being a "goddam negro" and failing to take up arms. They quarrel and fight; while scuffling, the cops come upon them and shoot them both. The play served not only as a plea for black men to defend themselves, but also as a critique of intra-racial quarreling: fighting among themselves when they should be fighting white racism could get black men killed.[83]

Like the Panthers, LeRoi Jones became enamored with the idea of revolution in the late 1960s. Revolution appealed to many black militants even though it was never a viable possibility. Several factors inhibited violent revolution in the United States in the 1960s. First, the United States government had not lost the allegiance or control of its armed forces—a key factor in internal revolutions. Second, Afro-Americans lacked a revolutionary majority; quite simply, there were not enough black people in the United States to carry off a coup d'état. Third, and most importantly, few blacks were willing to give up what they already had; only a handful were willing to trade the certainty of what America had to offer for the uncertainty of revolution. "A great number of blacks fail to see that there is any necessity to arm," a Black Panther informant would explain in 1971. "Others, awed by the obvious superiority in firepower available to the police, refuse to think in terms of armed conflict."[84]

It was widely believed by many whites that black revolutionaries were playing a game, or acting out a fantasy, and that they represented little danger to the community. White doubts about the earnestness of black revolutionaries vanished on the evening of July 23, 1968, when shooting erupted in the Glenville area of Cleveland's predominately black east side. Before the evening had ended, seven people were dead and fifteen wounded; three of the dead and eleven of those injured were police officers. In the next five days after the shooting, sixty businesses were destroyed or damaged by looting and arson. Property damage exceeded one million dollars.

Cleveland had been the first major American city to elect a black mayor, Carl B. Stokes. Personifying Black Power, Stokes symbolized a new breed of civil rights leader, taking the helm of public service. Plagued with the characteristically urban problems of choked thoroughfares, insufficient public transportation, crime, racial strife, poverty, inadequate housing, and corrupt politics, Cleveland was ripe for a leader sensitive to these issues.

Involved in the shooting were Fred (Ahmed) Evans and from fifteen to twenty of his group, the Black Nationalists of New Libya. Evans, like Robert Williams, was a soldier, a decorated Korean War veteran and two-hitch volunteer. Policemen characterized the incident as a "planned ambush," while black Clevelanders saw it as a classic example of police brutality. It came to light that Evans had received funds from a grant earmarked for an urban renewal project, "Cleveland: NOW!" Bureaucrats within Stokes' administration had allocated the grant money, and Stokes became known as a benefactor of cop-killing revolutionaries. An FBI informant allegedly reported that the Black Nationalists of New Libya were stockpiling weapons to carry out an assassination plot against moderate black leaders. The embarrassing incident tarnished the mayor's legacy.[85]

It is unclear why and how the shooting in Cleveland really began. No one knows who fired the first shots.[86] Because a situation existed in which any catalyst could have triggered bloodshed, it does not really matter. Both sides were primed for violence. Each expected a confrontation; each, to a certain degree, desired it. Cleveland's police officers, like those in Oakland, were white. Some had emigrated from the southern states and brought with them all the racial assumptions associated with that region; others descended from immigrants who had worked their way out of the slums. Many were not predisposed to empathize with the plight of blacks living in the ghetto.

On the other side, Ahmed Evans and his comrades-in-arms were itching for a fight. The shootout in Cleveland seemed to give credence to the notions that merely having weapons at hand created an impetus to use them, and that those who go looking for trouble often find it. It is certainly within the realm of possibility that Ahmed Evans and his band waylaid the Cleveland police. If so, this incident marked the complete metamorphosis of self-defense into an offensive action, or nondefensive assault. Evans' actions represented a severe deviation from the kind of defensive measures recommended by Malcolm X and by the Deacons for Defense and Justice a few years before. Perhaps the brand of self-defense practiced by Evans represented a necessary step toward a revolutionary consciousness. But it subsequently compromised any legitimate claim to self-defense, as understood in most legal and ethical frameworks, and it marked the end of an era of relative progress in black-white relations, especially compared to what would follow.

By 1968, self-defense as understood by the civil rights vanguard had come to signify something quite different than it had in 1955, and it only partially related to conventional notions of self-protection. Guns were flooding not only black communities but also white communities around the country, which geared up on both sides of the racial divide for a race war that never came.[87] The rhetoric of self-defense had assumed an ominous tone by 1968. A resolution adopted at the Black Students' Conference at Central State University of Ohio declared:

> We assert the right of Black students who are experiencing political and violent suppression to respond in kind. We see the Orangeburg Massacre as a lesson which teaches the necessity of self-defense. Our motto is: Avenge Orangeburg.[88]

Black nationalists outlined "black survival curriculums" that detailed self-defense and weaponry courses for children.[89] Members of US's paramilitary wing, Simba Wachanga, or "Young Lions," continued to develop their form of martial arts called Yangumi, "the way of the fist."[90] Even religious figures subscribed to a jaundiced philosophy of self-defense. Father James Groppi, a priest and youth advisor in Milwaukee, declared in *Ramparts* magazine: "I believe, with Malcolm X, in the absolute necessity of self-defense. I believe in what you might call the 'right to brick.' "[91] To like-minded revolutionaries in 1968, self-defense offered a license to "burn the mother down," or riot.

As the ugly repression of the Black Panthers by police and law enforcement personnel demonstrated, merely talking about violence could get a black person killed. The vast majority of white Americans and the police who served them neither identified with nor sympathized with the violent posturing and threatening rhetoric of this new phase of the struggle for black equality. It was this trend, in fact—the move from self-defense toward a position of more aggressive violence—that contributed to the end of what Brian Ward and Tony Badger define as the "classic southern civil rights era."[92] With the introduction of violent rhetoric, whites could no longer support the movement, and black activists could not effectively telegraph the distinctions between self-defense and violent revolution to the American public. The Black Power phase of the civil rights movement could not coalesce around such theoretical inconsistencies. Without clarifying the relationship between nonviolence, self-defense, and revolution, this latter phase of the movement faltered, and white support vanished.

Ironically, white southerners have always exhibited a unique tolerance of, if not admiration for, violent behavior. In "Below the Smith and Wesson Line," a chapter from his book *One South: An Ethnic Approach to Regional*

Culture (1982), John Shelton Reed has noted that, despite natural aversions to violence, some things are worth fighting for.

> There can be an exaggerated distaste for violence, it seems to me, which is as unwholesome in its own way as bloodlust. The pacifist merits our respect, but the coward does not. One says fighting is immoral (a defensible position, although we may disagree); the other say fighting is scary, or nasty, and nothing is worth fighting for, anyway. Whatever Southerners' faults in the matter (and they've usually been obvious), our people, black and white, have witnessed with some consistency and often at great cost to the belief that there are enemies who cannot or should not be appeased, conflicts that cannot or should not be negotiated, affronts that should not be ignored—in short, that there *are* things worth fighting for. We may disagree about what those things are, but I think we can use the reminder that they exist.[93]

As a white southerner attuned to what C. Vann Woodward has called "the burden of southern history," Reed might agree that civil rights and social justice fall into the category of "things worth fighting for." Conversely, by denying that violence was one way out of the South's racial mire, rationalists in the 1960s failed to provide constructive channels for minimizing its effects.[94] Lerone Bennett Jr. has further explored this aversion among otherwise supportive white liberals. White liberals, he explained in 1964, fear black violence more than anything else because it "illuminates the precarious ledge of their posture." Violence by whites, while deplorable, is endurable, "and white liberals endure it amazingly well." But black violence creates, or threatens to create, "a situation which forces white liberals to choose sides"; it "exposes their essential support of things as they are."[95] Bennett reasoned that the condemnation of any form of violence by blacks, in conjunction with anything less than militant opposition to violence by blacks, constituted a gross hypocrisy.

Erroneously, some scholars have claimed that the civil rights movement fell apart when activists lost faith in nonviolent direct action. Although the shift away from strict adherence to nonviolence contributed to the loss of white support and the eventual demise of the civil rights movement, at least two factors played even greater roles in derailing the movement. While willing to support the abolition of segregation and disfranchisement, most white Americans were not prepared to accept either economic justice or the redistribution of wealth, both of which activists began discussing in the late 1960s. Furthermore, when self-defense devolved from a pragmatic means of self-protection against white violence into an offensive weapon of first resort, then those involved in the Black Power phase of the civil rights movement could no longer claim the moral high ground in the struggle against white supremacy. More than disillusionment, frustration, burnout, fatigue, cooptation, and tribalism among civil rights organizations, it was these revolutionary trends—the expansion of the civil rights movement into economic realms, and the metamorphosis of self-defense into offensive violence—that caused the ultimate demise of the civil rights movement. As an expression of traditional American values and societal norms in the early and mid-1960s, self-defense proved to be a viable part of the black freedom struggle; as a platform for revolution in the late 1960s, it did not. By the time of Dr. King's assassination in 1968, self-defense did not resemble "self-defense" in a conventional sense at all, but it did speak to the angry, disillusioned, and desperate situation in which many black Americans found themselves.

There's a place for the Rap Browns and the Stokely Carmichaels. They've

instilled a lot of pride and dignity in a lot of Negroes—especially the young

Negroes. These guys have given many Negroes the courage to talk back.

CARL WASHINGTON, LONG BEACH, CALIFORNIA, 1968

CONCLUSION
THE COURAGE TO TALK BACK

In 1967, the new chairman of the SNCC told a crowd of black people in Cambridge, Maryland, why it was not only acceptable but imperative that they employ self-defense collectively: "You've got to understand what they [whites] are doing," H. Rap Brown explained. "America has laid out a plan to eliminate all black people who go against them." He saw a genocidal conspiracy in the backwaters of the South, where black people were starving; in the jungles of Vietnam, where a disproportionate number of black men were killed in combat; and wherever American diplomacy stretched across the globe. "A 19-year old boy shot thirty-nine times, four times in the head," he lamented, referring to recent rioting. "It don't take but one bullet to kill you. So they're really trying to tell you something else—how much they hate you, how much they hate black folks." For him, the only sensible course of action was to return fire.[1]

Like Brown, a number of black militants in the late 1960s embraced violence as a panacea for the tough problems facing Afro-Americans, but armed self-defense offered few easy solutions. In fact, it presented a number of problems, both concrete and abstract, for any black persons bold enough to espouse it. First, when black people said "self-defense," white people heard "violence" and reacted with fear and force. During this period, the actions of Robert Williams, Malcolm X, the Deacons for Defense, and particularly the Black Panthers all helped to transform self-defense from an individual prerogative into a socially conscious gesture, a unique kind of communalist behavior within Afro-American communities; however, their experiences, as well as that of Ahmed Evans, illustrate the difficulties in transforming self-defense from a course of individual prerogative into a programmatic course of action. When activists began to organize around the concept of self-defense, the threat of violence inherent in such an agenda often eclipsed its own practicality: only a few Americans—black or white—could distinguish between the violence of racial animosity and the necessary force of self-defense. Clearly, there was misunderstanding on two sides: those who advocated self-defense often seemed to misunderstand what Martin Luther King Jr. meant by the term "nonviolence," which they interpreted as passivity, and those who criticized self-defense often seemed to misunderstand what its proponents meant by the phrase, often misinterpreted as "violence." This misunderstanding was exacerbated by the print media; both mainstream publications and black newspapers seemed quick to characterize nonviolence as pacifism, and self-defense as "violence."

Second, the seemingly glaring contradiction of activists using firearms in a self-described "nonviolent movement" threatened to undo many of the gains that blacks had accomplished. As discussed earlier, self-defense and nonviolence often co-existed in an unlikely symbiosis, and many activists were able to believe in both self-defense and nonviolent direct action through a reconceptualization of each. To them, self-defense represented a direct means of combating physical assault, while nonviolence represented a tactic of protest and social reform, independent from moral discipline or piety. By being willing to fight and showing it, these activists felt they might not have to fight at all. A few noted that the nonviolent ideal was just that— an ideal, something toward which to strive; their dilemma centered upon what could be gained by abnegating self-defense and what could be lost. Finally, not all activists shared the vision of a nonviolent world in which blacks and whites could come together to mend their broken past. The rhetoric of Malcolm X, which coupled black separatism with an adamancy regarding self-defense, emphasized this latter point; like Robert Williams, Malcolm X could not relinquish self-defense in the quest for equal rights because, from his perspective, self-defense itself was central to the quest.

Third, in certain situations, resorting to force in self-defense could be gratuitous, shading into retribution, retaliation, and revenge. It is important to emphasize that the reason people own firearms is, at best, an imperfect indicator of how they actually use them.[2] Claiming one carries a gun for self-protection does not preclude malevolence, violent intent, or even criminal behavior. A burglar might honestly claim to carry a gun for protection, even though he is committing a crime and "defending himself" against a frightened homeowner wielding a firearm; accordingly, "self-defense," in some cases, represents a post-facto excuse rather than a morally justifiable response. As the Black Panther Party grew and expanded, the behavior of some BPP members exemplified this misappropriation of self-defense. Though they claimed they were defending themselves against racist police officers, at times their actions belied the requisite innocence necessary to the claim of self-defense. They acted not only from need but also from bravado, braggadocio, and anger.

As the old football aphorism goes, the best defense is a good offense. It is far better, according to this line of reasoning, to keep someone from attacking in the first place than to stop him once he has started; therefore, it is best to strike first and strike hard. As attractive as this option may be, the obvious flaw in its logic is that such "defense" is no longer defense: it is an offensive precaution. From a legal standpoint, such action is hardly justifiable; therefore, the preemptive actions of some Panthers and of Ahmed Evans are highly questionable. At best, Evans may be accused of defensive solicitation—at worst, cold-blooded ambush.

Fourth, it is quite plausible that the presence of weapons served not to deter conflict but to heighten tensions and feed violence. Interrogating David Hilliard in a television interview for CBS's "Face the Nation" in 1969, Bernard Nossiter wondered if storing caches of firearms was not "an invitation for the police to take action."[3] Hilliard denied stockpiling guns. By carrying guns, Nossiter implied, the Panthers put themselves in a position where sooner or later they would have to use them.[4] If weapons caches proved to be effective deterrents for some activists, such as the Deacons and Robert Williams, then they also provided an excuse for police to attack in other instances, as in Cleveland in 1968.

Fifth, and finally, the security gained from carrying guns was quite possibly more illusory than real. A firearm offers a defensive opportunity only if it is carried everywhere a person goes, even inside one's home, and only if an adversary somehow loses the advantage of surprise. It can be argued, as many pundits did in the late 1960s, that guns were more serviceable as rhetorical appendages than as tools of revolution, or even as devices of self-protection. In the absence of legal order, a firearm may be the most immediate means of thwarting criminal activity or preventing injury; however, in a civilized society, physical security is a collective responsibility, not an individual one. In fact, protesters did what they did to gain state protection that would preclude the need for carrying a gun in the first place. In other words, part of the reason the civil rights movement took place was to make "Negroes with guns" obsolete. Every American has the right to live without fear and without relying upon firearms for security. As one scholar has noted, civilization is characterized by "the gradual perfection of respectful procedure for moral violence [i.e., self-defense]." It is "the formalizing of moral violence under rule of law."[5] The civil rights movement itself represented a step toward a more civilized United States, obfuscating the need for armed camps, glaring at each other across the racial divide.

These considerations were enough to keep many folks from arming themselves. Of course, in a life-or-death confrontation, one tends to act first and rationalize later, and in such instances, self-defensive acts involve no forethought or deliberation (which, legally and ethically, is precisely what makes them qualify as self-defense). Still, if armed self-defense prefigured more problems than solutions, then these considerations might have been enough to deter a black person in the American South from keeping a gun handy.

But armed self-defense meant something else, something more, apart from its own practicality or feasibility. It meant showing fight. Self-defense brought about a radical re-alignment in Afro-American thinking, causing—to borrow Thomas Kuhn's theory of scientific revolution—a "paradigm shift" in black consciousness. Self-defense can be an analog of self-reliance.[6] Within the black struggle for equality, it became an expression of self-determination. Whether armed black southerners were safer than those who did not arm themselves seemed to matter less than whether they *felt* safer. Security was, more often than not, a state of mind, and self-defense was effective in a way violent political protest never could be—because the latter was all-too-successfully repressed. Violent expressions were simply illegal, beyond the pale of law and order, but self-defense, within the social and political matrices of American life, was both legal and justifiable, and it lent a sense of self-empowerment to those who employed it. Most importantly, it changed the way black people carried themselves and the way they interacted with whites.

The simple act of defending one's person in many ways came to symbolize the larger quest for Afro-American rights and racial equality. In defending oneself, one was helping to uplift the race. This "new" idea of the primacy of self-defense during the Black Power phase of the civil rights movement had deep roots in Afro-American history. When white people subjected black people to harsh, physical punishment, it often stemmed from some transgression in the region's unwritten code of etiquette: failing to yield the sidewalk, not averting one's eyes quickly enough or, in the case of Emmett Till, admiring a white woman.[7] To be black and southern in the mid-twentieth century meant, as it did in earlier times, having to live in a state of constant watchfulness (if not fear), and it meant being perpetually aware of racially defined prescriptions of behavior; however, the practice of self-defense in the 1950s and 1960s brought a new sensibility to these mores.

In practice and in spirit, self-defense reached beyond the mere need to protect one's person. Adopting a mindset of self-defense reflected an individual ultimatum, a kind of personal Maginot line, drawn in the sands of white southern contempt and hostility. It represented a quantum leap in the ability to define one's own space and identity and, when more than one black person decided on a course of self-defense, it represented a watershed in race relations. Deciding that one would fight back against racist intimidation meant an empowerment heretofore unknown among a people pestered by the lingering notions of self-doubt, reinforced by centuries of involuntary servitude.

At the heart of the issue of black self-defense was the issue of respect, or more accurately, *dis*respect, the refusal of whites to see Afro-Americans as individuals. Self-defense essentially represents an affirmation of self. As part of the civil rights struggle, it allowed black southerners to reaffirm their own humanity in a social order that repeatedly effaced the self-worth and individuality of black people. Black southerners were concerned not only with their status as American citizens possessing civil rights but also with their treatment as human beings with human rights. For example, black folks in the South had to struggle for the use of "courtesy titles" such as "sir," "ma'am," "mister," and "missus" in lieu of the more common (and often falsely familiar) "uncle" or "auntie." The disrespect implied in these latter terms represented one of many practices intended to reinforce the inferior status of Afro-Americans. In this sense, the quest for civil rights was part of a larger struggle for black equality, black freedom, and human dignity. Accordingly, the greatest challenge facing black people in the civil rights movement might not have been white racism or indifferent politicians or violence, but what one observer called "the gnawing inbred suspicion that they really are unqualified to make important decisions for themselves and must depend, in the end, on the benevolence of whites."[8] It was a time when even black people, who so recently had been "coloreds" or "Negroes," were themselves barely getting used to being called black. W. E. B. DuBois once illustrated this component of the black freedom struggle when he explained what made slavery so onerous. "It was in part psychological," he wrote, "the enforced personal feeling of inferiority, the calling of another Master; the standing with the hat in hand. It was the helplessness. It was the defenselessness of family life. It was the submergence below the arbitrary will of any sort of individual."[9] DuBois aptly captured the pain of deference to the white man's (and woman's) will, and his words spoke to the subservience that outlasted slavery and lived into the modern era.

This sense of subordination may have been particularly acute in black men, who shouldered the burden of defending not only themselves but also the women and children in their lives. Self-defense represented a man's prerogative and man's duty: it was a manly response to white transgressions. Consistently, male activists expressed the impulse to defend themselves in terms of gender roles and sexual divisions of labor. Most black men felt it was their responsibility to protect the women in their lives; in fact, they guardedly viewed self-defense as their domain, and theirs alone. But black men were not alone in feeling the sting of bigotry: black women continued to fight their own unique war on two fronts, against both racism and sexism. Out of necessity, and to their credit, women often subverted these traditional gender roles and implemented defensive measures themselves to protect their homes, bodies, and families.

Deciding that a white person could no longer physically threaten, bully, or intimidate represented a new mindset for many, many black individuals; collectively, these realizations signaled a new black consciousness. As one observer described the feeling in Robert Williams's hometown in 1961, after Williams had promised to "meet violence with violence":

> The morale of the Negroes in Union County is high. They carry them-
> selves with a dignity I have seen in no other southern community. Largely
> vanished are the slouching posture, the scratching head, and the indirect,
> mumbled speech that used to characterize the Negro male in the pres-
> ence of whites. It is as if, in facing up to their enemies, they have finally
> confronted a terrible reality and found it not so terrible after all. [10]

Realizing one could protect oneself allowed a person to look at his or her world in a new way, and this realization, as it spread in the 1960s, influenced multiple aspects of Afro-American culture. It affected how people carried themselves in public, talked to white employers, and confronted authority; in short, it affected how they interacted with the majority culture. Self-defense engendered confidence and self-esteem as it negated fear. It exponentially increased the self-assurance stunted by years of deference and servitude. For example, Williams recalled a college football player from Nashville named Leroy Wright who had come to Monroe to participate in demonstrations there. In an altercation outside a local drugstore, some "crackers," according to Williams, mistook Wright for a "pacifist nigger," and slapped him. Wright struck back. He was arrested and fined for assault. When he got out of jail, Wright came to Williams with his hand bandaged and sore and said:

> Man, let me tell you something . . . they put me in jail and it cost fifty
> dollars for hitting that cracker . . . but I never felt so good in all my life.
> I've been all over the South with these fellows [SNCC activists], and they've
> been beating my ass and putting cigarettes on me, and chains, and I have
> seen them hit girls, and this the first place I've been where you can hit a
> cracker. . . . [M]an, I hit that cracker with all my might, and when I hit
> that cracker . . . I damn near broke my hand . . . but it felt so good to see
> that cracker fall on his knees and his teeth fall out. . . . [M]an, you know
> what . . . I think you are right. I sure like Monroe. [11]

There had always been stereotypical "bad niggers": self-assured black men of folklore (such as Stagolee) and history (such as Nat Turner) who "brooked no shit" from anyone, including whites.[12] But during this period this same sort of mentality—that no white man could lay a finger on you—began to infuse the racial consciousnesses of everyday men and women who were far from "bad." Representing a sea change in black-white relations, the commonplace acceptance of self-defense did nothing short of reordering race relations in the United States. More than a physical act, self-defense was a frame of mind. As Carl Washington of Long Beach, California, expressed in 1968: "There's a place for the Rap Browns and the Stokely Carmichaels. They've instilled a lot of pride and dignity in a lot of Negroes—especially the young Negroes. These guys have given many Negroes the courage to talk back."[13]

In summary, self-defense, like nonviolence, represented a critical dimension of the fight for civil rights. A mentality of defiance infused the struggle for black equality, and self-defense, as a highly personal measure of defiance, came to symbolize the spirit of civil rights protest itself to many Afro-Americans. The absence of institutional protections, the reluctance of the federal government to commit fully to black equality, and the weak committal of most whites to the cause only heightened the need for self-reliance and, subsequently, for self-defense, which became an analog of self-determination and self-sufficiency for many black Americans in the 1960s. It substantiated citizenship; asserting one's rights, especially a right enshrined in the United States Constitution, was a very *American* thing to do.

During the period 1955–1968, the issue of self-defense by black Americans moved in two parallel and sometimes intertwining trajectories. It changed from a defensive measure to an offensive precaution and from an individual gesture to a collective action. It evolved alongside a third trajectory of protest in the struggle for black equality: nonviolent direct action, which in 1955 and 1956 was quickly becoming the normative method of protest in the burgeoning movement for black civil rights.

If self-defense proved effective in the struggle and complementary to nonviolence, then it did so at no small cost, and one must be careful not to romanticize the practice of self-defense in the civil rights movement. Armed self-defense provided no panacea capable of curing four hundred years of racial transgressions. It was a road paved with danger, a shortcut to martyrdom, and those individuals who practiced it, or even suggested it, risked everything, including their lives. Robert Williams spent much of his life on the lam. For every Charles Sims, triumphant in his bold posturing, there was a Robert Charles, shot down in a hail of bullets; for every Bogalusa, Louisiana there was a Rosewood, Florida, wiped from existence for the merest hint of defiance.

And yet the fact remains that few white supremacists were willing to die at the hands of those whom they saw as a bunch of crazy, gun-wielding "niggers." Malcolm X recognized this fact. "Whites will never correct the problem [of the color line] on moral, legal, or ethical reasons," he bluntly stated. "But they're realists enough to know that they don't want Negroes running around with rifles."[14] On the disadvantaged side of the South's racial divide, a significant proportion of black people felt they had little to lose and everything to gain in arming themselves and preparing to defend themselves in the name of protecting their constitutional freedoms.

[T]he only tired I was, was tired of giving in.

ROSA PARKS, 1992

POSTSCRIPT

THE ONLY TIRED

The story of Robert Williams's exile and return to the United States caps the history of civil rights and self-defense in a way nothing else can dramatize. His saga ends with an interesting twist that not only encapsulates the importance of self-defense in the struggle for black equality but also symbolically brings the civil rights movement full-circle to its humble beginnings in Montgomery, Alabama. While exiled in Cuba in the early 1960s, Robert Williams associated with Fidel Castro, Che Guevara, Alberto Pineira, Blas Roca, and other governmental officials, all of whom tried to convince him that "the race issue is due to class oppression . . . rather than racial struggle."[1] Cuban officials argued that the only chance for black advancement was for black and white workers to unite across racial boundaries. But Williams continued to see the greatest threat as coming from the same working-class whites championed by Communist doctrine. In 1964, when an interviewer asked him if he "preached hate" like the Muslims, Williams replied: "Yes, I teach and advocate hate. I teach and advocate hatred of all forms of oppression, tyranny, and exploitation. I teach and advocate hatred of the haters. Why should we be required to love our enemies?"[2]

Williams continued to agitate from abroad, using radio transmissions from Havana ("Radio Free Dixie") and his monthly newsletter the *Crusader* to encourage Afro-Americans to fight white oppression actively. He also sought to clear his name. His rhetoric took on an increasingly revolutionary, Marxist tone.[3] Such rhetoric prompted the editor of the *Charlotte Observer* to decry Williams's "scurrilous propaganda" and "anti-American diatribes of the rankest kind."[4]

After three years, Williams left Cuba for China. He had had differences with the Cuban Communist Party, which maintained that the race problem in the United States was strictly a class issue and that once the class problem had been solved through a socialist administration, racism would be abolished. Believing racism encompassed "more than just a class struggle," Williams left Cuba on relatively sour terms with government officials there.[5]

He traveled extensively in the People's Republic of China in 1964. He met with China's top-ranking officials (including Chairman Mao Tse-Tung), and studied Chinese economic development.[6] Though Williams claimed no political affiliation, his enemies in the United States associated him with communism in an attempt to tarnish his reputation further. One article in the *New York Times* emphasized the "lessons of discipline, commitment, and 'true militancy' he had learned in China." According to the article, he apparently "expressed much admiration for China's 'cultural revolution'."[7] But Williams, honoring anticommunist fervor in the United States, disavowed any association with the Communist Party. "I am not interested in promoting ideologies or philosophies. I am interested in justice and freedom. . . . It is not a matter of socialism, or what they call socialism or communism."[8] He denied any formal affiliation with the Communist Party. "This movement that I led was not a political organization," he repeated. "It had no political affiliations whatsoever. It was a movement of people who resented oppression."[9] Forced into exile, Williams became an expatriate, decrying American imperialism at home and abroad. During these years, he was not only a fugitive, but also a patriot: throughout this trying time, he still considered the United States "home."

Williams became more celebrated as a refugee than as a militant activist at home. During his exile, a number of domestic groups usurped his name and image to advance their own causes and to keep his cause alive in the United States. The Peace and Freedom Party suggested he run for President of the United States while in exile; he respectfully declined. He also served briefly as the honorary Prime Minister of the Provincial Government of the African-American Captive Nation, a short-lived separatist group advocating a separate nation within the U.S. for black Americans. While in Cuba, the Revolutionary Action Movement asked Williams to become its chairman; while in China, the Republic of New Africa made the same offer. Both titles were honorary, and Williams allowed both RAM and the RNA to use his name. Allowing these groups to use his name again put Williams on the radar screens of agencies such as the FBI, the Justice Department, and the CIA. Although Williams later resigned from these titular offices, and despite the fact that (according to his testimony) he was active neither in RAM nor the RNA, the government shadowed his every move thereafter.[10]

RAM was a Detroit-based, self-styled fusion of the Nation of Islam and the Student Nonviolent Coordinating Committee that "favored" Williams and his notions of armed self-defense. Max Stanford of RAM called for a self-defense-oriented "National Youth Movement," or "Black Guard," to "protect the true interest of Black America" by "cleans[ing] itself of the Black Nation's enemies."[11] The group made a media splash in 1965 when it bungled plans to blow up the nation's most symbolic monuments, including the Statue of Liberty and the Liberty Bell.

Like the Provincial Government of the African-American Captive Nation, the RNA sought to create a separate political state for blacks within the United States by occupying northern cities and the southern Black Belt. Strong neither in numbers nor in resources, the RNA came into existence on March 31, 1968, when over two hundred black people from all over the United States met at the Twenty-Grand Motel in Detroit to sign a "Declaration of Independence." Its leaders included, among others, Betty Shabazz and H. Rap Brown.[12]

Hoping to clear his name and tired of living in exile, Williams returned to the United States in 1969. He lived in Michigan and faced extradition to North Carolina. Williams testified before the U.S. Senate Judiciary Committee, chaired by Senator James Eastland of Mississippi, after being subpoenaed by its "Subcommittee to Investigate the Administration of the Internal Security Act and Other Internal Security Laws." The sub-committee, with Senator Strom Thurmond of South Carolina presiding, grilled Williams for three days in February and March 1970. In an amazing exchange, the details of Williams's exile slowly emerged. Thurmond asked Williams a series of pointed questions. Hinting at treason, Thurmond asked: "Were you advocating or did you suggest that they [black Americans] initiate a revolution?" Williams responded:

No. I advocated that they resist violence, racist violence and racist oppression, that they resist it with violence, but some people thought that I had advocated revolution, but the fact was that they did not read the pamphlets very well because I had always stipulated that I was for the support of the U.S. Constitution, that you would see if you read these all the way through from the very beginning that my complaint was because the Constitution was not being extended to us and that we should fight for the enforcement of the Constitution of the United States. And I also stated that what would happen, what could possibly happen in America, if these changes for justice and these changes for righteousness did not come about.

When asked if he abetted communists "to conspire against the United States," he replied: "When I was in Cuba I was probably having more trouble out of the Communists than the United States was having." Exasperated, Thurmond again asked if Williams "had taken any steps to inspire or foster a black revolution in this country while you were within the country or without the country?" Williams replied:

No. Not to inspire black revolution, but I did do everything I could to inspire black men to defend their homes, their women and children when there is a breakdown of law, and I always specified in everything I wrote and everything I said that this was the last resort when the law fails to protect our people, when the law fails to protect our women and children, and I hoped to inspire black men to defend themselves, their families, and to defend their communities against aggression, and this is what I advocated.[13]

He was loyal only to the cause of challenging white supremacy when and where he found it: beyond this immediate cause, he seemed oblivious to political ideology or social activism. Through this dialectic exchange, a composite of Williams's beliefs gradually evolved:

"I see self-determination not as just a separation of the races, but I see it as the right of a people to determine their own destiny. . . . I think people who are oppressed have a right to relieve themselves in whatever measure. I think it should be legal if possible, but if they can't do it legally I think it is the American way to do it with violence. . . . If I had been white in America I never would have been hounded and harassed and treated the way I have been treated. And I resent this. And there are some whites, whether they are in the law or on the outside, that just hate black people. And they hate me most of all. They hate me more . . . because I have resisted, and also because I have constantly advocated the enforcement of the Constitution."[14]

Williams was quick to associate gun owning with hunting and the outdoors. "I organized a charter group for the National Rifle Association there," he testified, "and we used to do quite a bit of shooting in the South. . . . And also I did quite a bit of hunting, and now I am a licensed hunter in Michigan."[15] Williams evoked the nation's most revered gun club, the National Rifle Association, to show how his own gun ownership was more mainstream than marginal. He realized how threatening black gun ownership remained to the white public, and he respected the power of the committee to persecute him further. He hoped to impress them as a red-blooded American.[16]

While the Senate hearings did not break his spirit, they certainly deflated Williams's defiance. Afterward, he shifted his energies in different directions. He took a position as an expert on Chinese-American relations at the Center for Asian Studies at the University of Michigan. Shortly thereafter, a book about Williams went to press. Williams had had a falling out with the ghostwriter of this book, Robert C. Cohen, after recording forty-six hours of interviews while in exile. Cohen had power of attorney over the book and had proceeded with plans to publish the autobiography with Bantam Books while Williams was out of the country. According to Williams, Cohen failed to get the book out on schedule (upon Williams's return to the United States in 1969); therefore, Williams repudiated their agreement. At the time of the Senate Judiciary hearings, he had received no royalties (agreed at eight cents per copy) for the book.[17] The book, entitled *Black Crusader* (1973), essentially became an unauthorized biography.

Williams served as a research associate in the Center for Chinese Studies at the University of Michigan from 1970 to 1971. Drawing from his first-hand experience in China, he advised Allen Whiting, a political scientist who in turn advised Henry Kissinger shortly before Kissinger's first trip to China. He also served as director of the Detroit East Side Citizens Against Drug Abuse Clinic. Despite Williams's relocation to Michigan, Klan members in North Carolina did not forget him. Klan members marched in Monroe in 1972, and during the march the Grand Dragon, Virgil Lee Griffin, said they wanted "to bring that nigger Robert Williams back so we can hang him."[18] Williams did return briefly to North Carolina in December 1975, after Governor William Milliken of Michigan extradited him to face the 1961 kidnapping charges; by then, the state of North Carolina had lost interest and dropped all charges against him.

Despite his efforts to resume a normal life, Williams remained the leading apostle of armed black resistance. As his wife Mabel observed:

> People like to blow up the fact that Robert was a violent man or believed in violence. But he didn't believe in doing violence other than in defense of his own. The powers-that-be were much more threatened by that gun than they were by the nonviolent protests he organized. Once they couldn't do violence and be immune to violence, they didn't do as much violence.[19]

The extent to which Robert Williams and self-defense were inextricably linked is illustrated by a letter written by Julian Mayfield to Williams on June 7, 1980, ostensibly to critique a reissue of the *Crusader* newsletter. The letter quickly turned from editorial advice to an excited discussion of armed resistance. Writing from a college campus in Adelphi, Maryland, Mayfield described the resurgence of the Ku Klux Klan on the East Coast, and the "middle-class blacks standing around who do not know what to do against racist violence." He coached his students on what to do. The Klansmen "have a right to burn a cross," he told them. "You have a right to kick their asses." Mayfield informed Williams that he had told his students about Williams's experience in Monroe, and "emphasized the fact that any black man who didn't have a gun was stupid"; but Mayfield worried that he "wasn't getting through," and implored Williams to resurrect his message of self-defense. "Please," he wrote, "in *The Crusader* tell every black man to get himself a gun, and *learn how to use it*. Even if he makes $30,000 a year." Mayfield concluded, "I don't have to tell you that racism is as deep now as it was when we left in 1961. It is only more sophisticated."[20] Williams likely agreed.

Williams enjoyed a final homecoming in 1995—thirty-five years after being forced to leave North Carolina—when he visited Monroe to lead a parade. He resided in Baldwin, Michigan, until his death on October 15, 1996, at the age of 71.[21] Interestingly, Rosa Parks delivered the eulogy at his funeral, and a tribute at Wayne State University honored him on November 1.[22]

Rosa Parks's eulogy of Robert Williams might seem to be a discordant note in the final coda of the civil rights movement. Here, after all, was the paragon of the civil rights movement—a woman who had come to symbolize nonviolence itself—eulogizing a man who had come to symbolize racial violence. But Rosa Parks never wholeheartedly endorsed nonviolence, and the solidarity she felt with Williams represented a kind of quiet assurance in the power of self-defense. Her tacit approval of self-defense is plain to anyone who has read her autobiography. "We always felt that if you talked violently and said what you would do if they [aggressors] did something to you, that did more good than nonviolence," she explained. "Most of the black people in Montgomery had similar feelings. . . . To this day I am not an absolute supporter of nonviolence in all situations."[23] In recounting her famous arrest, she included a most telling remembrance, which reveals her thoughts on self-defense. Thirty-seven years after the bus driver instructed her to give up her seat and "make it light on yourself," she remembered:

I could not see how standing up was going to "make it light" for me. The more we gave in and complied, the worse they treated us.

I thought back to the time when I used to sit up all night and didn't sleep, and my grandfather would have his gun right by the fireplace, or if he had his one-horse wagon going anywhere, he always had his gun in the back of the wagon. People always say that I didn't give up my seat because I was tired, but that isn't true. I was not tired physically, or no more tired than I usually was at the end of a working day. I was not old, although some people have an image of me as being old then. I was forty-two. No, the only tired I was, was tired of giving in.

The driver of the bus saw me still sitting there, and he asked was I going to stand up. I said, "No." He said, "Well, I'm going to have you arrested." Then I said, "You may do that."[24]

Mrs. Parks included the seemingly random remembrance of her grandfather's gun in her recollection of her arrest because, in her mind, civil rights and self-defense were indistinguishable. In considering her own activism, she could not help but think of her grandfather and his preparedness to defend himself and his family. "Dr. King used to say that black people should receive brutality with love, and I believed that was a goal to work for," she stated. "But I couldn't reach that point in my mind at all, even though I know that the strategy Dr. King used probably was the better one for the masses of people in Montgomery than trying to retaliate without any weapons or ammunition."[25]

NOTES

Introduction. Pure Fire

1. Powledge, *Free at Last?*, 33; Payne, *I've Got the Light of Freedom*.

2. It would be impossible to list here the vast number of works devoted to nonviolence; I offer a few of the most helpful. Martin Luther King Jr. himself has provided the best explanation of nonviolence within the context of the civil rights movement in *Stride toward Freedom*, 101–107; and in his famous "Letter from Birmingham City Jail," 3–14. For a comprehensive look at nonviolence in American history, see Lynd, *Nonviolence in America*. For a discussion of Gandhian nonviolence, see Bondurant, *Conquest of Violence*; see also Gandhi, *The Story of My Experiments with Truth*.

3. The most recent (and best) studies of this phase of the civil rights movement include Woodard, *A Nation within a Nation*; Van Deburg, *New Day in Babylon*; Jones, *Black Panther Party Reconsidered*; Kelley, *Freedom Dreams*; and Cleaver and Katsiaficas, *Liberation*.

4. See Sorel, *Reflections on Violence*; Lukács, *History and Class Consciousness*; and Fanon, *Les damnés de la terre*. See also Gandhi, *My Experiments with Truth*; King, "Letter from Birmingham City Jail"; and Arrendt, *On Violence*. This literature incorporates profound discussions of revolution, different forms of resistance, pacifism, and nonresistance, and many formidable thinkers have treated these topics. Georges Sorel and Georg Lukács each embraced proletarian violence as a function of socialist revolution in the early years of the twentieth century. In his classic analysis of colonial and post-colonial societies, Frantz Fanon celebrated the cathartic effect of violence by the oppressed against their oppressors. Mohandas K. Gandhi first articulated the moral imperative and power of nonviolence, or *satyagraha*, which he defined as "truth-strength" or "love-power." In an American context, Martin Luther King Jr. linked Gandhi's theories of nonviolence not only to civil disobedience but also to Christian love. And in her collection of essays on the subject, Hannah Arrendt distinguished between violence and power as she reconceptualized the entire issue.

5. See Wexler, *The Civil Rights Movement*, 228. Sanford Wexler notes that "the civil rights movement changed directions after 1965," explaining, "The movement for racial equality that first gained momentum in the mid-1950s with the Montgomery bus boycott and again in the early 1960s with the sit-ins and Freedom Rides did not come to an end in Selma, it only transformed itself into a new movement." Anna Kosof ends her discussion of the civil rights movement with Selma and the Voting Rights Act of 1965, after which the "moderate wing of the

civil rights movement," represented by King, gave way to young militants and their violent ways. "The late sixties saw a different kind of civil rights movement," she notes. "The mood of the country had shifted." See Kosof, *Civil Rights Movement*, 66. Brian Ward and Tony Badger define the "classic southern civil rights era" as 1955–1965. See Ward and Badger, *Making of Martin Luther King*, 4. William T. Martin Riches calls Selma "a crucial turning point" for those involved in the movement; see Riches, *The Civil Rights Movement*, 86. Steven F. Lawson allows that "black protest took a violent course with the outbreak of urban riots in the mid-1960s." See Lawson, *Running for Freedom*, 146. The year 1965, and the Watts riot, in particular, is a watershed for Harvard Sitkoff in his classic study of the movement. "The era of nonviolence ended," he writes, and "the age of Malcolm X's angry heirs began." See Sitkoff, *Struggle for Black Equality*, 185. Peter Levy agrees, noting, "To a large extent, the civil rights movement of the latter half of the 1960s represented the ascendancy of Malcolm X's black nationalist vision." See Levy, *The Civil Rights Movement*, 29. Vincent Harding also notes that what happened in Selma and in Watts in 1965 marked a break or shift. "In a sense, the rounding off of the classic southern phase of the movement in Selma that spring and the summertime explosion in black Los Angeles (as well as in places like Chicago and Philadelphia) proved to mark a turning point," he writes. See Harding et al., *Eyes on the Prize*, 180.

6. James Robert Ross's study of tactics and strategies in the civil rights movement, while not historicized, represents a classic dichotimization of violence and nonviolence. See Ross, *The War Within*. For contemporaneous examples from the 1960s, see J. H. Griffin, "On Either Side of Violence," *Saturday Review* 45 (October 27, 1962): 38. For examples in black periodicals, see "Violence versus Non-violence [photo editorial]," *Ebony* 20 (April 1965): 168–169. Textbooks—perhaps out of a need for conciseness—often use this model of discussing the movement's aims and tactics. For example, one college-level U.S. history textbook presents on facing pages "The Case for Violence" and "The Case Against Violence" as explained by Huey P. Newton and Martin Luther King Jr., respectively; see Blum and Woodward, *National Experience*, 854–855. Not all analyses follow this model. For example, Richard P. Young pointed out in 1970 that "black unrest," which many scholars noted as a new phenomenon in the mid- to late-1960s, was not new: "During most of our nation's past," he wrote, "black violence was contained only through systems of ruthless repression." See Young, *Roots of Rebellion*, 2.

7. A growing number of authors have alluded to the importance of this issue. For example, see Payne, *I've Got the Light of Freedom*; Shapiro, *White Violence and Black Response*; Tyson, *Radio Free Dixie*; de Jong, *A Different Day*; Crosby, " 'This nonviolent stuff ain't no good. It'll get you killed': Teaching About Self-Defense in the African-American Freedom Struggle," in Armstrong et al., *Teaching*;

Umoja, "Ballots and Bullets: A Comparative Analysis of Armed Resistance in the Civil Rights Movement," *Journal of Black Studies* 29, no. 4 (March 1999):558–578; and Umoja, "'We Will Shoot Back': The Natchez Model and Para-Military Organization in the Mississippi Freedom Movement," *Journal of Black Studies* 32, no. 3 (January 2002): 267–290.

8. See Cruse, *Crisis of the Negro Intellectual*, 347–401. In this epochal (and sometimes problematic) work on black thought in the 1960s, Cruse includes a chapter entitled "The Intellectuals and Force and Violence," which briefly discusses the phenomenon of armed self-defense. "The issue of armed self-defense," he writes, "as projected by [Robert] Williams in 1959, presaged the emergence of other factors deeply hidden within the Negro movement," namely latent revolutionary nationalism. Cruse at one point mischaracterizes self-defense as "retaliatory," but shrewdly points out that, as essentially a "holding action," it cannot be revolutionary by itself. He also includes a chapter entitled "From Monroe to Watts," in which he asserts (without explanation) that the "Watts uprising carried the concept of armed self-defense to its logical and ultimate extreme." Cruse calls for a scholarly treatment of the subject. "The faulty analysis of the meaning of armed self-defense has encouraged an extreme form of one-sided activism that leads to blind alleys and dead ends." He suggests that a failure to understand the implications of self-defense contributed to the undoing of the civil rights movement itself. "Faulty analysis of self-defense as a tactic has served to block a serious consideration of the necessity to cultivate strategies on the political, economic, and cultural fronts," he writes. "It has inspired such premature organizations as revolutionary action movements and black liberation fronts, which come into being with naively one-sided, limited programs, all proving to be abortive and short-lived." See also Ross, *The War Within*.

9. Payne, *I've Got the Light of Freedom*, 205.

10. Halbrook, *That Every Man Be Armed*, 28; see also Locke, *Two Treatises on Government*.

11. Storey, *Our Unalienable Rights*, 32–33. See also Spinard, *Civil Liberties*, 6.

12. See *Model Penal Code* § 3.04(1); see also Brown, *No Duty to Retreat*. For more, see Kwei Yung Lee, "Race and Self-Defense: Toward a Normative Conception of Reasonableness," *Minnesota Law Review* 81 (December 1996): 377–398; Uniacke, *Permissable Killing*; and Baum and Baum, *Law of Self-Defense*.

13. Raymond and Alice Bauer, "Day to Day Resistance to Slavery," *Journal of Negro History* 27 (1942): 388–419; see also Scott, *Weapons of the Weak*.

Chapter 1. Gon' Be Treated Right

1. See Tushnet, *American Law of Slavery, 1810–1860*, for more on the legal claim of slaves to self-defense.

2. See Stampp, *The Peculiar Institution,* for more on this notion.

3. Campbell and Rice, *Before Freedom Came,* 92.

4. Ibid.

5. Ibid., 110.

6. Cottrol, *Gun Control and the Constitution,* xv, xxv. In feudal England, lords emancipated villeins by giving them weapons, which became symbolic of the restoration of all rights previously denied them. See Halbrook, *That Every Man Be Armed,* 100.

7. Walker, *David Walker's Appeal,* 45–46.

8. McFeely, *Frederick Douglass,* 106.

9. Garnet, quoted in Shiffrin, "Rhetoric of Black Violence," 45–56.

10. Douglass, quoted in Martin, *Mind of Frederick Douglass,* 14.

11. Huggins, *Slave and Citizen,* 58.

12. McFeely, *Frederick Douglass,* 189.

13. Martin, *Mind of Frederick Douglass,* 188; see also Takaki, *Violence in the Black Imagination,* 17–35.

14. Huggins, *Frederick Douglass: Slave and Citizen,* 58–59.

15. Douglass, "A Terror to Kidnappers," reprinted in Foner, *Life and Writings,* 302.

16. Ibid.

17. Douglass, "The True Remedy for the Fugitive Slave Bill," reprinted in Foner, *Life and Writings,* 326. Emphasis in the original.

18. Douglass, quoted in Silberman, *Criminal Violence, Criminal Justice,* 48.

19. Clay, quoted in Stanley Harrold, "Violence and Nonviolence in Kentucky Abolitionism," 19–21.

20. A number of scholars have treated the subject of southern honor. For example, see Wyatt-Brown, *Honor and Violence in the Old South,* an abridged edition of *Southern Honor;* see also Ayers, *Vengeance and Justice.* Such patterns lasted well into the twentieth century. David Hilliard, Chief of Staff of the Black Panther Party, described his "proclivity to violence" as a "southern trait." See Hilliard and Cole, *This Side of Glory,* 40.

21. *Campbell v. People,* 16 Ill. 17 (1854).

22. United States Supreme Court, *Report of the Decision of the Supreme Court.*

23. Campbell and Rice, *Before Freedom Came,* 99.

24. See Shapiro, *White Violence and Black Response* for a thorough discussion. Many authors have treated this trend.

25. For more on the Black Codes, see Wilson, *The Black Codes of the South;* Foner, *Reconstruction,* 199–201, 208–209; and Litwack, *Been in the Storm So Long,* 366–371. The Codes were abolished after three years.

26. Reprinted in Halbrook, *That Every Man Be Armed,* 128.

27. Halbrook, *That Every Man Be Armed,* 237, note 57. Florida's Black Codes

were severe; they were also sometimes redundant and confusing. For example, one statute prohibited owning a firearm; the next forbade hunting with a gun "on the premises of another." See Wilson, *Black Codes of the South*, 98.

28. A few constitutional scholars have touched on this issue. For example, Stephen P. Halbrook's *That Every Man Be Armed,* which is partisan but not polemic, essentially represents a defense of the right to bear arms. Of most interest, for the purposes of this study, is how Halbrook reconstructs the intimate ties between Afro-Americans, gun ownership, and civil rights in congressional debates over the Fourteenth Amendment. Halbrook argues that the right of Afro-Americans to bear arms lies at the crux of congressional debates on the Fourteenth Amendment and the Civil Rights Act of 1866. See also Cottrol and Diamond, " 'Never Intended,' " 1307–1335, and Cramer, "The Racist Roots of Gun Control,"17–25.

29. Halbrook, *That Every Man Be Armed,* 111.

30. Ibid., 113.

31. Ibid., 118.

32. See Foner, *Reconstruction,* 119–123; and Litwack, *Been in the Storm So Long,* 276–280, for examples of how such fear prompted violence against freedmen.

33. Cottrol, *Gun Control and the Constitution,* xliv–xlv, note 39.

34. Ibid.

35. See Halbrook, *That Every Man Be Armed,* 108–115, 148–152; Litwack, *Been in the Storm So Long,* and Foner, *Reconstruction.* Numerous authors have treated this trend. Halbrook argues that the Fourteenth Amendment was designed, in large part, to insure that no state would disarm a freedman. He cites the thirteen-volume report of the hearings of the Joint Select Committee on the Condition of Affairs in the Late Insurrectionary States, a congressional subcommittee whose findings led directly to passage of the Civil Rights Act of 1875, to illustrate the widespread nature of the disarmament of blacks by white militia or Klansmen in the late 1860s and early 1870s. The index to volumes eight and nine of the hearings refers to over twenty pages under the topic "Arms, colored people deprived of." Both Leon Litwack and Eric Foner have extensively documented armed response by blacks during Reconstruction. It should be noted that both Litwack and Foner have emphasized that while blacks did resort to self-defense during Reconstruction, it was quite limited in scope and, more often than not, futile.

36. *United States v. Cruikshank et al.,* reprinted in Cottrol, *Gun Control and the Constitution,* 542–569. For a succinct explanation of the *Cruikshank* decision, see Cramer and Covey, *For the Defense of Themselves and the State,* 124–126.

37. See Woodward, *Strange Career of Jim Crow* and Litwack, *Trouble in Mind* for more on this episode in American history.

38. Fortune, quoted in Emma Lou Thornbrough, "T. Thomas Fortune: Militant

Editor in the Age of Accomodation" in Franklin and Meier, *Black Leaders of the Twentieth Century*, 22–23.

39. Wells, *Southern Horrors and Other Writings*, 70.

40. Ibid.

41. Gilbert, *Selected Writings of John Edward Bruce*, 31, 32.

42. See David Lodge, "Buddie Shang," Shelby County Black History Segment, written in June 1988; available at http://www.shelbycountyhistory.org/schs/blackhistory/buddieschang.htm. For more on Walker, see http://www.nlbpa.com/walker_moses_fleetwood.html.

43. See Johnson and Dunn, *A True Likeness*, 34 for examples of middle-class, black Southerners brandishing pistols while posing for portraits in the 1920s.

44. Tolnay and Beck, *A Festival of Violence*, 209.

45. Ibid., 210–211.

46. See Litwack, *Trouble in Mind*, 280–283 for a detailed account of the Sam Hose lynching.

47. Hair, *Carnival of Fury*, remains the definitive account of Robert Charles and the New Orleans riot remains; for briefer accounts, see Williamson, *A Rage for Order*, 133–141, and Litwack, *Trouble in Mind*, 405–410.

48. The details of the incident differ in different sources. See "High School Boy Killed," *Kansas City Star* (April 12, 1904) and "Cold Blooded Murder," *Wyandotte (KS) Herald* (April 12, 1904); Susan D. Greenbaum, *The Afro-American Community*, 64–68; and http://www.arthes.com/community/shooting/.

49. *Crisis*, May 1916, 43 and October 1934, 294; reprinted in Tolnay and Beck, *A Festival of Violence*, 208, 210.

50. DuBois, "Let Us Reason Together," *Crisis* 18 (September 1919):231.

51. Claude McKay, "If We Must Die," *Liberator,* July 1919. One writer has termed "If We Must Die" the poem "most often judged to be the inaugural address of the Harlem Renaissance." See Maxwell, *New Negro, Old Left*, ___ .

52. McKay, *A Long Way Home*, ___ .

53. *St. Louis Post-Dispatch*, October 20, 1899. For the historical basis of the ballad, see *The African-American Heritage of St. Louis: A Guide* (St. Louis: St. Louis Public Library, 1992); for lyrics, see Godfrey, *American Tramp and Underworld Slang*.

54. For more on Leadbelly, see Wolfe and Lornell, *Life and Legend*, 73–98; see also Lomax and Lomax, *Negro Folk Songs*. Freed after serving eight years, Leadbelly ran afoul of the law again in 1930 when he was forced to defend himself against a white man after failing to yield the sidewalk.

55. Lawrence Levine, "Marcus Garvey and the Politics of Revitalization" in Franklin and Meier, *Black Leaders of the Twentieth Century*, 113.

56. See Ellsworth, *Death in a Promised Land*, for more on the Tulsa Race Riot of 1921.

57. Ibid., 211.

58. DuBois, "The Arkansas Riots," reprinted in Lewis, *W. E. B. DuBois: A Reader*, 451.

59. See Martin, *Race First*, 187–188 for more on the UNIA. Of particular interest is the so-called Chattanooga Outrage on August 4, 1927, when police raided a UNIA meeting in Chattanooga, Tennessee. Members of the Universal African Legion stationed at the door requested that the police produce warrants authorizing entry, whereupon the police refused and opened fire. The Legionnaires returned fire, resulting in a number of casualties on both sides. Four UNIA members were subsequently tried and convicted on charges stemming from the incident.

60. For more on the Sweet trial, see the Transcript of the Henry Sweet Trial, Burton Historical Collection, Detroit Public Library; see also Joseph Turrini, "Sweet Justice," 22–27, and Tierney, *Darrow: A Biography*. Additionally, Douglas Linder has assembled an excellent website at http://www.law.umkc.edu/faculty/projects/ftrials/sweet/sweet.html.

61. Howard Odum, the renowned UNC social scientist, documented and analyzed these rumors from July 1942 to July 1943, and published his findings in 1943; see Odum, *Race and Rumors of Race*.

62. See O'Brien, *The Color of the Law* for an account of the events in Columbia.

63. For more on Rosa Lee Ingram, see "Rosa Lee Ingram," File, Papers of the Civil Rights Congress, Part 1: Case Files, Manuscript Collection, Shomburg Center for Research in Black Culture, New York Public Library, and "Sojourners for Truth and Justice" File, Matthews (J. B.) Papers, 1862–1986, Rare Book, Manuscript and Special Collections Library, Duke University. See also Virginia Shadron, "Popular Protest and Legal Authority."

Chapter 2. The Other Cheek

(Clayborne Carson's *The Papers of Martin Luther King Jr.* will be referred to in these notes as simply *Papers*.)

1. Virginia Durr to Clark Foreman, March 1955, in Sullivan, *Freedom Writer*, 84.

2. Virginia Durr to Jessica Mitford, May 6, 1955, in Sullivan, *Freedom Writer*, 87.

3. Oates, *Let the Trumpet Sound*, 65.

4. Sitkoff, *Struggle for Black Equality*, 43.

5. See Fairclough, "Martin Luther King Jr.," 3. Adam Fairclough has pointed out the difficulties in disaggregating King's philosophical tenets.

6. Branch, *Parting the Waters*, 161–162.

7. Oates, *Let the Trumpet Sound*, 89.

8. Ibid., 89–91. See also King, *Stride toward Freedom*, 137–138.

9. Abernathy, quoted in Garrow, *Bearing the Cross*, 62.

10. King, quoted in *Time*, Jan. 3, 1964, 27; see Garrow, *Bearing the Cross*, 62, 642 n. 48. Glenn E. Smiley to John Swomley and Al Hassler, February 29, 1956, in Carson, *Papers*, 3:14 n. 60.

11. King, quoted in Garrow, *Bearing the Cross*, 62.

12. *Papers*, 3:40.

13. "Negro Leader Fails to Get Pistol Permit," *Montgomery Advertiser*, sec. 3b, February 4, 1956.

14. The story of Rustin and Worthy's meeting with King has been retold in several sources. See Garrow, *Bearing the Cross*, 59–62, 72–73; Branch, *Parting the Waters*, 173–180; and Oates, *Let the Trumpet Sound*, 89–92.

15. King, quoted in Lynd, *Nonviolence in America*, 385.

16. King, *Stride toward Freedom*, 96.

17. Smiley, quoted in Garrow, *Bearing the Cross*, 68.

18. *Papers*, 3:19.

19. For more, see Gregg, *Power of Nonviolence*. King maintained a vibrant correspondence with Gregg. The two exchanged ideas regarding their books. In 1959, Gregg instructed King on the particulars of travel in India. Gregg to King, January 23, 1959, Box 27, IV, 1, Correspondence "G," Martin Luther King Collection, Department of Special Collections, Boston University. Gregg also educated King about Gandhi, sending him a copy of Joan Bondurant's *Conquest of Violence* and a two-volume set by Gandhi's secretary, Pyarelal. Gregg to King, December 20, 1958, Box 27, IV, 1, Correspondence "G," Martin Luther King Collection, Department of Special Collections, Boston University.

20. Glenn Smiley to Swomley and Hassler, February 29, 1956, in *Papers*, 3:20.

21. Rustin, "Report on Montgomery, Alabama," March 21, 1956, in *Papers*, 3:20.

22. Smiley to Swomley, March 2, 1956, in *Papers*, 3:18.

23. Rustin, *Strategies for Freedom*, 24.

24. See Seshachari, *Gandhi and the American Scene*, 83–101 for more on Gandhi's teachings.

25. Ibid., 84, 89.

26. Rustin, *Strategies for Freedom*, 24.

27. See Shridharani, *War without Violence*.

28. King, "How My Mind Has Changed in the Last Decade," undated manuscript draft, Box 4, I-21, Martin Luther King Collection, Department of Special Collections, Boston University.

29. Seshachari, *Gandhi and the American Scene*, 127, 130; see *Papers*, 2:139–140, 141–151, 222. Clayborne Carson downplays the extent of King's intellectual engagement with Niehbur; however, he also concedes that King had not only

written about Niehbur in graduate school but also corresponded with him in 1953.

30. King, *Stride toward Freedom*, 85.

31. Ibid.; see Baldwin, *To Make the Wounded Whole*, 61–62, for more on King's understanding of nonviolence. See Baldwin, *There Is a Balm in Gilead*, 11–14, for a full explanation of the controversy surrounding the accuracy of King's published works. David Garrow has pointed out that King's published works were heavily edited and partially ghostwritten, and he has warned against scholars' "naive overreliance" on these texts. According to him, the King portrayed in many scholarly works is a "spiritual stick-figure" compared to the actual man, and he has implored scholars to use only King's unedited, unpublished writings as primary sources. Garrow's scholarship is valuable (he has written the most comprehensive and insightful biography of King to date in *Bearing the Cross*), though I see little reason to treat King's edited, published works as anything other than King's own testimony. Certainly King's personality and the heart of his philosophy are expressed in his published books and essays, as well as in his extemporaneous writings.

32. Box 82, Folder 58, Martin Luther King Collection, Department of Special Collections, Boston University. King, *Stride toward Freedom*, 102–104, offers a more polished articulation of King's understanding of nonviolence. See also Boesak, "Coming In out of the Wilderness," 36, reprinted in Garrow, *Martin Luther King, Jr.*, 94; and Colaiaco, "Martin Luther King, Jr., and the Paradox of Nonviolent Direct Action," *Phylon* 47 (1986):18, reprinted in Garrow, *Martin Luther King, Jr.*, 191. For more on *sarvodaya*, see Bondurant, *Conquest of Violence*, 6.

33. See Otis Turner, "Nonviolence and the Politics of Liberation," *Journal of the Interdenominational Theological Center* 4 (Spring 1977): 49–60, reprinted in Garrow, *Martin Luther King, Jr.*, 985–999; Steinkraus, "The Dangerous Ideas of Martin Luther King, Jr.," *Scottish Journal of Religious Studies* 6 (1985): 20, reprinted in Garrow, *Martin Luther King, Jr.*, 925. See also Garrow, *Bearing the Cross*, 927.

34. Baldwin, *Balm in Gilead*, 175.

35. Ibid., 186.

36. Abernathy, *And the Walls Came Tumbling Down*, 162.

37. *Ibid.*, 160.

38. See *Papers*, 3:122 n. 7.

39. King, *Stride toward Freedom*, 88.

40. King to Bayard Rustin, September 20, 1956, Box 67, VIII, 34, Correspondence "W," Martin Luther King Collection, Department of Special Collections, Boston University.

41. King, "The Most Durable Power," *Christian Century*, 74 (June 5, 1957): 708.

42. See Adam Roberts, "Martin Luther King, Jr., and Nonviolent Resistance,"

The World Today, June 24, 1968, 232; reprinted in Garrow, *Martin Luther King, Jr.,* 765.

43. See Mulford Q. Sibley, "Negro Revolution and Non-violent Action: Martin Luther King, Jr.," *Political Science Review* 9 (1–6/70): 181; reprinted in Garrow, *Martin Luther King, Jr.,* 805.

44. "Elijah Muhammad Cautions on Use of Nonviolence," *New Pittsburgh Courier,* October 5, 1963, 1.

45. King, "Nonviolence: The Only Road to Freedom," *Ebony* 21 (October 1966):27–30.

46. King, *Where Do We Go from Here?,* 53.

47. J. Pius Barbour to Martin Luther King Jr., January 11, 1957, Box 63, VIII-16 (Correspondence "N"), Martin Luther King Collection, Department of Special Collections, Boston University.

Chapter 3. People with Strength

1. P. L. Prattis, "Nonviolence," pt. 1, *Pittsburgh Courier,* November 30, 1957, and "Nonviolence," pt. 2, *Pittsburgh Courier,* December 7, 1957.

2. Ibid.; see also Prattis, "Nonviolence," pt. 3, *Pittsburgh Courier,* December 14, 1957; "Nonviolence," pt. 5, *Pittsburgh Courier,* December 28, 1957; and "Nonviolence," pt. 4, *Pittsburgh Courier,* December 21, 1957.

3. Williams, *Negroes with Guns,* 122.

4. For more on Little Rock, see Record and Cassels, *Little Rock U.S.A.*

5. DuBois, "Martin Luther King's Life," 8.

6. Robert F. Williams, "Should Negroes Resort to Violence?," *Liberation,* September 1959, Schomburg Center Clipping File, 1925–1974, New York Public Library.

7. See Cohen, *Black Crusader,* 1–83 for more information on Williams's youth, and his experience in the armed services.

8. Williams, "1957," 70–72.

9. Cohen, *Black Crusader,* 46, 90.

10. Ibid., 90–91.

11. Whether or not the branch's predominately working-class membership made it unique is questionable. Tyson, like Williams, has argued that it did; however, some memoirs from the black freedom struggle in the 1940s and 1950s suggest that rural poor and working-class black people were major participants in civil rights organizations, including the NAACP. Many members of the traditional black middle class (teachers, ministers, professionals) may have remained aloof from civil rights activity. "In theory, these would be the very persons who would lead and staff a voter registration effort," J. L. Chestnut has written. "But the ties they had to the white ruling hierarchy . . . made them the most least likely group of

all to become involved. They had the most—the best jobs, the largest homes, the most prestige—and therefore the most to lose." See Chestnut and Cass, *Black in Selma*, 154.

12. See Williams, *Negroes with Guns*, 51, 66.

13. Cohen, *Black Crusader*, 46–47.

14. Ibid.

15. Ibid.

16. Robert F. Williams, interview by James Mosby, July 22, 1970, transcript, Ralph J. Bunche Oral History Collection (Civil Rights Documentation Project), Moorland-Spingarn Research Center, Howard University.

17. See Sitkoff, "African-American Militancy," in McMillen, *Re-Making Dixie*, 661–681. Numerous authors have treated this trend and have disagreed as to whether World War II was an interruption of legal battles and direct action in the 1930s or a catalyst of black protest in the post-war years.

18. Williams, interview by James Mosby.

19. Williams, *Negroes with Guns*, 51.

20. Ibid., 54.

21. "What Happened in Monroe, North Carolina," undated manuscript, printed by the Committee to Aid the Monroe Defendants; " 'Kidnapping' Papers" Folder, Box 3, Robert F. Williams Collection, Bentley Historical Library, University of Michigan.

22. For example, see "Citizens Fire Back at Klan," *Journal and Guide* [Carolina Edition], October 12, 1957, 1.

23. George L. Weissman, "The Kissing Case," *Nation* 188, no. 3 (January 17, 1959): 46–49.

24. Ibid. See also Williams, *Negroes with Guns*, 21–24.

25. For more on the "Kissing Case," see "Lesson of the Kissing Case," [Baltimore] *Afro-American*, February 28, 1959, 7; and "Tragic Plight of Negroes in Monroe, NC: Town of the 'Kissing Case' Involving a White Girl and 2 Negro Boys," *Jet*, February 12, 1959, 12–15.

26. *Crusader* 1, no. 1 (June 26, 1959): 1.

27. *Crusader* 1, no. 3 (July 11, 1959): 2.

28. Williams, quoted in "The Robert Williams Case," *Crisis* 66, no. 6 (June–July 1959): 326.

29. King, "The Social Organization of Nonviolence," *Liberation* 4, no. 7 (October 1959): 5–6.

30. Williams, *Negroes with Guns*, 41.

31. Ibid., 40.

32. King, "The Social Organization," 5.

33. Williams, *Negroes with Guns*, 78.

34. King, "The Social Organization," 6.

35. See "The Robert Williams Case," *Crisis* 66, no. 6 (June–July, 1959): 325–329 for the official account of Williams's suspension (provided by the NAACP); for another version, see Julian Mayfield, "Challenge to Negro Leadership," *Commentary* 31 (April 1961): 297–305.

36. Robert A. Fraser to Roy Wilkins, May 29, 1959, "Correspondence 1959" Folder, Box 1, Robert F. Williams Collection, Bentley Historical Library, University of Michigan.

37. Williams, *Negroes with Guns*, 111.

38. Myers, "When Violence Met Violence," 12–13.

39. See Powledge, *Free at Last?*, 151–152. Fred Powledge has described the many faces of white resistance by categorizing the different, oratorical rationales of white supremacists, from "integration-will-close-our-schools" to "federal-government-as-ogre" to "outside-agitator" to "they're-going-to-marry-your sister" to "our-colored-are-happy" to "we-must-protect-our-way-of-life." Perhaps most intriguing is the "blood-in-our-streets" rationale of southern politicians, who argued under the auspices of law and order that rapid desegregation would prompt violence by whites resorting to vigilantism.

40. The NRA was apparently unaware that its new chapter was primarily black because Williams aggrandized occupational data on his application. For example, on the NRA charter application, Williams listed brick masons as "contractors," and dishwashers as "restauranteurs." Williams, interview by James Mosby, July 22, 1970, transcript, Ralph J. Bunche Oral History Collection (Civil Rights Documentation Project), Moorland-Spingarn Research Center, Howard University.

41. McCord, *Life Styles in the Black Ghetto*, 239.

42. "400 Hear Debate on 'Violence,'" [Baltimore] *Afro-American*, October 17, 1959, 1.

43. "Monroe, N. C. Editor Defies Bigots Who Threaten Life," *Pittsburgh Courier*, August 4, 1961, 2.

44. "Robert Williams asks U. S. To Support War on South," [Baltimore] *Afro-American*, April 29, 1961, 1.

45. John Boardman, letter to the *Crusader*, January 10, 1961; Correspondence, Jan.–Sept. 1961, Box 1, Robert F. Williams Collection, Bentley Historical Library, University of Michigan.

46. Williams, quoted in Julian Mayfield, "Challenge to Negro Leadership," 300.

47. See Myers, "When Violence Met Violence," 18. The NAACP used the threat of a lawsuit to pressure local officials to desegregate. According to Andrew Myers, this incident shows that Williams "initially tried to work within the traditional NAACP framework of change through legal action."

48. Williams, *Negroes with Guns*, 46.

49. For examples, see Correspondence, Jan.–Sept. 1961, Box 1, Robert F. Williams Collection, Bentley Historical Library, University of Michigan.

50. See William Worthy, "Black Muslims NAACP Target: Raise Funds for Arms for Carolinian," [Baltimore] *Afro-American*, July 22, 1961, 1. The Williams article overshadowed an article on Martin Luther King Jr. in the headlines.

51. Langston Hughes, "Week by Week: Simple at the Golden Gate," *Tri-State Defender*, [Memphis] July 29, 1961, 6; for more on Jesse B. Simple (sometimes spelled "Semple"), see Hughes, *The Best of Simple*.

52. Williams, "Freedom Struggle in the 'Free World,' Part II," unpublished manuscript, Box 2, Undated Folder 1, Robert F. Williams Collection, Bentley Historical Library, University of Michigan.

53. Williams, "Neo-Barbarism: Inside the U.S.A.," unpublished manuscript, Box 2, Undated Folder 1, Robert F. Williams Collection, Bentley Historical Library, University of Michigan.

54. Williams, "Reflections of an Exiled Freedom Fighter," unpublished manuscript, Box 2, Undated Folder 2, Robert F. Williams Collection, Bentley Historical Library, University of Michigan.

55. Williams, "An Interview with Robert F. Williams," *Studies on the Left* 2 (1962): 3, 57, Box 2, "Published Articles" Folder, Robert F. Williams Collection, Bentley Historical Library, University of Michigan.

56. Williams, interview by James Mosby, July 22, 1970, transcript, Ralph J. Bunche Oral History Collection (Civil Rights Documentation Project), Moorland-Spingarn Research Center, Howard University.

57. Ernest R. Bromley, "Two New Publications: Pacifist, Nonpacifist," *Peacemaker* 15, no. 12 (September 8, 1962): 3.

58. Williams, "U.S.A.: Revolution without Violence?," *Revolution*, March 1964, 112.

59. Williams, *Negroes with Guns*, 121.

60. Ibid., 68.

61. For more on the sit-ins in Monroe, see Myers, "When Violence Met Violence," 27.

62. Williams, "U.S.A.: Revolution without Violence?," 110.

63. Williams, "Reflections of an Exiled Freedom Fighter," unpublished manuscript, Box 2, Undated Folder 1, Robert F. Williams Collection, Bentley Historical Library, University of Michigan.

64. Williams, *Negroes with Guns*, 75, 77. Stokely Carmichael noted in a speech at the University of California at Berkeley in 1965: "People ought to understand that we were never fighting for the right to integrate, *we were fighting against white supremacy*." See Carmichael, *Stokely Speaks*, 56.

65. Williams, *Negroes with Guns*, 112–113.

66. U.S. Senate Judiciary Hearings, testimony of Robert F. Williams, 4. In subsequent notes, this testimony will be referred to simply as "U.S. Senate Judiciary Hearings."

67. Williams, untitled, unpublished manuscript, Box 2, Undated Folder 1, Robert F. Williams Collection, Bentley Historical Library, University of Michigan.

68. Williams, interview by James Mosby, July 22, 1970, transcript, Ralph J. Bunche Oral History Collection (Civil Rights Documentation Project), Moorland-Spingarn Research Center, Howard University.

69. See "Jury Indicts Williams on Kidnapping Charge," *Charlotte Observer*, August 29, 1961, 1; see also Williams, *Negroes with Guns*, 83–90.

70. Berta Green, "Monroe Needs Help [letter to the editor]," [Baltimore] *Afro American*, October 21, 1961, 4.

71. See Williams, *Negroes with Guns*, 91–92; see also Truman Nelson, "The Resistant Spirit," in *Negroes with Guns*, 18. The U.S. Justice Department, in collaboration with Monroe Chief of Police A. A. Mauney, released 250,000 circulars describing Williams as "schizophrenic." Williams, of sound mind, had never undergone psychiatric evaluation, nor had he ever been diagnosed with schizophrenia.

72. See Jones, *Home*, 11–62. LeRoi Jones expertly described this trip in a 1960 essay entitled "Cuba Libre." Williams greatly impressed LeRoi Jones, who counted among his fellow travelers "one strange tall man in a straw hat and feathery beard (whom I later got to know as Robert Williams and who later figured very largely in the trip, certainly in my impressions of it)."

73. Sylvester Leaks, " 'Negroes with Guns' Powerful, Provocative: Author Attacks Credo of Passive Resistance," *Muhammad Speaks*, January 31, 1963, 14–15.

74. Lincoln, *The Black Muslims in America*, 4.

75. Morris Renek, "Portrait of a 'Wretched' Man: Robert Williams—Wanted by the FBI," *New Republic*, September 30, 1967, 12, Box 4, "Articles Concerning Robert Williams—1967" Folder, Robert F. Williams Collection, Bentley Historical Library, University of Michigan.

76. Forman, *The Making of Black Revolutionaries*, 158–211. Preferring the rhetoric of self-defense, Forman criticizes Williams's use of the phrase "meet violence with violence." Forman also argues that the civil rights movement could have been effectively organized around the concept of self-defense. See pp. 159, 376.

77. Sitkoff, *The Struggle for Black Equality*, 143. With Malcolm X, Williams "provided a sharp cutting edge to the black struggle. They kept the pressure on civil-rights leaders to be bolder, more militant," according to historian Harvard Sitkoff. "Simultaneously, their radicalism made the movement's leadership and objectives appear responsible and moderate. And they scared some white leaders

into accepting the civil rights demands as the only effective way to avert potential disaster."

78. For example, see *Liberation* 9, no. 2 (February 1969): 11.

79. Malcolm X, interview by A. B. Spellman, March 19, 1964, New York, reproduced in Malcolm X, *By Any Means Necessary*, 11.

80. Malcolm X, interviewed by Joe Rainey, March 8, 1964, WDAS Radio, Philadelphia, transcript, reprinted in Gallen, *Malcolm X: As They Knew Him*, 164.

81. Newton, *Revolutionary Suicide*, 112.

82. Cleaver, "The Land Question and Black Liberation" in *Post-Prison Writings and Speeches*, 71. According to William McCord, Williams "had some roots in the black community" (unlike earlier blacks associated with the radical left) and "did not deal solely in esoteric ideology." He evolved "a set of strategies and tactics intended for the here and now." For these reasons, his immediacy appealed to the revolutionary outlook of the Panthers. McCord, *Life Styles in the Black Ghetto*, 240, 242.

83. C. Timothy Heaton, undated letter to Robert F. Williams, Box 1, Undated Folder 1, Robert F. Williams Collection, Bentley Historical Library, University of Michigan.

84. Powledge, *Free at Last?*, 311. General histories of the civil rights movement tend to marginalize Williams. For example, Harvard Sitkoff has provided an accurate synopsis of Williams's activism, describing both his counterpoint to King and his fearful image in the media; however, Sitkoff, like most civil rights historians, treats him as tangential to the larger movement. See Sitkoff, *The Struggle for Black Equality*, 141, 143.

85. See Myers, "When Violence Met Violence," 82, 86. Andrew Myers's close examination of the Williams case forces both a re-consideration of Williams's role in the civil rights movement and a re-evaluation of prevailing assumptions about this early phase of the movement. Myers has pointed out that Williams's militant image in the press caused more moderate civil rights leaders to define their own limits of acceptable protest, and that the waves Williams sent through the international community as a dissident helped to "shame" the United States government into confronting the problem of the color line.

86. See Tyson, *Radio Free Dixie*. This recently published study of Williams represents the most comprehensive and thorough study of Williams to date. Tyson characterizes Williams as the founding father of Black Power: "one of the South's most dynamic race rebels" and "one of the most influential African American radicals of a generation that toppled Jim Crow." See also Tyson, "Robert F. Williams, NAACP Warrior and Rebel," *Crisis*, December–January 1998, 14–18, and Tyson, "Robert F. Williams, 'Black Power,' and the Roots of the African-American Freedom Struggle," *Journal of American History* 85, no. 2 (September

1998):540–570. Scholars have customarily portrayed the civil rights movement as a nonviolent appeal to the collective conscience of white Americans and portrayed the subsequent rise of Black Power as a violent repudiation of Martin Luther King's dream of a "beloved community." But *Radio Free Dixie* reveals that both strains of protest "emerged from the same soil, confronted the same predicaments, and reflected the same quest for African American freedom." Williams was a homegrown patriot, not an "outside agitator," as southern whites often termed civil rights activists from the North. As Tyson's scholarship demonstrates, independent black political action, black cultural pride, and armed self-reliance operated in the South in conjunction with legal efforts and nonviolent protest.

87. Williams, "Reflections of an Exiled Freedom Fighter," unpublished manuscript, Box 2, Undated Folder 1, Robert F. Williams Collection, Bentley Historical Library, University of Michigan.

88. See Cohen, *Black Crusader*, 47–56. Williams did attend college. Taking advantage of the GI Bill, he decided to go to college near Monroe to be near his family. After brief stints at both West Virginia State College and North Carolina College at Durham, he settled at Johnson C. Smith College in Charlotte until his GI benefits ran out in 1952. Financial need forced him to leave college and find work to support his family.

89. See Lipsitz, *A Life in the Struggle*, 9–11; see also Gramsci, *Selections from the Prison Notebooks*, 9, 10. In describing the life of civil rights activist Ivory Perry, George Lipsitz has applied the ideas of Antonio Gramsci, Italian theorist and Marxist, to the civil rights movement. Using Gramsci's concept of the "organic intellectual," Lipsitz has described how Perry held no formal status as intellectual or theorist, but still shaped the ideas and actions of an entire population group through his activism and by involving people in "social contestation." Organic intellectuals learn about the world by trying to change it. Like Perry, Williams personifies the quintessential organic intellectual.

90. Marc Schleifer, "Epilogue," in Williams, *Negroes with Guns*, 127–128. As Schleifer pointed out: "He [Williams] is unique only in that sheltered white consciousness that never read of the slave revolts in its history textbooks, and knows exactly who Booker T. Washington is, but only vaguely if at all of W. E. B. DuBois."

91. Oakley, letter to King, September 5, 1961, Box 7, I, 47, Martin Luther King Collection, Department of Special Collections, Boston University.

92. Williams, interview by James Mosby, July 22, 1970, transcript, Ralph J. Bunche Oral History Collection (Civil Rights Documentation Project), Moorland-Spingarn Research Center, Howard University. For more on Mabel Williams, see Tyson, *Radio Free Dixie.*

93. The best example remains Angela Davis. See her autobiography.

94. Mabel Williams in David Cecelski, "Mabel Williams: Standing Up to the Klan," Raleigh *News & Observer*, November 14, 1999; available online as an interview included in the University of North Carolina's Southern Oral History Program at http://www.sohp.org/research/lfac/N&O/6.5bl8-Mabel_Williams.html.

95. [Baltimore] *Afro-American*, September 15, 1962, 1.

96. Ibid.

97. William Kennedy, "Violence at Peak in Georgia," *New Pittsburgh Courier*, September 22, 1962, 1.

98. Bell, *CORE and the Strategy of Nonviolence*, 57.

99. San Francisco *Chronicle*, September 19, 1962.

100. Hayes and Zinn, interview in Emily S. Stoper, "The Student Nonviolent Coordinating Committee," 37–38. Stoper reported that whatever discussion about nonviolence there was in Mississippi in the early 1960s tended to center around what she called "marginal issues," such as "whether a SNCC member who was staying in the home of local black people should use the family's gun to protect them if they came under attack while the man in the family was not at home."

Chapter 4. We Assert and Affirm

1. "See His Gun, Seggies Run," [Baltimore] *Afro-American*, February 2, 1963, 1.

2. "Postman Slain in Ala. Was CORE Picket Line Veteran," *Tri-State Defender*, May 4, 1963, 1.

3. M. L. Reid, "He Avowed to 'Go Down Shooting' and 'Die with My Boots On,'" *Tri-State Defender*, June 29, 1963, 1; see also "Funeral Held for Pastor Who Died Shooting," *Tri-State Defender*, July 6, 1963, 1.

4. P. Giddings, *When and Where I Enter: The Impact of Black Women on Race and Sex in America* (New York: William Morrow, 1984), 291.

5. Sandra Y. Millner, "Recasting Civil Rights Leadership: Gloria Richardson and the Cambridge Movement," *Journal of Black Studies* 26, no. 6 (July 1996): 680. See also Anita K. Foeman, "Gloria Richardson: Breaking the Mold," *Journal of Black Studies* 26, no. 5 (May 1996): 604–615, and Peter B. Levy, *Civil War on Race Street: The Civil Rights Movement in Cambridge, Maryland* (Gainesville: University Press of Florida, 2003).

6. Richardson, quoted in "Lady General of Civil Rights," *Ebony* (July 1964), 25.

7. Thaddeus T. Stokes, "Notwithstanding: Body Guards for Civil Rights Leaders," *Tri-State Defender*, July 13, 1963, 6.

8. "Powell Says Nonviolence OK, But 'White House Dragging Feet on Rights,'" *New Pittsburgh Courier*, September 28, 1963, 16.

9. *Newsweek*, July 29, 1963. The survey was reprinted as Brink and Harris, *The Negro Revolution in America*, 71–75.

10. For more, see Malcolm X with Alex Haley, *The Autobiography of Malcolm X*.

11. "Elijah Muhammad Cautions on Use of Nonviolence," *New Pittsburgh Courier*, October 5, 1963, 1.

12. Thelwell, quoted in Gallen, *Malcolm X: As They Knew Him*, 33.

13. Farmer, quoted in Meier and Rudwick, *CORE*, 206.

14. Clarke, *Malcolm X: The Man and His Times*, 197.

15. See King, *Where Do We Go from Here?*, 58–59 for more on King's sense of the futility of revolution, which he called "blatantly illogical."

16. Published works concerning Malcolm X constitute a mixed bag of elegy, recollection, sensationalism, and scholarship. The definitive work by and about Malcolm X remains his autobiography; see Malcolm X with Alex Haley, *The Autobiography of Malcolm X*. An essential work of American autobiography, it has been reprinted numerous times. Other works about Malcolm X include Lomax, *To Kill a Black Man*; Clarke, *Malcolm X: The Man and His Times*; Breitman, *The Assassination of Malcolm X*; Goldman, *The Death and Life of Malcolm X*; Cone, *Martin and Malcolm and America: A Dream or a Nightmare*; Bruce Perry, *Malcolm: The Life of a Man Who Changed Black America*; Gallen, *Malcolm X: As They Knew Him*; Wood, *Malcolm X: In Our Own Image*; Dyson, *Making Malcolm*; and Theresa Perry, *Teaching Malcolm X*. Of these, Goldman's *Death and Life of Malcolm X*, Gallen's *Malcolm X: As They Knew Him*, and Clarke's *Malcolm X: The Man and His Times* are the most helpful. Goldman's book is the single best critical work regarding Malcolm. Well-written and incisive, it nicely complements the *Autobiography*; however, the author cannot resist dipping, in the second half of the book, into the speculative intrigue surrounding the unanswered questions of Malcolm's assassination. His annotated bibliography, "Notes on Sources," is quite helpful to those researching Malcolm's life; see Goldman, *Death and Life of Malcolm X*, 437–442. Gallen provides first-hand reminiscences of Malcolm; Clarke's collection of essays, more academic in tone, gropes for an understanding of his legacy. Clarke and Gallen both include important primary sources such as speeches and interviews; Gallen also includes a chronological timeline of Malcolm's life. This list contains only a sampling of the works about Malcolm X; it is by no means exhaustive.

17. Many of Malcolm X's speeches were collected and published posthumously. See the bibliographic entries for Malcolm X.

18. See Malcolm X, *Autobiography*, 251; Goldman, *Death and Life of Malcolm X*, 183. According to Malcolm, Elijah Muhammad was the first black leader with the courage to identify the enemy of black people. "Our enemy," Malcolm reiterated, "is the white man!" Some scholars have noted that Malcolm's racial preconceptions changed during his pilgrimage to Mecca; however, this realignment can be

overemphasized. As one historian has noted, his racial philosophy changed in Mecca, but only to the extent that his brother Muslims of every color had treated him like a human being; he saw little possibility of anything like that happening in America, short of a mass conversion to Islam, and in the meantime the chance that there might be a few "good" whites wasn't going to alter his judgment that, collectively, the lot of them was bad.

19. Malcolm X was aware of Robert Williams. See chapter 3, notes 79 and 80.

20. Malcolm X, "Message to the Grass Roots," speech, Northern Grass Roots Leadership Conference, King Solomon Baptist Church, November 10, 1963. This speech has been reproduced in a number of formats, including a recording published by the Afro-American Broadcasting and Recording Company, Detroit; see also *Malcolm X Speaks* and Clarke, *Malcolm X: The Man and His Times*. In his famous interview with Alex Haley for *Playboy* magazine, Malcolm said, "Islam is a religion that teaches us never to attack, never to be the aggressor—but you can waste somebody if he attacks you." Malcolm X, interview by Alex Haley, *Playboy*, May 1963, reprinted in Gallen, *Malcolm X: As They Knew Him*, 109–130.

21. Malcolm X, "Communication and Reality," Speech to Domestic Peace Corps, December 12, 1964, reprinted in Clarke, *Malcolm X: The Man and His Times*, 307–320.

22. Ibid.

23. Killens, quoted in C. S. King, *My Life with Martin Luther King, Jr.*, 226.

24. Malcolm X, interview by Kenneth B. Clark, June, 1963, reprinted in Clarke, *Malcolm X: The Man and His Times*, 168–181; see also "Malcolm X Disputes Nonviolence Policy," *New York Times*, June 5, 1963, 29.

25. Malcolm X, interview by Kenneth B. Clark.

26. Malcolm X, "The Ballot or the Bullet" in *Malcolm X Speaks*, 23–44.

27. Malcolm X, quoted in Goldman, *The Death and Life of Malcolm X*, 135.

28. King, "Letter from Birmingham Jail" in *Why We Can't Wait*, 87. This letter has been reprinted numerous times in various sources.

29. Zellner and Robinson, quoted in Belfrage, *Freedom Summer*, 174–176.

30. Mary King, *Freedom Song*, 319, 322.

31. The entirety of this discussion can be found in King, *Freedom Song*, 311–323.

32. Ibid.

33. Ibid. See Carson, *In Struggle*, 164; and Haines, *Black Radicals*, 53–54, 157–159.

34. Davis, quoted in Gallen, *Malcolm X: As They Knew Him*, 95.

35. Ibid., 94.

36. See Davis, *Malcolm X: The Great Photographs*, 55, 92. With Elijah Muhammad's approval, Malcolm and hundreds of other Muslims protested the arrest of two Muslims selling *Muhammad Speaks* in Times Square on December 25, 1962; however, the following year Muhammad instructed Malcolm not to help or join in

any demonstrations sponsored by the various civil rights organizations—including the upcoming March on Washington.

37. "Malcolm X Disputes Nonviolence Policy," *New York Times*, June 5, 1963, 29.

38. Goldman, *Death and Life of Malcolm X*, 75, 101.

39. See Ralph, *Northern Protest*; and Garrow, *Chicago 1966*. Chicago represented a turning point for King in this regard. After the open-housing protests in Chicago in 1966, he increasingly recognized that legislative reform was not enough.

40. King, "In a Word: Now," *New York Times Magazine*, September 29, 1963, 91–92.

41. King, *Letter from Birmingham City Jail*.

42. C. S. King, *My Life with Martin Luther King, Jr.*, 259.

43. Malcolm, quoted in Davis, *Malcolm X: The Great Photographs*, 44.

44. Ibid.

45. Ibid. Malcolm X, quoted in Warren, *Who Speaks for the Negro?*, 258.

46. Goldman, *The Death and Life of Malcolm X*, 187.

47. Clarke, *Malcolm X: The Man and His Times*, 90.

48. Goldman, *The Death and Life of Malcolm X*, 155. Peter Goldman has surmised that Malcolm posed for this photo "precisely for melodramatic effect, as a deterrent to his enemies."

49. Malcolm X, *The Speeches of Malcolm X at Harvard*, 161–175.

50. Ibid.

Chapter 5. A Brand New Negro

(Roy Reed's articles in the *New York Times Magazine* and the *New York Times*, respectively, will be referred to simply as "The Deacons" and "Armed Negro Unit.")

1. Grant, *Black Protest*, 359.

2. Roy Reed, "The Deacons, Too, Ride by Night," *New York Times Magazine*, August 15, 1965, 10(L++); and Roy Reed, "Armed Negro Unit Spreads in South," *New York Times*, June 6, 1965, 1(L++). Roy Reed, Atlanta correspondent for the *New York Times*, was the only writer to take an interest in the Deacons during their heyday. I have relied heavily on his insight into the Deacons' activities. Reed respected and understood the Deacons, but paradoxically viewed them as misguided and "foolhardy."

3. "Murder in Mississippi," *Sepia*, May 1967, 78.

4. Sellers, quoted in Hampton and Fayer, *Voices of Freedom*, 286.

5. Grant, *Black Protest*, 357.

6. Fairclough, *Race and Democracy*, 358.

7. Fred Powledge, "Armed Negroes Make Jonesboro an Unusual Town," *New York Times*, February 21, 1965, 52.

8. Fred Brooks, interview by John Britton, Nashville, Tennessee, November 29, 1967 Ralph J. Bunche Oral History Collection (Civil Rights Documentation Project), Moorland Spingarn Research Center, Howard University.

9. "Armed Negro Unit," 25; "The Deacons," 10–11.

10. "Armed Negro Unit," 25; "The Deacons," 10–11.

11. For more on Earnest Thomas and the founding of the Deacons, see Lance Hill, "The Deacons for Defense and Justice," 20–28. Hill's dissertation represents an excellent, in-depth study of the Deacons.

12. Radio bulletin from New Orleans FBI Office to FBI Director, January 6, 1965, Declassified Documents, Deacons for Defense and Justice FBI Files, Part 1a, 6.

13. Report from United States Department of Justice Office, New Orleans, to FBI Director, January 6, 1965 Declassified Documents, Deacons for Defense and Justice FBI Files, Part 1a, 8.

14. "Negroes Demonstrate in Bogalusa," *Southern School News* 11, no. 11 (May 1965): 5.

15. Raines, *My Soul Is Rested*, 416.

16. "Klantown, USA," *The Nation*, February 1, 1964, 112.

17. "Background on Bogalusa" in "Chapters: Bogalusa, Louisiana, 1965 and undated" File, Folder 6865, Floyd B. McKissick Papers, Special Collections, Wilson Library, University of North Carolina at Chapel Hill.

18. Ibid.

19. Ibid.

20. Ibid.

21. Untitled memo to CORE Chapters, March 1, 1965, in "Chapters: Bogalusa, Louisiana, 1965 and undated."

22. *Southern School News* 11, no. 11 (May 1965): 5; "Bogalusa Mayor Announces End of City Segregation Ordinances," *Southern School News* 11, no. 12 (June 1965): 14.

23. "Bogalusa Promises," *Facts on File*, May 1965, 197; *Southern School News* June 1965, 14; Cutrer and Farmer quoted in *New York Times* May 24, 1965, 1, 18.

24. "Bogalusa Killing," *Facts on File*, July 1–7, 1965, 246–247.

25. Cutrer, quoted in *New York Times*, May 24, 1965, 1, 18; *Facts on File*, July 1–7, 1965, 246–247.

26. "Armed Negro Unit," 25; Farmer, *Lay Bare the Heart*, 287–291.

27. "Armed Negro Unit," 25; "Marchers Upset by Apathy," *New York Times*, June 14, 1966, 19; Grant, *Black Protest*, 63.

28. "The Deacons," 10(L++).

29. Ibid.; see also "The Deacons and Their Impact," *National Guardian*, September 4, 1965, 4 for another photo of Sims.

30. "The Deacons," 11; Grant, *Black Protest*, 359; "Armed Negro Unit," 25.

31. Thomas, quoted in "Armed Negro Unit"; Sims, quoted in Raines, *My Soul Is Rested*, 418; and in Grant, *Black Protest*, 361.

32. Sonia Sanchez, formerly associated with the Black Panther Party, has noted: "The whole image that went around the world of Panthers going into the [California state] assembly with guns was something that said, simply, 'Don't mess with me.' And I remember talking to some old folks at the time. They said, 'Well, girl, that ain't nothing new. We always owned guns. We just kept them in our top drawer, you see.' The whole point of the newspaper articles was simply that this was a new phenomenon, that we never thought black men had guns. But if you went south or out west, black folks always had guns someplace in the house." Sanchez quoted in Hampton and Fayer, *Voices of Freedom*, 370.

33. "Armed Negro Unit," 25; "The Deacons," 10–11.

34. Thomas, quoted in "Armed Negro Unit," 1 (L++).

35. Sims, quoted in "Rights Activities Spread in South," *New York Times*, August 1, 1965.

36. "Jonesboro 'Deacons' Offer Example for Rights Forces," *The Militant* 29, no. 9 (March 1, 1965): 8.

37. Sims, quoted in Grant, *Black Protest*, 358; see also "Deacons Organize Chicago Chapter," *New York Times*, April 6, 1966, 29.

38. For Sims's misnomers, see "The Deacons," 22; and Raines, *My Soul Is Rested*, 420.

39. Robinson, "Bus Driver Learns Not to Call Negro Man 'Boy,'" *New Pittsburgh Courier* 6, no. 23 (June 19, 1965): 8. As a syndicated columnist, Robinson wrote articles for several black dailies, including the New York *Post*, the New York *Citizen-Call*, the *New Pittsburgh Courier*, and, from 1962 to 1969, the New York *Amsterdam News*; see Rampersad, *Jackie Robinson*.

40. Robinson, "Deacons Will Stay Unless U.S. Moves," *New Pittsburgh Courier* 6, no. 29 (July 31, 1965): 8.

41. Ibid.

42. Roy Reed, "White Man is Shot by Negro in Clash in Bogalusa, La.," *New York Times*, July 9, 1965, 1, 13. See also "Tension in Bogalusa, La.," *Facts on File*, July 7, 1965, 255.

43. Roy Reed, "Moderates Fail to Aid Bogalusa," *New York Times*, July 11, 1965, 46.

44. John C. Martzell, quoted in Roy Reed, "U.S. Court Enjoins Bogalusa Police," *New York Times*, July 11, 1965, 1, 46.

45. James Farmer, "Deacons for Defense," *New York Amsterdam News*, July 10, 1965, 15.

46. A. Z. Young, quoted in Lipsitz, *A Life in the Struggle*, 95.

47. Fred L. Zimmerman, "Race and Violence: More Dixie Negroes Buy Arms

to Retaliate against White Attacks," *Wall Street Journal* 73, no. 7 (July 12, 1965): 1, 15.

48. Ibid.

49. Ibid.

50. Roy Reed, "Negroes Reject Bogalusa Truce," *New York Times*, July 14, 1965, 1, 22.

51. Zimmerman, "Race and Violence," *Wall Street Journal*, July 12, 1965, 15.

52. Roy Reed, "Negroes Reject Bogalusa Truce," *New York Times*, July 14, 1965, 1, 22.

53. Deposition by A. Z. Young, Washington Parish, Louisiana, July 14, 1965, in "Chapters: Bogalusa, Louisiana, 1965 and undated" File, Folder 6865.

54. See "Deacons Defy Whites, Stay Armed Thruout, [sic]" *New York Amsterdam News*, July 24, 1965, 9.

55. See "Form New Group to Aid 'Deacons,'" *New York Amsterdam News*, August 14, 1965, 13. Auxiliary groups, such as the Austin group and, later, the "Friends of the Deacons" in New York City, cropped up outside the South. See "Deacons Organize Chicago Chapter," *New York Times*, April 6, 1966, 29.

56. Zimmerman, "Race and Violence," *Wall Street Journal*, July 12, 1965, 1.

57. Sims, quoted in Roy Reed, "Deacons, in Mississippi Visits, Implore Negroes 'to Wake Up,'" *New York Times*, August 30, 1965.

58. Lance Hill, "The Deacons for Defense and Justice," 57; see also Akinyele Umoja, "Eye for an Eye," 188. Hill and Umoja have both expertly discussed the role of women in the Deacons.

59. Sims, quoted in Raines, *My Soul Is Rested*, 421.

60. Burris, quoted in "The Deacons," 11.

61. Tucker, quoted in "Marchers Upset by Apathy," *New York Times*, June 14, 1966, 19.

62. Thomas, quoted in "Marchers' Ranks Expand to 1,200," *New York Times*, June 20, 1966, 20.

63. Sims, quoted in Grant, *Black Protest*, 362.

64. Salenger, quoted in "The Deacons," 22.

65. Quoted in *Wall Street Journal*, July 12, 1965.

66. Umoja, "Eye for an Eye," 189.

67. "Train People in Realities," *New Pittsburgh Courier* 6, no. 36 (September 18, 1965): 8.

68. "No Money for Deacons in Harlem," *New Pittsburgh Courier* 6, no. 42 (October 30, 1965): 1.

69. Herman Porter, "An Interview with Deacon for Defense," *Militant* 29, no. 42 (November 22, 1965): 1–2.

70. Ibid.

71. Ibid.

72. Ibid.

73. Austan's notion that violence must at times be restrained by force has grounding in Christian teachings. Thomas Merton, a Christian theologian, argued in 1968 that denying force in all instances is immoral, and that sometimes the only way to protect human life and rights effectively is by "forcible resistance" against unjust encroachment. Merton questioned placing the onus of responsibility for utilizing nonviolence on oppressed minorities struggling for equality. "Instead of preaching the Cross *for others* and advising them to suffer patiently the violence which we sweetly impose on them, with the aid of armies and police, we might conceivably recognize the right of the less fortunate to use force, and study more seriously the practice of nonviolence and humane methods on our own part. . . ." Merton, *Faith and Violence*, 3–10.

74. "Freedom Fighter Hits Dirty Roxbury Streets," *Bay State [Roxbury, Mass.] Banner* 1, no. 24 (March 5, 1966): 3.

75. "Charles Sims Speaks," *Bay State Banner* 1, no. 25 (March 12, 1966): 1.

76. "Bogalusa Deacons Seek Emergency Funds," *Bay State Banner* 1, no. 33 (May 28, 1966): 8.

77. Gene Roberts, "Mississippi March Gains Momentum," *New York Times*, June 10, 1966, 1, 35.

78. Sellers, *The River of No Return*, 162.

79. Oates, *Let the Trumpet Sound*, 397–398. According to Oates, King "pleaded with his Deacon brothers to remain true to nonviolence," but "the Deacons didn't 'believe in that naked shit no way,'" and would not be swayed by King.

80. Ibid. King confirmed this account of the contested debate in his final book. See King, *Where Do We Go from Here?*.

81. Garrow, *Bearing the Cross*, 477; Sellers, *The River of No Return*, 166. Adam Fairclough has suggested that Carmichael encouraged animosity between King and Wilkins "to ensure that SNCC did not become absorbed in a broad coalition that watered down its more radical aims." He also has suggested that King allowed his long-standing dislike of Wilkins to influence his judgment regarding the Deacons. See Fairclough, *To Redeem the Soul of America*, 313–315.

82. Sims, quoted in Raines, *My Soul Is Rested*, 422.

83. Sims quoted in Raines, *My Soul Is Rested*, 421–422, and in *New York Times Magazine*, August 15, 1965, 24.

84. Gene Roberts, "Mississippi March Gains Momentum," *New York Times*, June 10, 1966, 35. See also Sellers, *The River of No Return*, 165–166.

85. "Marchers Upset by Apathy," *New York Times*, June 14, 1966, 19.

86. "Philadelphia, Miss. Whites and Negroes Trade Shots," *New York Times*, June 22, 1966, 1, 24, 25.

87. Ibid.

88. Sellers, *The River of No Return*, 169.

89. "Sims Defends Black Power," *Bay State Banner* 1, no. 40 (July 16, 1966): 2.

90. For a full treatment of Black Power ideology, see Carmichael and Hamilton, *Black Power*. Sims, quoted in Raines, *My Soul Is Rested*, 423.

91. See "Bogalusa Official Asks Investigation," *New York Times*, September 17, 1966, 26.

92. "Deacons for Defense Spokesman To Speak at Bridge Meeting," *The Bay State Banner* 2, no. 17 (January 21, 1967):1.

93. Ibid.

94. "Mississippi March by Negroes Halted," *New York Times*, September 5, 1967, 31.

95. The Declassified Documents, FBI Counterintelligence Program (COINTELPRO) File (August 27, 1964–April 28, 1971), Deacons for Defense and Justice File, serial 5; see also O'Reilly, *Racial Matters*.

96. Sims, quoted in Grant, *Black Protest*, 361.

97. Ibid.

98. Sims, quoted in Raines, *My Soul Is Rested*, 419.

99. See "The Deacons," 22. Noting that the Deacons toed the line of aggressive violence, Roy Reed termed the Deacons' means of dealing with the oppressor "noble belligerence."

100. Lance Hill maintains that the Bogalusa Deacons ceased activities at the end of 1965 because the Klan there had died, no longer able to intimidate local blacks. He also notes that city officials in Bogalusa used the courts to "neutralize," through grand-jury indictments and injunctions, the BCVL (Bogalusa Civic Voters League) and the Deacons. City officials also sued several Deacons and BCVL members in the fall of 1966; see Hill, "The Deacons for Defense and Justice," 421, 425.

101. For example, see Justice Department Memorandum, March 16, 1966, Declassified Documents, Deacons for Defense and Justice FBI Files, Part 2d, 6; see also "Negroes Plan Armed Unit on Rights, *Sunday Star [Washington, D.C.]*, February 27, 1966, B5.

102. FBI Memorandum, July 12, 1966, Declassified Documents, Deacons for Defense and Justice FBI Files, Part 3b, 6.

103. Robert Hicks, interview by Robert Wright, August 10, 1969, Bogalusa, Louisiana, Ralph J. Bunche Oral History Collection (Civil Rights Documentation Project), Moorland-Spingarn Research Center, Howard University.

104. Sims, quoted in Raines, *My Soul Is Rested*, 421. Adam Fairclough has noted that the Deacons deliberately inflated their numbers and armament for the purpose of deterring the Klan. He estimates their membership to be "in the dozens rather than the hundreds, and certainly not in the thousands." See Fairclough, *Race and Democracy*, 359.

105. Sims, quoted in Grant, *Black Protest*, 363.

106. Compare with Malcolm X's definition of a Muslim: "A Muslim to us is somebody who is for the black man: I don't care if he goes to the Baptist church seven days a week." Malcolm X, "The *Playboy* Interview: Malcolm X Speaks with Alex Haley," *Playboy*, May 1963, reprinted in Gallen, *Malcolm X: As They Knew Him*, 112.

107. Sims, quoted in Grant, *Black Protest*, 358.

108. "Philadelphia, Miss., Whites and Negroes Trade Shots," *New York Times*, June 22, 1965, 25.

109. Sims, quoted in Grant, *Black Protest*, 364.

110. Farmer, quoted in "White Man is Shot by Negro in Clash in Bogalusa, La.," *New York Times*, July 9, 1965, 13.

111. Lynd, *Nonviolence in America*, 397.

112. Haines, *My Soul Is Rested*, 54.

113. Meier and Rudwick, *CORE*, 402.

114. Resolutions for the Resolution Committee of the National Convention of CORE, July 1–July 4, from the Northeast Region, Papers of the Congress of Racial Equality (microfilm), Reel 9, Doe Library, UC Berkeley. Lance Hill credits CORE with helping to establish the Deacons. He writes, "Despite their failures in Jonesboro, CORE had inadvertently made one significant accomplishment: they had facilitated the formation of the first formally organized paramilitary organization in the civil rights movement. CORE's tolerance for self-defense had contributed to the formation of Jonesboro's permanent self-defense organization." See Hill, "The Deacons for Defense and Justice," 48.

115. Olsen, *Last Man Standing*, 25–26.

116. Fred Brooks, interview by John Britton, Nashville, Tennessee, November 29, 1967, Ralph J. Bunche Oral History Collection (Civil Rights Documentation Project), Moorland Spingarn Research Center, Howard University.

117. Grant, *Black Protest*, 359, 362.

118. Lipsitz, *A Life in the Struggle*, 96.

Chapter 6. Code 1199, Officer Needs Help

(The papers of the Governor's Commission on the Los Angeles Riots will be referred to simply as the "McCone Report." Related archival material is referred to as the "McCone Papers," and an abridged, published version of the report, *Violence in the City*, is also referred to. The investigating body was called the "McCone Commission.")

1. Sears and McConahay, *The Politics of Violence*, 3.

2. Papers of the Governor's Commission on the Los Angeles Riots, "Testimony of William H. Parker," Sept. 16, 1965, Carton 24, 115; Manuscripts Division, Bancroft Library, UC Berkeley.

3. "Watts: Riot or Revolt?" CBS Television Network, December 7, 1965, 10–11 P.M. EST; Bancroft Library, UC Berkeley.

4. "Watts: Riot or Revolt?"

5. Week's News in Review, *Los Angeles Times Perspective*, sec. G, August 22, 1965, 4.

6. For statistics, see Horne, *Fire This Time*, 1; Sears and McConahay, *The Politics of Violence*, 9, 13; and Cohen and Murphy, *Burn, Baby, Burn!*, 254–56, 317–318.

7. Cohen and Murphy, *Burn, Baby, Burn!*, 278–280.

8. McCone, *Violence in the City*, 1.

9. Ibid., 3.

10. "Transcripts of Witness' Testimony," Carton 24, 115, McCone Papers.

11. McCone, *Violence in the City*, 4–5, 81, 82. The testimony of interviewed arrestees and the many complaints logged against the LAPD led the McCone Commission to begin its explication of the causes of the riot with what the Commission called the "problem" of law enforcement. The Commission acknowledged the "deep and long-standing schism" between the black community and the police department. See McCone, *Violence in the City*, 27.

12. For critiques of the McCone Commission's report, see Blauner, "Whitewash Over Watts: The Failure of the McCone Commission Report," in Fogleson, *The Los Angeles Riots*; see also *An Analysis of the McCone Report by the California Advisory Commission to the United States Commission on Civil Rights* (January 1966), 2.

13. Harding, *Anarchy Los Angeles*, 1, 14. Compare this statement to Chief Parker's "monkeys in a zoo" comment, supra note 7.

14. For standard explanations of the riot, see Cohen and Murphy, *Burn, Baby, Burn!*, 287, and Sears and McConahay, *The Politics of Violence*, 163–164.

15. See Lee Rainwater, "Open Letter on White Justice and the Riots," in Rossi, *Ghetto Revolts*, 127.

16. "Transcripts of Witness Testimony," Carton 24, 115, McCone Papers.

17. Gerald Horne's exhaustive *Fire this Time*, while excellent in most respects, is typical of this trend. A comprehensive, in-depth study of the Watts riot, Horne's book more than makes up for the scanty analysis of the McCone Report; however, in giving consideration to the unique conditions of Los Angeles life and politics, it widens the lens so much that any and every aspect of life in L.A. can be seen as contributing to the riot. For example, Horne discusses Communist organizing in L.A. in the 1940s—the relevance of which to the Watts conflagration is unclear.

18. Sears and McConahay, *The Politics of Violence*, 4; Cohen and Murphy, *Burn, Baby, Burn!*, 29.

19. "Arrestee Data," Carton 6, 12a, Folders 5, 6, 10, 11, and 17, McCone Papers.

20. "Arrestee Data," Carton 6, 12a, Folders 7 and 12, McCone Papers.

21. Charles Hillinger and Jack Jones, "Residents Put Blame on Police for Uproar," *Los Angeles Times*, August 13, 1965, 3.

22. Ibid.

23. McCone Report, Vol. 15, Doe Library, uc Berkeley.

24. "Watts: Riot or Revolt?"

25. "Testimony of Edmund G. Brown," Carton 24, 115, McCone Papers.

26. "Testimony of Bradford Crittenden," Carton 26, 115, McCone Papers. Crittenden added that he was not surprised to learn of allegations of "ungentlemanly language" by his chp officers in the heat of the Frye arrest; Officer Minikus had had his shirt torn off, he noted, and the arrest "wasn't pleasant."

27. Horne, *Fire This Time*, 104.

28. Ibid., 241.

29. Hillinger and Jones, "Residents Put Blame on Police for Uproar," *Los Angeles Times*, August 13, 1965, 3.

30. McCone Report, Vol. 15, Doe Library.

31. Jerry Cohen, "Viewpoint of Rioters Hard to Find, But Here's How One of Them Sees It," *Los Angeles Times*, August 22, 1965, 1.

32. Ibid.

33. "Watts: Riot or Revolt?"

34. "Transcripts of Witness' Testimony," Carton 24, 115, McCone Papers.

35. Ibid.

36. "Supplemental Information Requested by Phone This Date on Area Training, re: Area Training, Mob and Riot Control," September 13, 1965; Committee Exhibit: Field Extension and Area Training Program, File: Crittenden, Carton 18, 105, McCone Papers. The memorandum was apparently written by A. E. Allen, Lieutenant Acting Commander of the chp.

37. Interview by Bill Brown, with Jack Latham (knbc Reporter) and Elmer Peterson (nbc Correspondent), knbc News Conference Transcript, September 25, 1965 in "Exhibits Presented by Committee by Witnesses," File: Parker, Carton 19, 105, McCone Papers.

38. "The Los Angeles Ghetto Uprising," *People's World*, August 21, 1965, 3.

39. Joe, quoted in Cohen and Murphy, *Burn, Baby, Burn!*, 72.

40. "Arrestee Data," Carton 6, 12a, Folder 15, McCone Papers. Emphasis added.

41. "Arrestee Data," Carton 6, 12a, Folder 7, McCone Papers. Emphasis added.

42. Reese, quoted in Horne, *Fire This Time*, 56.

43. "Arrestee Data," Carton 6, 12a, Folder 9, McCone Papers. Emphasis added.

44. J.B., quoted in Cohen and Murphy, *Burn, Baby, Burn!*, 173. Emphasis added.

45. Cohen and Murphy, *Burn, Baby, Burn!*, 59, 124.

46. Rosa, *Why Watts Exploded*, 20.

47. See Horne, *Fire This Time*, 167. It has been suggested that the Watts riot gave birth to the Black Panther Party: a statement with perhaps more literary flair and poetic appeal than historical accuracy. Metaphorically, the BPP rose like a phoenix from the flames of Watts to symbolize a new kind of black nationalism, but it did so in 1967, two years after the flames were extinguished in Watts, and it did so several hundred miles to the north, in a community with striking similarities to—and important differences from—Watts. Certainly the Panthers' primary concern was protection from police brutality.

48. "Testimony of William H. Parker," September 16–17, Carton 24, 115, McCone Papers.

49. Ibid.

50. Crump, *Black Riot in Los Angeles*, 7.

51. For the self-destructive nature of rage and self-hatred in the black ghettoes of the 1960s, see Hendin, *Black Suicide*.

52. Cohen and Murphy, *Burn, Baby, Burn!*, 211–213.

Chapter 7. Blood to the Horse's Brow

1. Andrew Kopkind, "The Lair of the Black Panther," *New Republic* 155 (August 13, 1966): 10–13.

2. Ibid.

3. John Jackson, interview by Robert Wright, August 3, 1968, Hayneville, Alabama, transcript, Ralph J. Bunche Oral History Collection (Civil Rights Documentation Project), Moorland-Spingarn Research Center, Howard University.

4. See Stanton, *From Selma to Sorrow* for more on Liuzzo.

5. Jones, in *Lowndes County Freedom Organization*, video.

6. Moore, in *Lowndes County Freedom Organization*, video.

7. Mants, in *Lowndes County Freedom Organization*, video.

8. Jackson, interview by Wright, August 3, 1968.

9. See Carson, *In Struggle*, 209. As Carson has written, Carmichael and Ricks "touched a nerve in a very nervous white America." He has pointed out, "Ricks provided Carmichael with a new weapon in his ideological struggle with King when he demonstrated the enormous appeal of the slogan 'Black Power'—a shortened version of 'black power for black people,' a phrase used by SNCC workers in Alabama." "Black Power" had been used before as a political expression. Novelist Richard Wright used "Black Power" as the title of his book on African politics written in the 1950s. Black activist Paul Robeson spoke of black power during the 1950s, as did Harlem political leaders Jesse Gray and Congressman Adam Clayton Powell even earlier. "But combined with Ricks' infectious contempt for Mississippi's white authorities," Manning Marable has observed, "and in the context of the Meredith March, the slogan captured the mood of the majority of

CORE and SNCC activists and most rural blacks as well." Manning Marable, *Race, Reform and Rebellion*, 104.

10. Hall, quoted in Hampton and Fayer, *Voices of Freedom*, 305.

11. See Carson, *In Struggle*, 288–289. Black Power became tightly entangled in what he has termed "white fears and black fantasies."

12. Carmichael, *Stokely Speaks*, 18.

13. Young, quoted in Hampton and Fayer, *Voices of Freedom*, 299. Henry Hampton has written: "The Panthers insisted that 'picking up the gun' was a political act designed to galvanize the black community. But the image of young black men carrying guns on the streets of American cities also galvanized the white establishment." Hampton and Fayer, *Voices of Freedom*, 351.

14. See Carmichael and Hamilton, *Black Power*. Stokely Carmichael and Charles V. Hamilton offered the best (though still cloudy) interpretation of Black Power in their book; unfortunately, this book complicated the meaning of Black Power to the civil rights movement in the United States by incorporating Third World nationalist movements and ideology and by defining Black Power in terms of international struggle. Other helpful works, written at the time, include Scott and Brockriede, *The Rhetoric of Black Power* and Cone, *Black Theology and Black Power*. For white perspectives, see Fager, *White Reflections on Black Power* and Hough, *Black Power and White Protestants*.

15. Carmichael, quoted in Sitkoff, *Struggle for Black Equality*, 202.

16. Carmichael and Hamilton, *Black Power*, 52.

17. Ibid., 53.

18. Brown, *Fighting for US*, 51.

19. Sitkoff, *The Struggle for Black Equality*, 202.

20. Carmichael, quoted in Carson, *In Struggle*, 205.

21. King, *Where Do We Go from Here?*, 64, 66.

22. Killens, quoted in McCord et al., *Life Styles in the Black Ghetto*, 281.

23. Ibid.

24. See Carson, *In Struggle*, 278. Carson has noted that SNCC inspired Newton and Seale who, after reading a pamphlet about "how the people in Lowndes County chose to arm themselves," adopted the black panther symbol of the Lowndes County Freedom Organization as their own.

25. Seale, quoted in Mark Kitchell (dir.), *Berkeley in the Sixties* [film] (San Francisco: California Newsreel, 1990).

26. Newton, *Revolutionary Suicide*, 112. Newton listed Robert Williams among his "idols," including Marcus Garvey, Ernesto "Che" Guevara, Kwame Nkrumah, Regis Dubray, and Mao Tse-Tung; see Rush Greenlee, "A Revolutionary Talks From Cell," *San Francisco Examiner*, June 30, 1968, 1.

27. Seale, *A Lonely Rage*, 130.

28. See Howard in McCord et al., *Lifestyles in the Black Ghetto*, 241. Afro-Americans had traditionally carried weapons (usually in anticipation of attack by other blacks), but the Panthers were the first to carry weapons in anticipation of attack by police. "In essence, [the Panthers] have simply taken over the 'self-defense' position advocated by Robert Williams a decade earlier," explained John Howard, professor of sociology at City College of New York, in 1969. "Most whites would view the Panthers as revolutionary because they choose to arm themselves, but many of their goals are distinctly nonrevolutionary." Reginald Major recognized the Panthers as "a logical development of earlier black revolutionary programs, particularly that of Robert Williams, the Muslims, Malcolm X, and the more activist civil rights organizations like SNCC." See Major, *A Panther Is a Black Cat*, 63. Clayborne Carson has argued that while Newton and Seale claimed to have been inspired by SNCC's accomplishments in the Deep South, "their evolving attitudes about SNCC revealed little understanding of its history." Carson, *In Struggle*, 278.

29. Seale, *A Lonely Rage*, 151.

30. Ibid., 135.

31. Newton, *Revolutionary Suicide*, 113.

32. Newton, quoted in Hampton and Fayer, *Voices of Freedom*, 353.

33. For example, see *Huey* [video].

34. Seale, *Seize the Time*, 71.

35. Ibid., 116–117.

36. See Jerry Belcher, "Oakland Black Panthers Wear Guns, Talk Revolution," *San Francisco Examiner*, April 30, 1967.

37. "Guns Baby Guns," in *Black Panther* 1, no. 5 (July 20, 1967): 9.

38. Brown, *A Taste of Power*, 107. Emphasis added.

39. Seale, *A Lonely Rage*, 154.

40. Ibid., 418.

41. See Tucker, *For Blacks Only*, 40. Sterling Tucker, Executive Director of the Urban League in Washington, D.C., argued in 1971 that "no discussion of black violence can be undertaken without reference to white America's shield and defender: the police." He noted: "In virtually every situation where blacks have advocated the carrying of arms, it has been for the purposes of self-defense against the violence of white America's cops. In consequence, the issue of black 'violence' cannot be understood separately from that of the police, their practices and policies, and their relations with the ghetto community."

42. See O'Reilly, *Racial Matters*, 296. Kenneth O'Reilly has noted: "For many of the young men and women who joined the Party, all social ills could be traced back to the police who patrolled the ghettoes. . . . 'Off the pig!' became the Black Panther slogan, and it suggested to some, [J. Edgar] Hoover included, that

the party had assumed the right to liberate black people from a police army of occupation by murdering anyone who wore a badge."

43. See Howard in McCord, *Life Styles in the Black Ghetto*, 242, 240. "[The Panthers'] ideas about self-defense grew out of the realities of their own lives," explained Howard. "That they reached the position [Robert] Williams had come to a decade before was due more to circumstance than design." Williams, who evolved "a set of strategies and tactics intended for the here and now," appealed to Newton's impetuous nature.

44. Newton, quoted in Earl Ofari, *Black Liberation*.

45. Hilliard and Cole, *This Side of Glory*, 40.

46. Ibid., 23–97.

47. Newton, *Revolutionary Suicide*, 89. Newton was paraphrasing Seale; see Seale, *Seize the Time*, 15.

48. Seale, *Seize the Time*, 418.

49. Newton, *Revolutionary Suicide*, 188–189.

50. Seale, *Seize the Time*, 418. Reginald Major attempted to express the Panthers' mindset: "Few people can reasonably be expected to engage in warfare with police. But anyone, if he has any self-respect, recognizes that there is some form of provocation, some threat to his person, that will elicit a furious response. No one—a legislature, a court, a police department, or an army—can take away or confer the right to self-defense. This is part of the message of the gun." Major saw the superior firepower of police as "another way of saying that black people are poor." Major, *A Panther Is a Black Cat*, 32.

51. Anonymous, *I Was a Black Panther*, 90. The author of this book concealed his identity for fear of reprisals for telling his story.

52. Cox, quoted in U.S. Congress, "The Black Panther Party," 26.

53. Landon Williams, panel discussion, Berkeley Graduate Assembly, Booth Auditorium, Boalt Hall, University of California, October 25, 1990, video recording, Media Resource Center, UC Berkeley.

54. *Huey* [video].

55. Newton, *Revolutionary Suicide*, 74.

56. Cox and Hilliard, quoted in U.S. Congress, "The Black Panther Party," 17. Expletives deleted in original text.

57. *Black Panther*, April 25, 1970.

58. See Fanon, *Les damnés de la terre* [*The Wretched of the Earth*]; see also Seale, *Seize the Time*, 25–26, 34. Fanon, a black psychiatrist from Martinique who worked in Algeria for the National Liberation Front in its fight against the French, considered violence a necessary function of the liberation of the oppressed. Newton and Seale digested Fanon's theories of violence and, in the BPP's latter stages, argued that spontaneous violence educates those "who are in a position with skills to lead the people to what needs to be done."

59. Bakunin, *Catechism of the Revolutionist*.

60. Skolnick, *The Politics of Protest*, 116.

61. Ibid.

62. Hilliard and Cole, *This Side of Glory*, 180.

63. *Black Panther*, March 23, 1968.

64. Foner, *The Black Panther Speaks*, 180.

65. *Black Panther*, January 17, 1969.

66. Hilliard, quoted in U.S. Congress, "The Black Panther Party," 17. For more on this incident, see "U.S. Agents Hold Hilliard—'Threat to the President,'" *San Francisco Chronicle*, December 4, 1969; see also Hilliard and Cole, *This Side of Glory*, 264–265.

67. Major, *A Panther Is a Black Cat*, 61.

68. See Hoover, quoted in Major, *A Panther Is a Black Cat*, 300. On June 15, 1969, J. Edgar Hoover, FBI Director, declared, "the Black Panther Party, without question, represents the greatest threat to the internal security of the country." Kenneth O'Reilly has observed: "Hoover's pursuit of the Black Panther Party was unique only in its total disregard for human rights and life itself." O'Reilly, *Racial Matters*, 294.

69. *Black Panther*, May 4, 1968, 17.

70. See Series 4, Box 5, Folder 51, Huey P. Newton Foundation Records, 1968–1994, Black Panther Party Research Project, Department of Special Collections, Stanford University; see also Series 4, Box 1, Folder 1. By September 13, 1968, the FBI had infiltrated the Party and begun collecting informant reports; by early 1969, it was running wiretaps on the BPP. For more information on the detrimental effect of the FBI on the Black Panther Party, see Leroy F. Aarons and Robert C. Maynard, "Panther Leadership Hurt by Sweeping FBI Raids," *Washington Post* (June 25, 1969) and "How the FBI Poked and Pried at Dissidents," *San Francisco Examiner* [City Edition] (March 9, 1976). Books on the subject include Kenneth O'Reilly, *Racial Matters*; Churchill, *Agents of Repression*; and Wilkins and Clark, *Search and Destroy*.

71. Landon Williams, panel discussion, Berkeley Graduate Assembly, Booth Auditorium, Boalt Hall, University of California, October 25, 1990, video recording, Media Resource Center, UC Berkeley.

72. One scholar has discussed the Black Panther Party's rank-and-file membership, drawn from whom Karl Marx called the "lumpen proletariat": the unemployed, unskilled, and impoverished. He argues that Newton and Seale's decision to rely on the lumpen "placed the organization on a course of instability" and that the emphasis on the lumpen was "a decisive factor in the BPP's eventual decline as a national political force." In other words, the Panthers' practice of recruiting those whom Bobby Seale called "brothers off the block" (often undisciplined and sometimes criminally inclined) heightened

violence; undercut alliances with Students for a Democratic Society (SDS), SNCC and other organizations; reinforced misogynistic behavior; and invited government repression. See Chris Booker, "Lumpenization: A Critical Error of the Black Panther Party," in Jones, *The Black Panther Party Reconsidered*, 337–362. In this same volume, Ollie Johnson asserts, "The rise of the Party was rapid and dramatic; its fall, slow and embarrassing. . . . The confluence of three internal factors (intra-party conflict, strategic organization errors, and a rise in party authoritarianism) contributed directly to the demise of the BPP." See Ollie A. Johnson III, "Explaining the Demise of the Black Panther Party: The Role of Internal Factors," in Jones, *The Black Panther Party Reconsidered*, 391–409.

73. Newton, *The Original Vision*. In actuality, the Ten Point Program contained twenty points, with practice expressed in the section "What We Want" and theory expressed in "What We Believe."

74. Ibid.

75. Ibid.

76. FBI report, November 26, 1973, Series 4, Box 14, Folder 20, Huey P. Newton Foundation Records, 1968–94, Black Panther Party Research Project, Department of Special Collections, Stanford University Libraries.

77. Carl Miller, quoted in Pearson, *The Shadow of the Panther*, 328.

78. Melvin Newton, quoted in Hilliard and Cole, *This Side of Glory*, 6–7.

79. Scholars have tended to differentiate between the civil rights movement and the more "militant" Black Power movement; however, recent scholarship has begun to blur these familiar distinctions as part of a larger attempt to emphasize the continuities from the civil rights phase to the Black Power phase of the struggle for black equality. For example, see Collier-Thomas and Franklin, *Sisters in the Struggle* and Peniel Joseph, "Black Power Studies: Rethinking the Civil Rights/Black Power Era, 1955–1975" (presented at the November 2003 conference "The Black Power Movement in Historical Perspective: Dialogues on Race and American Society" at the University of Connecticut).

80. For more on these studies, see the President's Commission on Law Enforcement and the Administration of Justice, *Task Force Report: The Police* (Washington, D.C.: U.S. Government Printing Office, 1967), especially Chapter 6; see also Skolnick, *The Politics of Protest*, 97–135.

81. The literature concerning riots in the 1960s is too extensive to discuss in this context. For an introduction, see the U.S. Commission on Civil Disorders, *Report of the National Advisory Commission on Civil Disorders* and Conot, *Rivers of Blood, Years of Darkness*.

82. Jones, *Arm Yourself or Harm Yourself*.

83. Ibid.

84. Major, *A Panther Is a Black Cat*, 31–32.

85. For more on Mayor Stokes and the Ahmed Evans incident, see Zannes, *Checkmate in Cleveland*.

86. See Masotti and Corsi, *Shootout in Cleveland*. An exhaustive investigation by the Civil Violence Research Center at Case Western Reserve University, under the direction of Louis H. Masotti and Jerome R. Corsi, proved inconclusive as to who instigated the violence. Masotti and Corsi's report soundly condemned police conduct in Cleveland's black neighborhoods.

87. See "Guns!," *Sepia* 17 (August 1968): 22–26.

88. Reprinted in Lincoln, *Is Anybody Listening to Black America?*, 150.

89. Ibid., 122–123.

90. Brown, *Fighting for US*, 53–55.

91. Lincoln, *Is Anybody Listening to Black America?*, 225.

92. Ward and Badger, *The Making of Martin Luther King*, 4.

93. Reed, *One South*, 153.

94. Bruno Bettelheim, "Violence: A Neglected Mode of Behavior," in Endleman, ed., *Violence in the Streets*, 42.

95. Bennett, *The Black Mood and Other Essays*, 82.

Conclusion. The Courage to Talk Back

1. H. Rap Brown, quoted in Patrick C. Kennicott and Wayne E. Page, "H. Rap Brown: The Cambridge Incident," *Quarterly Journal of Speech* 58, no. 3 (October 1971): 329.

2. Hastings, *The Fire this Time*, 125. As one British journalist has noted, "A marital quarrel can have a very speedy end indeed if both parties know that there is a loaded revolver 'to protect against burglars' in the top drawer of the bureau."

3. Nossiter, quoted in Hilliard and Cole, *This Side of Glory*, 272.

4. See Burner, *And Gently He Shall Lead Them*, 7. In discussing Bob Moses's appreciation for Albert Camus, Eric Burner captures the giddy lure of the gun when he writes that "violence in good causes has within it a capacity for oppression," and "within the rebel there lurks the oppressor."

5. Robert Ginsberg, "The Paradoxes of Violence, Moral Violence, and Nonviolence," in Kool, *Perspectives on Nonviolence*, 162.

6. As Preston K. Covey, Director of the Center for the Advancement of Applied Ethics at Carnegie Mellon University, has observed: "The actuarial success of armed self-defense is one matter; the residual moral value of having the personal responsibility and prerogative of armed self-defense is quite another." Quoted in Cramer and Covey, *For the Defense of Themselves and the State*, viii.

7. For more on racial etiquette in the jim crow South, see Doyle, *The Etiquette of Race Relations*.

8. Frank Millspaugh, "Black Power," *Commonweal* 84, no. 18 (August 5, 1966): 502.

9. DuBois, *Black Reconstruction in America*, 8–9.

10. Julian Mayfield, "Challenge to Negro Leadership: The Case of Robert Williams," *Commentary* 31 (April 1961): 297–305.

11. Williams, interview by James Mosby, July 22, 1970, transcript, Ralph J. Bunche Oral History Collection (Civil Rights Documentation Project), Moorland-Spingarn Research Center, Howard University. James Forman has also described this incident. See Forman, *The Making of Black Revolutionaries*, 190.

12. Seale, *A Lonely Rage*, 153. The stereotypical "bad nigger" is a ubiquitous figure in Afro-American folklore and culture. Ready to fight at the slightest provocation, characters such as Stagolee would kill a black person or a white person without hesitation. Such figures attained status not only from their pugilistic skills but also from their grandiloquent boasts about their exploits. Bobby Seale indicated in his autobiography that he and Huey Newton were "Stagolees." For a discussion of this stereotype, see Arthur Raper, "Race and Class Pressures," unpublished manuscript, Raper Papers, Wilson Library, Special Collections, University of North Carolina.

13. Carl Washington, quoted in Lincoln, *Is Anybody Listening to Black America?*, 173.

14. Malcolm X, quoted in Goldman, *The Death and Life of Malcolm X*, 156.

Postscript. The Only Tired

1. Testimony of Robert F. Williams, U.S. Senate Judiciary Hearings, Subcommittee on Internal Security, 91st Congress, Second Session, February 16, 1970 (Washington, D.C.: U.S. Government Printing Office, 1971), 3–4, 12.

2. Williams, "An Interview with Robert Williams," *Marxist Leninist Quarterly* 2 (1964): 1, 60.

3. For example, see Williams, "USA: The Potential for a Minority Revolution," *The Crusader* 7, no. 1 (August 1965): 1–8.

4. "Moment of Truth for Williams?," *Charlotte Observer*, February 2, 1965; "Articles Concerning Williams, 1965" Folder, Box 4, Bentley Collection.

5. Williams, "*The Black Scholar* Interviews: Robert F. Williams," *Black Scholar* 1 (May 1970): 7, 5.

6. See "Inside China: The Odyssey of Robert Williams," *Muhammad Speaks*, June 5, 1964, 11–15; see also William Worthy, "The Red Chinese American Negro," *Esquire*, October 1964, 132 ff.

7. Thomas A. Johnson, "Militant Hopeful on Racial Justice," *New York Times*, September 15, 1969, 67.

8. Williams, quoted in Robert C. Maynard, "Williams Says Duty Called Him Back," *Washington Post*, September 15, 1969, 1, A4.

9. Williams, *Negroes with Guns*, 119.

10. U.S. Senate Judiciary Hearings, 10, 18, 29, 44–45. Williams claimed no affiliation; however, his papers collected at the Bentley Historical Library contain a number of items from his personal files related to both RAM and the RNA.

11. Max Stanford, "Calling All Black People," undated pamphlet, published by the Black Liberation (RAM) Party, Box 3, "Republic of New Africa" Folder 1, Robert F. Williams Collection, Bentley Historical Library, University of Michigan.

12. For more on the Republic of New Africa, see Van Deburg, *New Day in Babylon*, 144–149.

13. U.S. Senate Judiciary Hearings, 9, 11, 12.

14. U.S. Senate Judiciary Hearings, 83, 84, 89.

15. U.S. Senate Judiciary Hearings, 76.

16. See "Interview with Robert Williams," *Marxist Leninist Quarterly* 2, no. 1 (1964): 53. In an interview published in the *Marxist Leninist Quarterly*, Williams drew parallels between his bearing arms and soldiers' bearing arms while fighting for the United States in Vietnam.

17. U.S. Senate Judiciary Hearings, 24–28.

18. Griffin, quoted in Southern Conference Educational Fund (SCEF) newsletter, February 4, 1972, Box 3, Miscellenea Folder 1, Robert F. Williams Collection, Bentley Historical Library, University of Michigan.

19. Mabel Williams in David Cecelski, "Mabel Williams: Standing Up to the Klan," Raleigh *News and Observer*, November 14, 1999; available online as an interview included in the University of North Carolina's Southern Oral History Program at http://www.sohp.org/research/lfac/N&O/6.5bl8-Mabel_Williams.html.

20. Julian Mayfield to Robert Williams, June 7, 1980, Correspondence, Box 6, Folder 20, Julian Mayfield Papers, Schomburg Center for Research in Black Culture, Harlem, New York. Emphasis in the original.

21. See "Robert F. Williams, 71, Civil Rights Leader and Revolutionary" [obituary], *New York Times*, October 19, 1996, 52.

22. "Community Gives Rights Activist Hero's Welcome," *Charlotte Observer*, August 20, 1995, 1B, 4B.

23. Parks, *Rosa Parks: My Story*, 174–175.

24. Ibid., 115–116.

25. Ibid., 178.

SELECTED BIBLIOGRAPHY

Manuscripts and Archival Collections

Boston University, Boston, Massachusetts. Department of Special Collections.

Duke University, Durham, North Carolina. Rare Book, Manuscript and Special Collections Library. Matthews (J. B.) Papers, 1862–1986.

Moorland-Spingarn Archives, Howard University, Washington, D.C. Ralph J. Bunche Oral History Collection (Civil Rights Documentation Project).

Schomburg Center for Research in Black Culture, New York City Public Library, New York, New York. General Research and Reference Collections. Manuscripts, Archives, and Rare Books Division.

Stanford University, Palo Alto, California. Martin Luther King Jr. Papers Project. Black Panther Party Research Project, Huey P. Newton Foundation Records, 1968–1994.

University of California at Berkeley, Berkeley, California. Doe Library and Bancroft Library. NAACP Papers and CORE Papers. Bancroft Collection on Social Protest Movements. Papers of the Governor's Commission on the Los Angeles Riots (McCone Papers).

University of Michigan, Ann Arbor, Michigan. Bentley Historical Library. Robert F. Williams Papers.

University of North Carolina at Chapel Hill, Chapel Hill, North Carolina. Wilson Library. Floyd B. McKissick Papers.

Newspapers and Periodicals

Afro-American (Baltimore, Maryland)
Bay State Banner (Roxbury, Massachusetts)
Black Panther
Charlotte Observer
Commentary
Crisis
Crusader
Ebony
Esquire
Facts on File
Jet
Journal and Guide (Norfolk, Virginia)
Kansas City Star
Liberation

Life
London News Chronicle
Los Angeles Times
Los Angeles Times Perspective
Militant
Monroe Enquirer (North Carolina)
Montgomery Advertiser
Muhammad Speaks
Nation
National Guardian
New Republic
New York Amsterdam News
New York Post
New York Times
New York Times Magazine
New York World
Newsweek
Peacemaker
Phylon
Pittsburgh Courier
Revolution
St. Louis Post-Dispatch
San Francisco Chronicle
San Francisco Examiner
Saturday Review
Sepia
Southern School News
Sunday Star (Washington, D.C.)
Time
Tri-State Defender (Memphis, Tennessee)
Wall Street Journal
Washington Post
Wyandotte Herald (Kansas)

Other Sources

Abernathy, Ralph David. *And the Walls Came Tumbling Down.* New York: Harper and Row, 1989.
Anonymous, as told to Chuck Moore. *I Was a Black Panther.* Garden City, N.Y.: Doubleday, 1970.
Armstrong, Julie Buckner, Houston B. Robertson, and Rhonda Y. Williams.

Teaching the American Civil Rights Movement: Freedom's Bittersweet Song. New York: Routledge, 2002.

Arrendt, Hannah. *On Violence.* New York: Harcourt Brace Jovanovich, 1969.

Ayers, Edward L. *Vengeance and Justice: Crime and Punishment in the 19th-Century American South.* New York: Oxford University Press, 1984.

Bakunin, Mikhail Aleksandrovich. *Catechism of the Revolutionist* [pamphlet]. Oakland: Black Panther Party for Self-Defense, [196?]; Bancroft Collection on Social Protest Movements, Bancroft Library, University of California, Berkeley.

Baldwin, Lewis V. *There Is a Balm in Gilead.* Minneapolis: Fortress, 1991.

———. *To Make the Wounded Whole: The Cultural Legacy of Martin Luther King, Jr.* Minneapolis: Fortress, 1992.

Baum, Frederic S., and Joan Baum. *Law of Self-Defense.* Dobbs Ferry, N.Y.: Oceana Publications, 1970.

Belfrage, Sally. *Freedom Summer.* New York: Viking, 1965.

Bell, Inge Powell. *CORE and the Strategy of Nonviolence.* New York: Random House, 1968.

Bennett, Lerone, Jr. *The Black Mood and Other Essays.* New York: Johnson, 1964. Reprinted by Barnes and Noble, 1970.

Berkeley in the Sixties [video]. San Francisco: California Newsreel, 1990.

Blum, John M., and C. Vann Woodward. *The National Experience: A History of the United States.* 8th ed. New York: Harcourt Brace Jovanovich, 1993.

Bondurant, Joan V. *Conquest of Violence: The Gandhian Philosophy of Conflict.* Rev. ed. Princeton, New Jersey: Princeton University Press, 1988.

Branch, Taylor. *Parting the Waters: America in the King Years, 1954–63.* New York: Simon and Schuster, 1988.

Breitman, George, Herman Porter, and Baxter Smith. *The Assassination of Malcolm X.* Edited by Malik Miah. New York: Pathfinder, 1976.

Brink, William, and Louis Harris. *The Negro Revolution in America.* New York: Simon and Schuster, 1963.

Brown, Elaine. *A Taste of Power: A Black Woman's Story.* New York: Anchor Books, 1992.

Brown, Richard Maxwell. *No Duty to Retreat: Violence and Values in American History and Society.* Norman: University of Oklahoma Press, 1991.

Brown, Scot. *Fighting for US: Maulana Karenga, the US Organization, and Black Cultural Nationalism.* New York: New York University Press, 2003.

Burner, Eric. *And Gently He Shall Lead Them: Robert Parris Moses and Civil Rights in Mississippi.* New York: New York University Press, 1994.

California. Legislature. Assembly. Committee on Criminal Justice. *A Model Penal Code for the State of California: A Study and Recommendation.* Sacramento: California State Assembly, 1976.

Campbell, Edward D. C., Jr., with Kym S. Rice. *Before Freedom Came: African-American Life in the Antebellum South*. Charlottesville, Va.: The Museum of the Confederacy, 1991.

Carmichael, Stokely. *Stokely Speaks: Black Power/Back to Pan Africanism*. New York: Random House, 1965.

Carmichael, Stokely and Charles V. Hamilton. *Black Power: The Politics of Liberation in America*. New York: Vintage, 1967.

Carson, Clayborne. *In Struggle: SNCC and the Black Awakening of the 1960s*. Cambridge: Harvard University Press, 1981.

Carson, Clayborne, et al., eds. *The Papers of Martin Luther King, Jr.* Vols. 1–3. Berkeley: University of California Press, 1992–1997.

Chestnut, J. L., Jr., and Julia Cass. *Black in Selma: The Uncommon Life of J. L. Chestnut, Jr.* New York: Farrar, Strauss, Giroux, 1990.

Churchill, Ward. *Agents of Repression: The FBI's Secret Wars Against the Black Panther Party and the American Indian Movement*. Boston: South End, 1988.

Clarke, John Henrik, ed. *Malcolm X: The Man and His Times*. New York: Collier, 1969.

Cleaver, Eldridge. *The Genius of Huey P. Newton: Minister of Defense of the Black Panther Party* [pamphlet]. Oakland, Calif.: Black Panther Party, 1970.

———. *Post-Prison Writings and Speeches*. New York: Vintage Books, 1967.

Cleaver, Kathleen, and George Katsiaficas. *Liberation, Imagination, and the Black Panther Party*. New York: Routledge, 2001.

Cohen, Jerry, and William S. Murphy. *Burn, Baby, Burn!: The Los Angeles Race Riot*. New York: E. P. Dutton, 1966.

Cohen, Robert S. *Black Crusader*. New York: Lyle Stuart, 1972.

Collier-Thomas, Bettye, and V. P. Franklin, eds. *Sisters in the Struggle: African-American Women in the Civil Rights-Black Power Movement*. New York: New York University Press, 2001.

Cone, James H. *Black Theology and Black Power*. New York: Seabury, 1969.

———. *Martin and Malcolm and America: A Dream or a Nightmare*. Maryknoll, N.Y.: Orbis, 1991.

Conot, Robert. *Rivers of Blood, Years of Darkness*. New York: Bantam, 1967.

Cottrol, Robert J. *Gun Control and the Constitution: The Courts, Congress, and the Second Amendment*. New York: Garland Publishing, 1993.

Cottrol, Robert J., and Raymond T. Diamond. "'Never Intended to Be Applied to the White Population': Firearms Regulation and Racial Disparity—the Redeemed South's Legacy to a National Jurisprudence?" *Chicago-Kent Law Review* 70 (1995): 1307–1335.

Cramer, Clayton E. "The Racist Roots of Gun Control." *Kansas Journal of Law and Public Policy* 4 (1995): 17–25.

Cramer, Clayton E. and Preston K. Covey. *For the Defense of Themselves and the State: The Original Intent and Judicial Interpretation of the Right to Keep and Bear Arms*. Westport, Conn.: Praeger, 1994.

Crump, Spencer. *Black Riot in Los Angeles: The Story of the Watts Tragedy*. Los Angeles: Trans-Anglo Books, 1966.

Cruse, Harold. *The Crisis of the Negro Intellectual*. New York: William Morrow, 1967.

Davis, Thulani. *Malcolm X: The Great Photographs*. New York: Stewart, Tabori, and Chang, 1992.

de Jong, Greta. *A Different Day: African American Struggles for Justice in Rural Louisiana, 1900–1970*. Chapel Hill: University of North Carolina Press, 2002.

The Declassified Documents. FBI Counterintelligence Program (COINTELPRO) File. August 27, 1964–April 28, 1971, Deacons for Defense and Justice File, Serial 5.

Dick, James C. *Violence and Oppression*. Athens: University of Georgia Press, 1979.

Dittmer, John. *Local People: The Struggle for Civil Rights in Mississippi*. Urbana: University of Illinois Press, 1994.

Doyle, Bertram W. *The Etiquette of Race Relations: A Study in Social Control*. Chicago: University of Chicago Press, 1937.

DuBois, W. E. B. *Black Reconstruction in America*. New York: Russell and Russell, 1962.

———. "Martin Luther King's Life: Crusader without Violence." *National Guardian* 12, no. 4 (November 9, 1959): 8.

Dyson, Michael Eric. *Making Malcolm: The Myth and Meaning of Malcolm X*. New York: Oxford University Press, 1995.

Ellsworth, Scott. *Death in a Promised Land: The Tulsa Race Riot of 1921*. Baton Rouge: LSU Press, 1982.

Endleman, Shalom, ed., *Violence in the Streets*. Chicago: Quadrangle, 1968.

Fager, Charles E. *White Reflections on Black Power*. Grand Rapids, Mich.: William B. Eerdmans, 1967.

Fairclough, Adam. "Martin Luther King, Jr. and the Quest for Nonviolent Social Change." *Phylon* 47 (Spring 1986): 3.

———. *Race and Democracy: The Civil Rights Struggle in Louisiana, 1915–1972*. Athens: University of Georgia Press, 1995.

———. *To Redeem the Soul of America: The Southern Christian Leadership Conference and Martin Luther King Jr.* Athens: University of Georgia Press, 1987.

Fanon, Frantz. *Les damnés de la terre*. Paris: François Maspero, 1961. English reprint [*The Wretched of the Earth*], New York: Grove, 1968.

Farmer, James. *Lay Bare the Heart: An Autobiography of the Civil Rights Movement*. New York: Plume, 1985.

Fischer, Louis. *The Essential Gandhi: His Life, Work, and Ideas.* New York: Vintage, 1962.

Fogleson, Robert M., ed. *The Los Angeles Riots.* New York: Arno Press and the *New York Times,* 1969.

Foner, Eric. *Reconstruction: America's Unfinished Revolution, 1863–1877.* New York: Perennial Library, 1989.

Foner, Philip S., ed. *The Black Panther Speaks.* 2nd ed. New York: Da Capo, 1995.

———, ed. *The Life and Writings of Frederick Douglass.* Vol. 5. New York: International Publishers, 1975.

Forman, James. *The Making of Black Revolutionaries.* Seattle: Open Hand Publishing, 1985.

Franklin, John Hope and August Meier, eds. *Black Leaders of the Twentieth Century.* Urbana: University of Illinois Press, 1982.

Gallen, David, ed. *Malcolm X: As They Knew Him.* New York: Carroll and Graf, 1992.

Gandhi, Mohandas K. *The Story of My Experiments with Truth.* 2nd ed. Ahmedabad: Navajivan, 1940.

Garrow, David J. *Bearing the Cross: Martin Luther King Jr. and the Southern Christian Leadership Conference.* New York: William Morrow, 1986.

———. *Chicago 1966: Open Housing Marches Summit Negotiations and Operation Breadbasket.* Brooklyn, N.Y.: Carlson, 1989.

———. *Martin Luther King Jr.: Civil Rights Leader, Theologian, Orator.* Brooklyn, N.Y.: Carlson, 1989.

———. *Protest at Selma: Martin Luther King Jr., and the Voting Rights Act of 1965.* New Haven: Yale University Press, 1978.

Giddings, P. *When and Where I Enter: The Impact of Black Women on Race and Sex in America.* New York: William Morrow, 1984.

Gilbert, Peter, comp. and ed. *The Selected Writings of John Edward Bruce: Militant Black Journalist.* New York: Arno Press, 1971.

Godfrey, Irwin. *American Tramp and Underworld Slang.* New York: Gale Group, 1971.

Goldman, Peter. *The Death and Life of Malcolm X.* 2nd ed. Urbana: University of Illinois Press, 1979.

Gramsci, Antonio. *Selections from the Prison Notebooks.* Edited by Quintin Hoare and Geoffrey Nowell Smith. New York: International Publishers, 1971.

Grant, Joanne. *Black Protest: History, Documents, and Analyses; 1619 to the Present.* New York: Fawcett Premier, 1968.

Greenbaum, Susan D. *The Afro-American Community in Kansas City, Kansas.* Kansas City: City of Kansas City, 1982.

Gregg, Richard. *The Power of Nonviolence.* Rev. ed. London: George Routledge, 1938.

Haines, Herbert. *Black Radicals and the Civil Rights Mainstream, 1954–1970.* Knoxville: University of Tennessee Press, 1988.

Hair, William Ivy. *Carnival of Fury: Robert Charles and the New Orleans Race Riot of 1900.* Baton Rouge: Louisiana State University Press, 1976.

Halbrook, Stephen P. *That Every Man Be Armed: The Evolution of a Constitutional Right.* Albuquerque: University of New Mexico Press, 1984.

Hampton, Henry, and Steve Fayer with Sarah Flynn. *Voices of Freedom: An Oral History of the Civil Rights Movement from the 1950s Through the 1980s.* New York: Bantam, 1990.

Harding, Frank, ed. *Anarchy Los Angeles.* Los Angeles: Kimtex Corporation, 1965.

Harding, Vincent, with Clayborne Carson, David J. Garrow, and Darlene Clark Hine, eds. *Eyes on the Prize: A Reader and Guide.* New York: Penguin, 1987.

Harrold, Stanley. "Violence and Nonviolence in Kentucky Abolitionism." *Journal of Southern History* 57, no. 1 (February 1991): 19–21.

Hastings, Max. *The Fire This Time: America's Year of Crisis.* New York: Taplinger, 1969.

Hendin, Herbert. *Black Suicide.* New York: Basic, 1969.

Hill, Lance. "The Deacons for Defense and Justice: Armed Self Defense in the Civil Rights Movement." Ph.D. diss., Tulane, 1997.

Hilliard, David, and Lewis Cole. *This Side of Glory: The Autobiography of David Hilliard and the Story of the Black Panther Party.* Boston: Back Bay, 1993.

Hodgson, Godfrey. *America in Our Time: From World War II to Nixon, What Happened and Why.* New York: Vintage, 1976.

Horne, Gerald. *Fire this Time: The Watts Uprising and the 1960s.* Charlottesville: University Press of Virginia, 1995.

Hough, Joseph C., Jr. *Black Power and White Protestants: A Christian Response to the New Negro Pluralism.* London: Oxford University Press, 1968.

Huey [video]. American Documentary Films in cooperation with the Black Panther Party. Chicago: International Historic Films, 1984.

Huggins, Nathan Irvin. *Slave and Citizen: The Life of Frederick Douglass.* Boston: Little, Brown, 1980.

Hughes, Langston. *The Best of Simple.* New York: Noonday Press, 1990.

Johnson, Thomas L., and Phillip C. Dunn, eds. *A True Likeness: The Black South of Richard Samuel Roberts, 1920–1936.* Chapel Hill, N.C.: Algonquin, 1986.

Jones, Charles, ed. *The Black Panther Party Reconsidered.* Baltimore: Black Classic, 1998.

Jones, LeRoi (Amiri Baraka). *Arm Yourself or Harm Yourself: A Message of Self-*

Defense to Black Men [one-act play]. Newark, N.J.: Jihad Publications, 196?;
Bancroft Collection on Social Protest Movements, Bancroft Library, University
of California, Berkeley.

————. *Home: Social Essays.* New York: William Morrow, 1966.

Kelley, Robin D. G. *Freedom Dreams: The Black Radical Imagination.* Boston:
Beacon, 2002.

Kennicott, Patrick C., and Wayne E. Page. "H. Rap Brown: The Cambridge
Incident." *The Quarterly Journal of Speech* 58, no. 3 (October 1971): 329.

King, Coretta Scott. *My Life with Martin Luther King, Jr.* New York: Holt,
Rinehart, and Winston, 1969.

King, Martin Luther, Jr. "Letter from Birmingham City Jail" [pamphlet].
Philadelphia: American Friends Service Committee, 1963.

————. "The Most Durable Power." *The Christian Century* 74 (June 5, 1957): 708.

————. *Stride Toward Freedom: The Montgomery Story.* New York: Harper and
Row, 1958.

————. *Where Do We Go from Here: Chaos or Community?* New York: Harper and
Row, 1967.

————. *Why We Can't Wait.* New York: Signet, 1963.

King, Mary. *Freedom Song: A Personal Story of the 1960s Civil Rights Movement.*
New York: William Morrow, 1987.

Kitchell, Mark, dir. *Berkeley in the Sixties* [Film]. San Francisco: California
Newreel, 1990.

Kool, V. K., ed. *Perspectives on Nonviolence.* New York: Springer Verlag, 1990.

Kosof, Anna. *The Civil Rights Movement and its Legacy.* New York: Franklin Watts,
1989.

Lane, Roger, and John J. Turner Jr., eds. *Riot, Rout, and Tumult: Readings in
American Social and Political Violence.* Westport, Conn.: Greenwood, 1978.

Lawson, Steven F. *Running for Freedom: Civil Rights and Black Politics in American
Since 1941* 2nd ed. New York: McGraw-Hill, 1997.

Lee, Cynthia Kwei Yung. "Race and Self-Defense: Toward a Normative
Conception of Reasonableness." *Minnesota Law Review* 81 (December 1996):
377–398.

Levy, Peter. *The Civil Rights Movement.* Westport, Conn.: Greenwood, 1998.

Lewis, David Levering. *W. E. B. DuBois: A Reader.* New York: Henry Holt, 1995.

Lincoln, C. Eric. *The Black Muslims in America.* Boston: Beacon, 1961.

————, ed. *Is Anybody Listening to Black America?* New York: Seabury, 1968.

Lipsitz, George. *A Life in the Struggle: Ivory Perry and the Culture of Opposition.*
Philadelphia: Temple University Press, 1988.

Litwack, Leon. *Been in the Storm So Long: The Aftermath of Slavery.* New York:
Vintage Books, 1979.

————. *Trouble in Mind: Black Southerners in the Age of Jim Crow*. New York: Alfred A. Knopf, 1998.

Litwack, Leon, and August Meier, eds. *Black Leaders of the Nineteenth Century*. Urbana: University of Illinois Press, 1988.

Locke, John. *Two Treatises on Government*. Edited by Peter Laslett. Cambridge, England: Cambridge University Press, 1960.

Lomax, John A., and Alan Lomax. *Negro Folk Songs as Sung by Lead Belly: "King of the Twelve-String Guitar Players of the World," Long-Time Convict in the Penitentiaries of Texas and Louisiana*. New York: Macmillan, 1936.

Lomax, Louis. *To Kill a Black Man*. Los Angeles: Holloway House, 1968.

Lowndes County Freedom Organization: The Rise of the Black Panthers [video]. University of Alabama Center for Public Television, reproduced by Films for the Humanities and Sciences, 1995.

Lukács, Georg. *History and Class Consciousness*. Reprint, Boston: MIT Press, 1972.

Luker, Ralph E. *Historical Dictionary of the Civil Rights Movement*. Vol. II, *Historical Dictionaries of Religions, Philosophies, and Movements*. Lanham, Md.: Scarecrow, 1997.

Lynd, Staughton, ed. *Nonviolence in America: A Documentary History*. Indianapolis: Bobbs-Merrill, 1966.

McCone, John A., and Warren M. Christopher, Earl S. Broady, Asa V. Call, Charles S. Cassasa, James Edward Jones, Sherman M. Mellinkoff, and Mrs. Robert G. Neumann. *Violence in the City—An End or Beginning?*. Report by the Governor's Commission on the Los Angeles Riots [abridged]. Los Angeles: Jeffries Banknote, 1965.

McCord, William, John Howard, Bernard Friedberg, and Edwin Harwood. *Life Styles in the Black Ghetto*. New York: W. W. Norton, 1969.

McFeely, William S. *Frederick Douglass*. New York: W. W. Norton, 1991.

McKay, Claude. *A Long Way Home*. New York: L. Furman, 1937.

McMillen, Neil, ed. *Re-Making Dixie: The Impact of World War II on the American South*. Jackson: University Press of Mississippi, 1997.

Major, Reginald. *A Panther Is a Black Cat*. New York: William Morrow, 1971.

Marable, Manning. *Race, Reform, and Rebellion*. Jackson: University Press of Mississippi, 1984.

Martin, Tony. *Race First: The Ideological and Organizational Struggles of Marcus Garvey and the Universal Negro Improvement Association*. Dover, Mass.: Majority Press, 1976.

Martin, Waldo E., Jr. *The Mind of Frederick Douglass*. Chapel Hill: University of North Carolina Press, 1984.

Masotti, Louis H., and Jerome R. Corsi. *Shootout in Cleveland: A Report Submitted to the National Commission on the Causes and Prevention of Violence*. New York: Bantam Books, 1969.

Maxwell, William. *New Negro, Old Left*. New York: Columbia University Press, 1999.

Mayfield, Julian. "Challenge to Negro Leadership." *Commentary* 31 (April 1961): 297–305.

Meier, August. *Negro Thought in America, 1880–1915*. Ann Arbor: University of Michigan Press, 1966.

———. *The Transformation of Activism*. Chicago: Aldine, 1970.

Meier, August, and Elliott Rudwick. *CORE: A Study in the Civil Rights Movement, 1942–1968*. New York: Oxford University Press, 1973.

Meier, August, Elliott Rudwick, and John Bracey. *Black Protest in the Sixties*. 2nd ed. New York: Markus Wiener, 1991.

Meier, August, Elliott Rudwick, and Francis L. Broderick. *Black Protest Thought in the Twentieth Century*. 2nd ed. Indianapolis: Bobbs-Merrill, 1971.

Merton, Thomas. *Faith and Violence: Christian Teaching and Christian Practice*. South Bend: University of Notre Dame Press, 1968.

Myers, Andrew. "When Violence Met Violence: Facts and Images of Robert F. Williams and the Black Freedom Struggle in Monroe, North Carolina." Master's thesis, University of Virginia, 1993.

Nelson, Truman. *People With Strength in Monroe, North Carolina* [pamphlet]. Monroe, N.C.: Committee to Aid the Monroe Defendants, 1963; Bancroft Collection on Social Protest Movements, Bancroft Library, University of California, Berkeley.

Newton, Huey P. *The Original Vision of the Black Panther Party* [pamphlet]. Oakland, Calif.: Black Panther Party, 1973; Bancroft Collection on Social Protest Movements, Bancroft Library, University of California, Berkeley.

———. *Revolutionary Suicide*. New York: Harcourt Brace Jovanovich, 1973.

———. *To Die for the People: The Writings of Huey P. Newton*. New York: Vintage Books, 1972.

O'Brien, Gail Williams. *The Color of the Law: Race, Violence, and Justice in the Post–World War II South*. Chapel Hill: University of North Carolina Press, 1999.

O'Reilly, Kenneth. *Racial Matters: The FBI's Secret File on Black America, 1960–1972*. New York: Free Press, 1989.

Oates, Stephen. *Let the Trumpet Sound: The Life of Martin Luther King Jr.* New York: Harper and Row, 1982.

Odum, Howard. *Race and Rumors of Race: The American South in the Early Forties*. Reprint, Baltimore: Johns Hopkins University Press, 1997.

Ofari, Earl. *Black Liberation: Cultural and Revolutionary Nationalism* [pamphlet].

Detroit: Radical Education Project, 1970; Bancroft Collection on Social Protest Movements, Bancroft Library, University of California, Berkeley.

Olsen, Jack. *Last Man Standing: The Tragedy and Triumph of Geronimo Pratt*. New York: Anchor Books, 2000.

Parks, Rosa. *Rosa Parks: My Story*. New York: Dial Books, 1992.

Payne, Charles M. *I've Got the Light of Freedom: The Organizing Tradition and the Mississippi Freedom Struggle*. Berkeley: University of California Press, 1995.

Pearson, Hugh. *The Shadow of the Panther: Huey Newton and the Price of Black Power in America*. Reading, Mass.: Addison-Wesley, 1994.

Perry, Bruce. *Malcolm: The Life of a Man Who Changed Black America*. Barrytown, N.Y.: Station Hill, 1991.

Perry, Theresa. *Teaching Malcolm X*. New York: Routledge, 1996.

Powledge, Fred. *Free at Last?: The Civil Rights Movement and the People Who Made It*. New York: Harper Perennial, 1991.

President's Commission on Law Enforcement and the Administration of Justice. *Task Force Report: The Police*. Washington, D.C.: U.S. Government Printing Office, 1967.

Raines, Howell. *My Soul Is Rested: Movement Days in the Deep South Remembered*. New York: Penguin, 1977.

Ralph, James R., Jr. *Northern Protest: Martin Luther King Jr., Chicago, and the Civil Rights Movement*. Cambridge: Harvard University Press, 1993.

Rampersad, Arnold. *Jackie Robinson: A Biography*. New York: Alfred A. Knopf, 1997.

Record, Wilson, and Jane Cassels, eds. *Little Rock U. S. A.: Materials for Analysis*. San Francisco: Chandler Publishing, 1960.

Reed, John Shelton. *One South: An Ethnic Approach to Regional Culture*. Baton Rouge: Louisiana State University Press, 1982.

Riches, William T. Martin. *The Civil Rights Movement: Struggle and Resistance*. New York: St. Martin's Press, 1997.

Robinson, Jo Ann. *The Montgomery Bus Boycott and the Women Who Started It: The Memoir of Jo Ann Gibson Robinson*. Knoxville: University of Tennessee Press, 1987.

Rosa, Della. *Why Watts Exploded: How the Ghetto Fought Back* [pamphlet]. 2nd printing. Socialist Workers Party Pamphlet. Los Angeles: Los Angeles Local, July 1966.

Ross, James Robert. *The War Within: Violence or Nonviolence in the Black Revolution*. New York: Sheed and Ward, 1971.

Rossi, Peter H., ed. *Ghetto Revolts*. 2nd ed. New Brunswick, N.J.: Transaction Books, 1973.

Rustin, Bayard. *Strategies for Freedom*. New York: Columbia University Press, 1976.

Scott, James C. *Weapons of the Weak: Everyday Forms of Peasant Resistance.* New Haven: Yale University Press, 1985.

Scott, Robert L., and Wayne Brockriede. *The Rhetoric of Black Power.* New York: Harper and Row, 1969.

Seale, Bobby. *A Lonely Rage: The Autobiography of Bobby Seale.* New York: Times Books, 1978.

———. *Seize the Time: The Story of the Black Panther Party and Huey P. Newton.* New York: Random House, 1968.

Sears, David O., and John B. McConahay. *The Politics of Violence: The New Urban Blacks and the Watts Riot.* Boston: Houghton Mifflin, 1973.

Sellers, Cleveland. *The River of No Return: The Autobiography of a Black Militant and the Life and Death of SNCC.* New York: William Morrow, 1973.

Seshachari, C. *Gandhi and the American Scene: An Intellectual History and Inquiry.* Bombay: Nachiketa Publications, 1969.

Shadron, Virginia. "Popular Protest and Legal Authority in Post-World War II Georgia: Race, Class, and Gender Politics in the Rosa Lee Ingram Case." Ph.D. diss., Emory University, 1991.

Shapiro, Herbert. *White Violence and Black Response: From Reconstruction to Montgomery.* Amherst: University of Massachusetts Press, 1988.

Shiffrin, Steven H. "The Rhetoric of Black Violence in the Antebellum Period." *Journal of Black Studies* 2, no. 1 (September 1971): 45–56.

Shridharani, Krishnalal. *War without Violence: A Study of Gandhi's Method and Its Accomplishments.* New York: Harcourt Brace Jovanovich, 1939.

Silberman, Charles E. *Criminal Violence, Criminal Justice.* New York: Vintage, 1978.

Sitkoff, Harvard. *The Struggle for Black Equality.* Rev. ed. New York: Hill and Wang, 1993.

Skolnick, Jerome H. *The Politics of Protest: Violent Aspects of Protest and Confrontation.* A Staff Report to the National Commission on the Causes and Prevention of Violence. Washington, D.C.: Superintendent of Documents, U.S. Government Printing Office, 1969.

Sorel, Georges. *Reflections on Violence.* Reprint, Cambridge: Cambridge University Press, 2000.

Spinard, William. *Civil Liberties.* Chicago: Quadrangle Books, 1970.

Stampp, Kenneth. *The Peculiar Institution: Slavery in the Ante-Bellum South.* New York: Alfred A. Knopf, 1956.

Stanton, Mary. *From Selma to Sorrow: The Life and Death of Viola Liuzzo.* Athens: University of Georgia Press, 1998.

Stoper, Emily S. "The Student Nonviolent Coordinating Committee: The Growth of Radicalism in a Civil Rights Organization." Ph.D. diss., Harvard University, 1968.

Storey, Robert Gerald. *Our Unalienable Rights*. Springfield, Illinois: Charles C. Thomas, 1965.

Sullivan, Patricia. *Freedom Writer: Virginia Durr, Letters from the Civil Rights Years*. New York: Routledge, 2003.

Supplemental Studies for the National Advisory Commission on Civil Disorders. Washington, D.C.: Superintendent of Documents, U.S. Government Printing Office, 1968.

Takaki, Ronald. *Violence in the Black Imagination: Essays and Documents*. Expanded ed. Oxford: Oxford University Press, 1993.

Tierney, Kevin. *Darrow: A Biography*. New York: Crowell, 1979.

Tolnay, Stewart E., and E. M. Beck. *A Festival of Violence: An Analysis of Southern Lynchings, 1882–1930*. Urbana: University of Illinois Press, 1995.

Tucker, Sterling. *For Blacks Only: Black Strategies for Change in America*. Grand Rapids, Michigan: William B. Eerdmans, 1971.

Turrini, Joseph. "Sweet Justice." *Michigan History Magazine*, July–August 1999, 22–27.

Tushnet, Mark V. *The American Law of Slavery, 1810–1860: Considerations of Humanity and Interest*. Princeton, New Jersey: Princeton University Press, 1981.

Tyson, Timothy B. *Radio Free Dixie: Robert F. Williams and the Roots of Black Power*. Chapel Hill: University of North Carolina Press, 1999.

————. "Robert F. Williams, 'Black Power,' and the Roots of the African American Freedom Struggle." *Journal of American History* 85, no. 2 (September 1998): 540–570.

Umoja, Akinyele O. "Ballots and Bullets: A Comparative Analysis of Armed Resistance in the Civil Rights Movement." *Journal of Black Studies* 29, no. 4 (March 1999): 558–578.

————. "Eye for an Eye: The Role of Armed Resistance in the Mississippi Freedom Movement." Ph.D. diss., Emory University, 1996.

————. " 'We Will Shoot Back': The Natchez Model and Para-Military Organization in the Mississippi Freedom Movement." *Journal of Black Studies* 32, no. 3 (January 2002): 267–290.

Uniacke, Suzanne. *Permissable Killing: The Self-Defense Justification of Homicide*. Cambridge: Cambridge University Press, 1994.

U.S. Commission on Civil Disorders. *Report of the National Advisory Commission on Civil Disorders*. Washington, D.C.: Kerner Commission, U.S. Government Printing Office, 1968.

U.S. Commission on Civil Rights. *Freedom to the Free: A Report to the President by the United States Commission on Civil Rights*. Washington, D.C.: U.S. Government Printing Office, 1963.

U.S. Commission on Civil Rights. *Law Enforcement: A Report on Equal Protection in the South*. Washington, D.C.: U.S. Government Printing Office, 1965.

U.S. Congress. House. Committee on Internal Security. "The Black Panther Party: Its Origin and Development as Reflected in Its Official Weekly Newspaper *The Black Panther Black Community News Service*," 91st Cong., 2nd sess., October 6, 1971. Washington, D.C.: U.S. Government Printing Office, 1971.

U.S. Congress. Senate Judiciary Hearings. Subcommittee on Internal Security. Testimony of Robert F. Williams. 91st Cong., 2nd sess., February 16, 1970. Washington, D.C.: U.S. Government Printing Office, 1971.

U.S. Supreme Court. *Report of the Decision of the Supreme Court of the United States, and the Opinions of the Judges Thereof, in the Case of Dred Scott versus John F. A. Sandford* (Washington, D.C.: C. Wendell, 1857), Bancroft Library, UC Berkeley.

Van Deburg, William. *New Day in Babylon: The Black Power Movement and American Culture, 1965–1975*. Chicago: University of Chicago Press, 1992.

Walker, David. *David Walker's Appeal to the Coloured Citizens of the World, but in Particular, and Very Expressly, to Those of the United States of America*. Black Classic Press Edition. Baltimore: Black Classic, 1993.

Ward, Brian, and Tony Badger. *The Making of Martin Luther King and the Civil Rights Movement*. New York: New York University Press, 1996.

Warren, Robert Penn. *Who Speaks for the Negro?* New York: Random House, 1965.

Washington, James M., ed. *A Testament of Hope: The Essential Writings and Speeches of Martin Luther King, Jr.* San Francisco: Harper, 1991.

Wells, Ida B. *Southern Horrors and Other Writings*. Edited by Jacqueline Jones Royster. Boston: Bedford Books, 1997.

Wexler, Sanford. *The Civil Rights Movement: An Eyewitness History*. New York: Facts on File, 1993.

Whitfield, Stephen J. *A Death in the Delta: The Story of Emmett Till*. New York: Free Press, 1988.

Wilkins, Roy, and Ramsey Clark. *Search and Destroy: A Report by the Commission of Inquiry into the Black Panthers and the Police*. Published by the NAACP and the Metropolitan Applied Research Center, Inc. New York: Harper and Row, NAACP and the Metropolitan Applied Research Center, Inc., 1973.

Williams, Robert F. "1957: The Swimming Pool Showdown." *Southern Exposure* 8, no. 2 (Summer 1980): 70–72.

———. *Negroes with Guns*. New York: Marzani and Munsell, 1962; 2nd ed. Chicago: Third World, 1973.

Williamson, Joel. *A Rage for Order: Black-White Relations in the American South since Emancipation*. New York: Oxford University Press, 1986.

Wilson, Theodore Brantner. *The Black Codes of the South*. Tuscaloosa: University of Alabama Press, 1965.

Wolfe, Charles, and Kip Lornell. *The Life and Legend of Leadbelly*. New York: HarperCollins, 1992.

Wood, Joe, ed. *Malcolm X: In Our Own Image*. New York: St. Martin's Press, 1992.

Woodard, Komozi. *A Nation Within a Nation: Amiri Baraka (LeRoi Jones) and Black Power Politics*. Chapel Hill: University of North Carolina Press, 1999.

Woodward, C. Vann. *The Strange Career of Jim Crow*. 2nd rev. ed. London: Oxford University Press, 1965.

Wyatt-Brown, Bertram. *Honor and Violence in the Old South*. New York: Oxford University Press, 1986.

———. *Southern Honor: Ethics and Behavior in the Old South*. New York: Oxford University Press, 1982.

X, Malcolm. *By Any Means Necessary: Speeches, Interviews, and a Letter by Malcolm X*. New York: Pathfinder, 1970.

———. *The End of White World Supremacy: Four Speeches*. Edited by Benjamin Goodman. New York: Merlin House, 1971.

———. *Malcolm X and the Negro Revolution*. London: Owen, 1969.

———. *Malcolm X on Afro-American History*. New York: Merit Book, 1970.

———. *Malcolm X Speaks: Selected Speeches and Statements*. New York: Merit Publishers, 1965.

———. *The Speeches of Malcolm X at Harvard*. New York: William Morrow, 1968; reprint, New York: Paragon House, 1991.

———. *Two Speeches by Malcolm X*. New York: Pioneer Publishers, 1965; reprint, New York: Pathfinder, 1970.

X, Malcolm, with Alex Haley. *The Autobiography of Malcolm X*. New York: Grove, 1964.

Young, Richard P. *Roots of Rebellion: The Evolution of Black Politics and Protest since World War II*. New York: Harper and Row, 1970.

Zannes, Estelle. *Checkmate in Cleveland: The Rhetoric of Confrontation During the Stokes Years*. Cleveland: Case Western University Press, 1972.

Zinn, Howard. *SNCC: The New Abolitionists*. Boston: Beacon, 1965.

INDEX